Further mathematics

II. Vectors and mechanics

Draft edition

The School Mathematics Project

Further mathematics

II. Vectors and mechanics

Draft edition

Cambridge at the University Press 1971

Published by the Syndics of the Cambridge University Press
Bentley House, 200 Euston Road, London N.W.1
American Branch: 32 East 57th Street, New York, N.Y. 10022

ISBN: 0 521 08045 2

Set in cold type by E.W.C. Wilkins and Associates Ltd.,
and printed in Great Britain by
Alden & Mowbray Ltd., at the Alden Press, Oxford

The School Mathematics Project

This project was founded on the belief, held by a group of practising school teachers, that there are serious shortcomings in traditional school mathematics syllabuses, and that there is a need for experiment in schools with the aim of developing syllabuses which are in line with up-to-date ideas and applications. To this end, they and their successors have co-operated in devising radically new syllabuses which more adequately reflect the nature and usages of mathematics and which, by spanning the whole secondary-school course, would lead to new examinations at all levels.

This is not the place to describe the complex arrangements which this simple objective has required; the printed annual reports of the Project deal with such matters and are available on request to the Director at Westfield College, University of London. But perhaps acknowledgement could gratefully be expressed here of the financial support which has enabled the work to be done.

As for the Project's series of publications, it is not claimed for one moment that the texts represent the best possible development of the subject – there is altogether too much of mathematics for that to be true of any course. For this reason, especially, the Further Mathematics books are published in experimental format, for the ground which they are breaking is indeed new at the G.C.E. A-level stage. It is anticipated that the books will remain in use in their present form for a period of perhaps three or four years, after which experience will show what revision is necessary. The Project always welcomes comments from teachers who have used the texts in order to improve on the material and its presentation.

Initially five books in this series are planned under the titles:

(i) Linear Algebra and Geometry,

(ii) Vectors and Mechanics,

(iii) Differential Equations and Circuits,

(iv) Extensions of Calculus,

(v) Statistics and Probability.

Later it may be appropriate to produce books on other topics. The examinations (common to all G.C.E. boards) are based on these texts, and the details of the arrangement of papers are available from the S.M.P. Office.

This text is based on the original contributions of

A. Hurrell

P.G.T. Lewis

A.T. Rogerson

I.C. Warburton

and is edited by P.G.T. Lewis.

Many other schoolteachers have been directly involved in the further development and revision of the material and the Project gratefully acknowledges the contributions which they and their schools have made.

Contents

	Page
Preface	ix
1. Differential Geometry	1
2. Polar Kinematics and Conics	27
3. Vector Products	52
4. Rigid Bodies	86
Miscellaneous exercises	133
Answers to exercises	139
Index	155

Preface

This book is designed to meet the needs of those working at the S.M.P. Further Mathematics section on Vectors and Mechanics. As such it has to serve a variety of users. In particular, some will wish to tackle the double subject 'in parallel', starting on the Further Mathematics and the single subject S.M.P. Mathematics at much the same time. Others may prefer to take the subjects 'in series', completing the single subject syllabus, and indeed even sitting the examination, before moving on to the double subject.

With this in mind, we have shaped this book to suit the former, on the grounds that it is better to have to skim through what you already know, rather than having to take a large body of knowledge on trust. Anyone with an elementary knowledge of cartesian kinematics and particle dynamics, for example, up to Additional Mathematics O-level standard, should be able to work through most of this text. Greater knowledge of integration would be helpful, otherwise answers given can only be verified by differentiation. Furthermore we have concentrated on getting the basic ideas clear rather than on excessive depth of treatment. Our aim has been to give an intuitive feel for each topic before formalising the work on it. There are numerous worked examples and exercises. Also this has undergone the test of classroom use.

The theme throughout is dynamic; force and motion, from the simplest plane particle to a glimpse of the general, capricious, rigid body.

The first chapter, differential geometry, is an investigation of motion along curves, both cartesian and polar. The distance travelled is closely related to the velocity. Likewise the curvature is related to the acceleration and hence to the forces involved. The opposite problem, that of determining the path travelled from a knowledge of the forces acting, is more difficult. The second chapter investigates this for a central force, such as gravitational attraction, and takes a closer look at the orbits (conics) obtained and their role in space-travel. This work is then extended to a consideration of the orientation of objects and the vector product is introduced in the third chapter as a convenient means of investigating rotation. In particular, angular velocity is seen to be a vector quantity.

Finally, the last chapter ties all the previous work together to develop a model of the motion of a rigid body. This is completely specified by two simple equations, of linear and rotational momentum. Their application, however, is not so simple, and is largely restricted to motion in a plane. The final section outlines the extension to three dimensions, and is particularly suited to those who have already done the linear algebra in the S.M.P. course.

There is a summary at the end of each chapter and a final collection of miscellaneous questions on all the work covered. Some sections are marked with an asterisk. The ideas and techniques they contain are of interest and are relevant, but not essential, to the development of the subject.

Vector methods are used extensively, and particular care has been taken to render the vector product palatable. It is hoped that this will be of wider use than its S.M.P. context, both in sixth forms and among first year undergraduates who wish to gain familiarity with vector methods or refresh their grasp of this work.

1. Differential Geometry

1. DIFFERENTIAL GEOMETRY

1.1 Kinematics

Fasten your seat belt and we shall be off. The flight path is given by: $x = t^2$, $y = 0{\cdot}01t^3$, where t is the time after take-off. We reach our cruising elevation after 100 seconds and level out at constant speed. How fast are we then travelling? Did the acceleration cause discomfort? What thrust must the engines provide? How far are we from the airport? How far have we actually travelled? Was the flight smooth? These are a few of the questions that we may be able to answer. (The units are metric.)

Example 1. Here

$$\mathbf{r} = t^2\hat{\mathbf{i}} + 0{\cdot}01t^3\,\hat{\mathbf{j}},$$
$$\mathbf{v} = \dot{\mathbf{r}} = 2t\hat{\mathbf{i}} + 0{\cdot}03t^2\,\hat{\mathbf{j}},$$
$$\mathbf{a} = \dot{\mathbf{v}} = \ddot{\mathbf{r}} = 2\hat{\mathbf{i}} + 0{\cdot}06t\,\hat{\mathbf{j}},$$

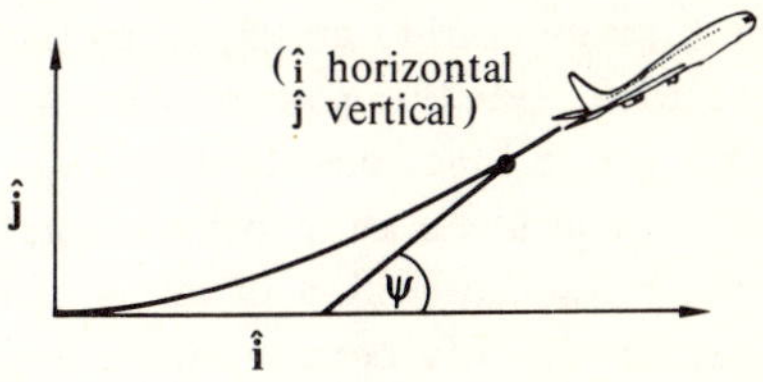

Fig. 1.

where dots denote differentiation with respect to time, and 'hats' are used to emphasise unit vectors. When $t = 100$, $\mathbf{r} = 10^4\,\hat{\mathbf{i}} + 10^4\,\hat{\mathbf{j}}$. So the altitude is 10 000 metres and the distance from the airport, assumed at sea level, is $r = 10^4\sqrt{2}$m. But this, of course, is much less than the distance we have in fact travelled. (See Section 3.) Also $\mathbf{v} = 200\hat{\mathbf{i}} + 300\hat{\mathbf{j}}$, so that the speed is $v = 100\sqrt{13}$ m/s along the path, which is at an angle $\psi = \tan^{-1}(\frac{3}{2}) = 56{\cdot}3°$ to the horizontal.

$\mathbf{a} = 2\hat{\mathbf{i}} + 0{\cdot}06t\,\hat{\mathbf{j}}$ at any time t and is thus at its greatest, $\mathbf{a} = 2\hat{\mathbf{i}} + 6\hat{\mathbf{j}}$ with $a = 2\sqrt{10}$ m/s², just before levelling out. This is comparable with the acceleration of an object falling freely under the earth's gravitational attraction, and might cause discomfort.

The engines would have to provide a thrust of

$$\begin{pmatrix} 0 \\ 9{\cdot}8m \end{pmatrix} + \begin{pmatrix} 2m \\ 6m \end{pmatrix} = \begin{pmatrix} 2m \\ 15{\cdot}8m \end{pmatrix} \quad \text{newtons}$$

to overcome the earth's attraction and give this acceleration, where m is the mass of the plane.

We are quite familiar with the fact that the position vector $\mathbf{r}$ of an object in a plane can be expressed in terms of the unit vectors $\hat{\mathbf{i}}$ and $\hat{\mathbf{j}}$ as $\mathbf{r} = x\hat{\mathbf{i}} + y\hat{\mathbf{j}}$. In general x and y may have any values (the object may be anywhere in the plane) and $\mathbf{r}$ is said to have two *degrees of freedom*. However, we were able to express the position of our object in terms of one *parameter* t by means of the two *parametric functions* $x = t^2$ and $y = 0{\cdot}01t^3$ so that the values of x and y, and hence $\mathbf{r}$, were known at any time t. Thus $\mathbf{r}$ had only one degree of freedom.

We shall confine our attention to functions which are continuous (unbroken) and differentiable (smooth), so that **r** is the position vector of a point on a continuous curve.

1.2 Parametric representation

$x = t^2$, $y = 0{\cdot}01t^3$ is a parametric representation of the curve $y = 0{\cdot}01(\sqrt{x})^3$, since $y = 0{\cdot}01t^3$ and $t = \sqrt{x}$, (or $-\sqrt{x}$ if t is negative, giving the branch $y = -0{\cdot}01(\sqrt{x})^3$).

Now it is easy to see that $x = 4p^2$, $y = 0{\cdot}08p^3$ represents the same curve, with parameter p. So there is no unique representation. Suggest another one.

Example 2. $x = \cos\alpha$, $y = \sin\alpha$. Here the parametric functions cosine and sine map the real numbers onto the circle $x^2 + y^2 = 1$. (See Figure 2.) Likewise $x = \cos 3\beta$, $y = \sin 3\beta$ also map the reals onto this circle.

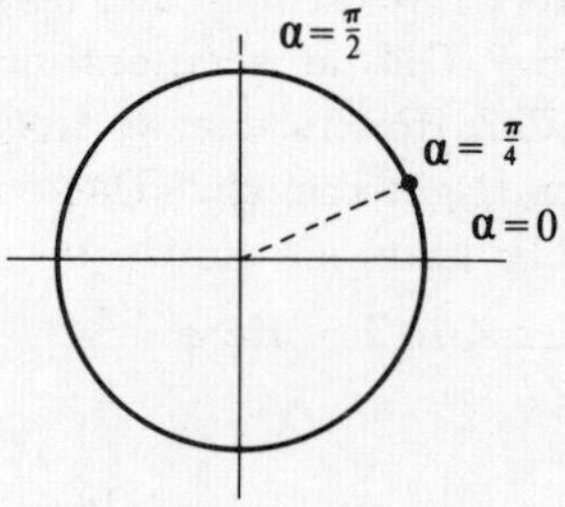

Fig. 2.

The circle is, of course, traced out more than once, since cosine and sine are both periodic functions. But the most significant fact is that there is no single function which maps x onto y or y onto x, and to be able to investigate such a curve through its expression in terms of two parametric *functions* is very convenient.

1.3 Finding parametric functions for curves

We are now faced with the question whether a given curve can be expressed in terms of parametric functions and, if so, with the problem of finding suitable functions.

Given any continuous curve, consider the position of an object which moves steadily along the curve. At any time t it has a unique position vector **r**. Thus the components of **r** are functions of the time t. Hence there are parametric functions f and g such that $x = f(t)$, and $y = g(t)$. It is thus always possible to express the position vector of a point on any continuous curve by two parametric functions, though it may be difficult to obtain the two functions explicitly in practice. We have already seen that such functions are not unique, and in obtaining a suitable pair much depends on the way in which the curve is specified.

Furthermore, although it has been convenient to think of our parameter t as representing the time, this is certainly not necessary. Suitable parametric functions may well express **r** as a function of the time, or in terms of the angle θ between the position vector and some fixed direction, or in terms of the distance s along the curve from some fixed point, or merely as a function of some parameter p to which no physical or geometric significance can be attached, but whose domain is a subset of the real numbers.

Example 3. To find the locus of the feet of a man standing at the centre of a ladder of length $2a$ which slips down, in a vertical plane, with its top against a vertical wall and its base on the horizontal ground. Let α be the acute angle between the ladder and the ground. (See Figure 3.) Then the coordinates of the mid-point of the ladder are: $x = a\cos\alpha$, $y = a\sin\alpha$. This curve is a circle, as we found in the previous example; but in this case only one quadrant of the circle is described, since α is restricted to lie in the interval $0 \leqslant \alpha \leqslant \frac{1}{2}\pi$.

What if he had been two-thirds of the way up the ladder?

What is the locus of his head if he remains vertical?

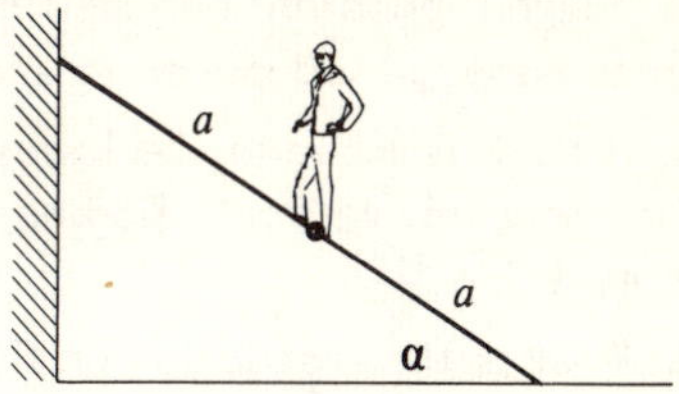

Fig. 3.

EXERCISE A

1. $$\mathbf{r} = t^2\hat{\mathbf{i}} + 2t\hat{\mathbf{j}}.$$

Draw a graph of the path for the first 5 seconds. Calculate r, v and a when $t = 3$ and show your results on your graph.

2. $$\mathbf{r} = 4\cos(0{\cdot}1\pi t)\,\hat{\mathbf{i}} + 3\sin(0{\cdot}1\pi t)\,\hat{\mathbf{j}}.$$

Describe the motion and find the direction of motion when $t = 12$. What is the greatest speed and when does it occur? When is the acceleration parallel to the x-axis?

3. Sketch the following loci, using cartesian coordinates. Regarding the parameter p as the time, find the velocity and acceleration after 2 seconds in each case and indicate your results in your sketch.

(a) $x = 2p,\ y = 8p + 3$; (b) $x = 5p - 1,\ y = 20p - 1$;

(c) $\mathbf{r} = 5p\hat{\mathbf{i}} + 12p\hat{\mathbf{j}}$; (d) $x = 2p^3,\ y = 3p^2$;

(e) $x = 3\sin p,\ y = 3\cos p$; (f) $\mathbf{r} = 3\begin{pmatrix}\sin 2p\\ \cos 2p\end{pmatrix}$;

(g) $(1 + p^2)\mathbf{r} = 6p\hat{\mathbf{i}} + (3 - 3p^2)\hat{\mathbf{j}}$; (h) $x = \sin^3 p,\ y = \cos^3 p$.

4. Find, by eliminating p, the equations connecting x and y in Question 3 above. In which cases can the relation be considered as a function mapping $x \to y$?

5. Write down a *unit* vector in the direction of the tangent at the point with parameter p for each of the curves in Question 3 above.

6. $$\mathbf{r} = 5\cos\omega t\,\hat{\mathbf{i}} + 5(1 + \sin\omega t)\,\hat{\mathbf{j}}.$$

Describe the motion and show that the acceleration is constant in magnitude. What can you say about the direction of the acceleration? If the motion is in a vertical plane with $\hat{\mathbf{j}}$ vertical, show that the object is travelling horizontally when $t = \pi/2\omega$ and that it appears weightless at this instant [i.e. there is no force acting on it] if $\omega = \sqrt{2}$, where the gravitational acceleration is taken as $10\,\text{m/s}^2$.

7. Express x and y as parametric functions of a parameter p:

(a) $y = 2x + 1$; (b) $y^2 = 4x$;

(c) $y^3 = 3x$; (d) $x^2 + y^2 = 4$;

(e) $x^2 - y^2 = 1$.

8. Sketch the curves in Question 7 above.

9. A car drives along the curve $y = 4x$, starting at the origin, so that its speed in the x direction is always 9 units/s. By choosing a suitable parametric function for x, find its speed in the y direction after 5s.

10. Suggest possible parametric functions for the motion of a point on a wind-screen wiper which moves to and fro along the arc of a circle.

11. A mark is made at the lowest point of a wheel of radius a. The wheel is then rolled forward, without slipping, through an angle α. What is now the position of the mark?

12. What is the restriction on the function h if parametric functions f and g can be replaced by the combined functions fh and gh? (See Example 2, where f, g, h are cos, sin and the trebling function.)

13. $x = \sin t, \qquad y = \cos t, \qquad z = t.$

Describe the path and show that the speed is constant.

*2. NODES AND CUSPS

Consider the curve traced by a light fixed to a wheel which rolls along a straight line without slipping. It is called a *trochoid*. Try to decide what it looks like by rolling a tin lid with a pencil stuck through it.

The most convenient form of trochoid is obtained if we roll a circle of radius a along the line $y = 2a$. (Figure 4.) When the circle has turned through an angle α the point B, initially on the radius CO distant b from C, will have been rotated about C through an angle α, also translated a distance MN = Arc $M'N = a\alpha$, in the direction of x. Thus the angle $B'C'L = \alpha$, and the position of B' is given by: $x = a\alpha + b \sin \alpha, \qquad y = a - b \cos \alpha.$

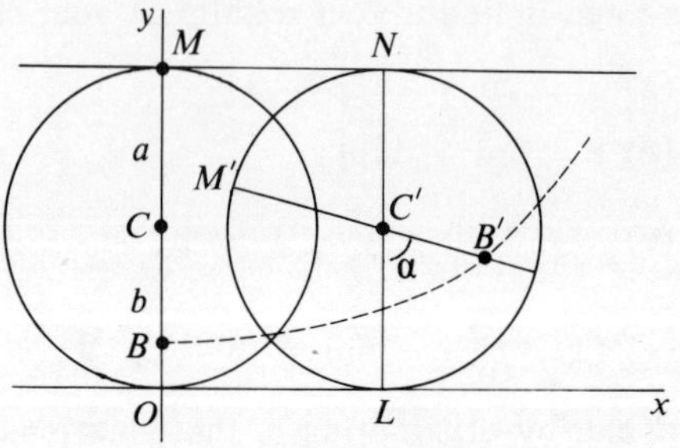

Fig. 4.

These are parametric functions for the curve traced out by B.

Consider the locus of a point on the flange of a wheel on a railway truck where $b > a$ for example. When $a = 1$ and $b = \frac{3}{2}$; then $x = \alpha + \frac{3}{2} \sin \alpha$, $y = 1 - \frac{3}{2} \cos \alpha$; and the curve has a series of loops with points, called *nodes*, where the curve crosses over itself.

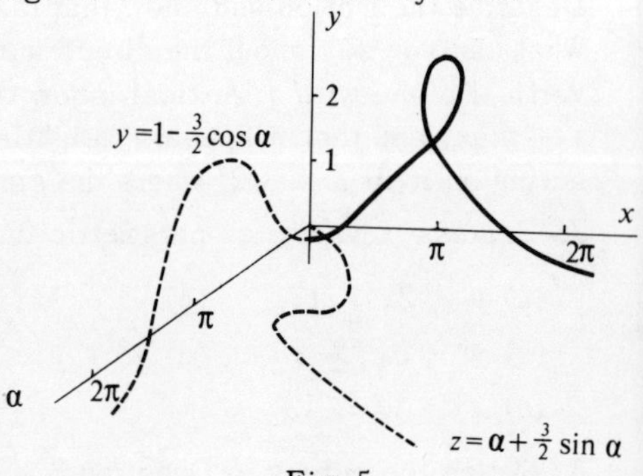

Fig. 5.

What features of the parametric functions give rise to a node? It is quite helpful mentally to move along the curve while tracing with a finger the components along the x or y axis. This will give an appreciation of how such a curve is generated by its parametric functions. For a node there must be two distinct values of the parameter which give rise to the same position vector; that the converse is not true can be seen from the circle of Example 2; here the parameters α and $\alpha + 2\pi$ give the same point, but this is not a node.

The diagram (Figure 5) shows only one period, or complete revolution, of the circle. We see that y first increases then decreases steadily. However, x, while generally increasing, decreases in the neighbourhood of $\alpha = \pi$ before continuing to increase. It is this 'wiggle' in the graph of the function for x which gives rise to the loop which characterises a node. In fact there are three values of α for which the value of $f(\alpha)$ is the same, two giving rise to the node and the third to the top of the loop. The graph of $f : \alpha \to x$ has point symmetry about the point where $\alpha = \pi$, while that of $g : \alpha \to y$ has line symmetry about the line $\alpha = \pi$. This point and line symmetry is a common feature of parametric functions of a curve with a node, when the axes are suitably chosen, if the curve is to have symmetry about its loop.

Next consider the trochoid with $a = 1$ and $b = \frac{1}{2}$. (Figure 6.) Here $x = \alpha + \frac{1}{2} \sin \alpha$, giving a curve which appears to have little in common with the previous one. The graph of g, of course, still has a turning point where $\alpha = \pi$. That of f still has an inflexion where $\alpha = \pi$, but the 'wiggle' has been smoothed out.

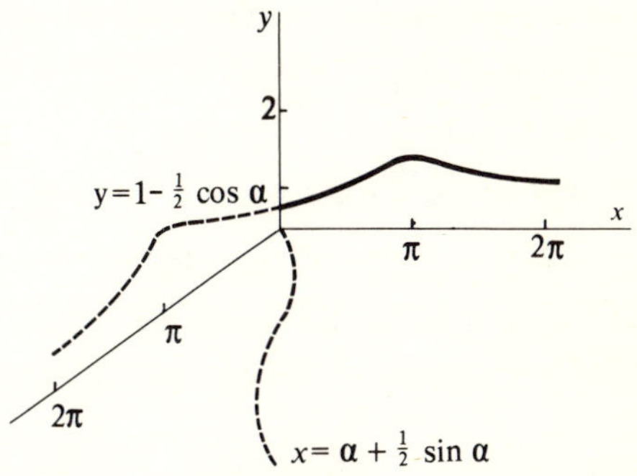

Fig. 6.

Finally, consider the situation with $a = 1$, $b = 1$. This is the *cycloid*, the locus of a point on the circumference of a rolling wheel. Here $x = \alpha + \sin \alpha$, $y = 1 - \cos \alpha$, giving a curve with a series of sharp points, or *cusps*, at which the direction of the curve is reversed. (Figure 7.)

This curve is really intermediate between the previous two. g has a turning point where $\alpha = \pi$ and f has a point of inflexion at which the gradient $f'(\pi)$ is zero. It is this simultaneous stationary value for x and y which often typifies the appearance of a cusp.

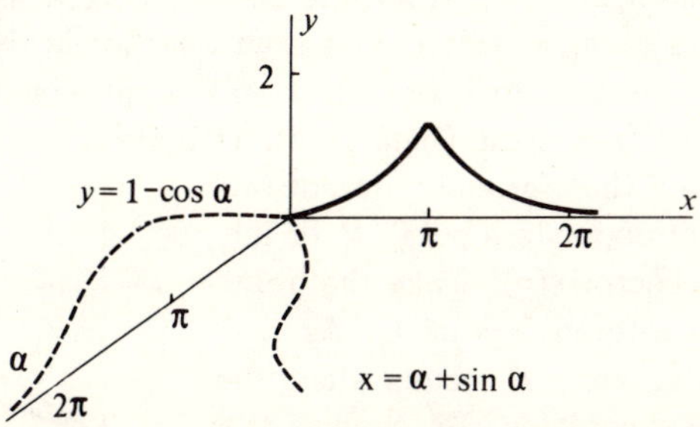

Fig. 7.

EXERCISE B

1. Sketch the motion along the curve $x = t^3$, $y = t^2$ and investigate the velocity at the cusp.

2. Sketch the motion along the curve $x = (t - 1)t(t + 1)$, $y = t^2$. Find the direction of the acceleration at the node.

3. Sketch the following curves:

(a) Trisectrix $x = \cos\alpha + \cos 2\alpha$, $y = \sin\alpha + \sin 2\alpha$.

(b) Cardioid $x = 2\cos\alpha + \cos 2\alpha$, $y = 2\sin\alpha + \sin 2\alpha$.

(c) Deltoid $x = 2\cos\alpha + \cos 2\alpha$, $y = 2\sin\alpha - \sin 2\alpha$.

4. Sketch the following curves. Find the velocity and acceleration at each crossing of the axes for motion along such switchbacks, where the parameter t is the time for the motion.

(a) Strophoid $x = (t^2 - 1)/(t^2 + 1)$, $y = t(t^2 - 1)/(t^2 + 1)$.

(b) Hyperbola $x = (1 + t^2)/(1 - t^2)$, $y = t/(1 - t^2)$.

(c) Folium $x = t/(1 + t^3)$, $y = t^2/(1 + t^3)$.

5. Sketch the curve $x = p - p^3$, $y = 1 - p^4$.

6. Make up your own parametric functions to give:

(a) a curve with a node at $p = 1$;

(b) a curve with a cusp at $p = 1$.

3. LENGTH OF CURVE

If we look back on our journey in Example 1, we were $10^4\sqrt{2}$ metres from the airport after 100 seconds. However, this tells us as little about the actual distance travelled as the knowledge that a point on a circle is 5m from the centre tells us of its distance along the circumference. To find the distance along a curve we shall have to look more closely at its direction.

Consider a point P on a curve, with position vector $\mathbf{r}$ given by a parameter p. Intuitively we see that a change in the value of p causes a change in the value of $\mathbf{r}$.

The *amount* by which $\mathbf{r}$ changes is the amount by which P moves which, for a small change, is the amount by which the curve changes in length. The direction of change of $\mathbf{r}$ is along $\hat{\mathbf{t}}$, where $\hat{\mathbf{t}}$ is a unit vector in the direction of the tangent to the curve. We can thus write $\delta\mathbf{r} = \delta s\hat{\mathbf{t}}$, approximately, where s denotes the length of the curve from some fixed point. (Figure 8.)

Formally, we state that for any value of the parameter p there corresponds a point P of the curve, with position vector $\mathbf{r}(p)$. Take the point for which $p = 0$ as a reference point C. As p changes from the value zero, P moves along the curve from C to a new position. We assume that with every point P we can associate a distance $s(p)$, measured along the curve from C to P,

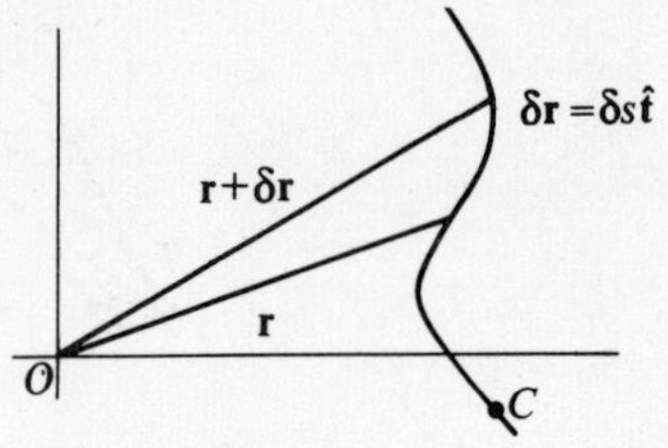

Fig. 8.

whose rate of change is *defined* to be the magnitude of the rate of change of position of P; that is,

$$\mathbf{r}' = s'\hat{\mathbf{t}},$$

where $\hat{\mathbf{t}}$ is a unit vector in the (variable) direction of change of P, that is, along the tangent to the curve at P. Dashes denote differentiation with respect to the parameter p.

Note: If time is taken as the parameter, this becomes:

$$\dot{\mathbf{r}} = v\hat{\mathbf{t}}$$

since $\dot{s}$ is then the speed v of P along the curve, i.e. P changes position with speed v in the direction of the tangent.

By expressing $\mathbf{r}$ in cartesian or polar form it is now possible to obtain expressions for s', and hence for the curve length s, in terms of the parameter p.

3.1 Cartesian coordinates

$$\begin{aligned} \mathbf{r} &= x\hat{\mathbf{i}} + y\hat{\mathbf{j}} \\ \Rightarrow \quad \mathbf{r}' &= x'\hat{\mathbf{i}} + y'\hat{\mathbf{j}} \\ \Rightarrow \quad s'\hat{\mathbf{t}} &= x'\hat{\mathbf{i}} + y'\hat{\mathbf{j}} \\ \Rightarrow \quad s'^2 &= x'^2 + y'^2, \text{ since } t \text{ is a unit vector,} \\ \Rightarrow \quad s &= \int \sqrt{(x'^2 + y'^2)}\, dp. \end{aligned}$$

This gives the curve length s, in terms of the parameter p.

Note: With time as the parameter we get the familiar expression:

$$v^2 = \dot{x}^2 + \dot{y}^2.$$

Example 4. Find the length from $p = 1$ to $p = 3$ of the curve:

$$x = 2p, \qquad y = 6p + 1.$$

Here

$$x' = 2, \qquad y' = 6$$

$$\begin{aligned} \Rightarrow \quad s &= \int_1^3 \sqrt{(4 + 36)}\, dp \\ &= [(\sqrt{40})p]_1^3 \\ &= 4\sqrt{10}. \end{aligned}$$

More generally, the length of this curve (the line $y = 3x + 1$) from the point $C(0, 1)$ with parameter $p = 0$, to the point $P(2p, 6p + 1)$ with parameter p, is $\sqrt{(40)}\,p$.

In this example, because the curve happens to be a *straight line*, we can verify this result by Pythagoras's Theorem:

$$\begin{aligned} CP^2 &= [2p - 0]^2 + [(6p + 1) - 1]^2 \\ &= 40p^2. \end{aligned}$$

3.2 Special parameters

Sometimes it is convenient to take x, or y, as the parameter, giving:

$$s = \int \sqrt{[1 + (dy/dx)^2]}\, dx.$$

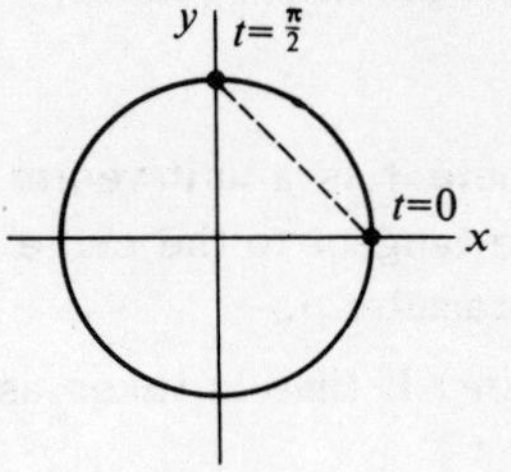

Fig. 9.

Example 4a (compare with Example 4). Find the length from (2, 7) to (6, 19) of the curve

$$y = 3x + 1.$$

Here $dy/dx = 3$, giving

$$s = \int_2^6 \sqrt{10}\, dx$$

$$= [(\sqrt{10})x]_2^6$$

$$= 4\sqrt{10}.$$

Example 5. The position of a particle at time t is given by $\mathbf{r} = (3\cos t)\hat{\mathbf{i}} + (3\sin t)\hat{\mathbf{j}}$ How far does it travel in the first $\frac{1}{2}\pi$ seconds?

$$s = \int_0^{\frac{1}{2}\pi} \sqrt{(\dot{x}^2 + \dot{y}^2)}\, dt$$

$$= \int_0^{\frac{1}{2}\pi} \sqrt{(9\sin^2 t + 9\cos^2 t)}\, dt$$

$$= \int_0^{\frac{1}{2}\pi} 3\, dt$$

$$= 3(\tfrac{1}{2}\pi).$$

However,

$$\mathbf{r}(\tfrac{1}{2}\pi) - \mathbf{r}(0) = \begin{pmatrix}0\\1\end{pmatrix} - \begin{pmatrix}1\\0\end{pmatrix} = \begin{pmatrix}-1\\1\end{pmatrix},$$

so that the displacement is only $\sqrt{2}$. The particle has of course moved with speed 3, one quarter of the way round a circle.

3.3 Sign convention

It is necessary to evaluate a square root to obtain s. It seems most reasonable to choose the sign of s so that an increase in the parameter p gives an increase in the value of s. This we shall assume throughout. However, it should be noted that a change in the choice of parameter can thereby sometimes reverse the direction of s. For example, consider the line $x + y = 1$. (Figure 10.) Taking x as parameter, as x increases we move *down* the line from left to right. Taking y as parameter, as y increases we move *up* the line from right to left.

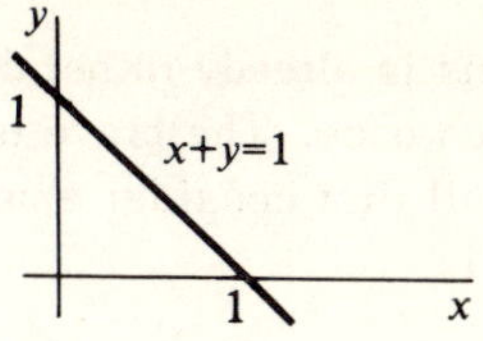

Fig. 10.

Note: There are in fact very few curves for which it is possible to evaluate the integral for their arc length explicitly and in practice they must often be tackled by numerical approximations, such as Simpson's rule. (e.g. Exercise C, Question 10.)

EXERCISE C

Find general expressions for the lengths of the curves given in the first 6 questions.

1. $y = 4x + 3$.

2. $x = 2p^3$, $y = 3p^2$.

3. $x = 3 \sin p$, $y = 3 \cos p$.

4. $x = 5p$, $y = 12p$.

5. The circumference of a circle of radius c.

6. The curve, a cycloid, traced out by the mark in Exercise A, Question 11: $x = \alpha + \sin \alpha$, $y = 1 - \cos \alpha$.

7. Calculate the actual distance travelled by the 'plane (see Example 1) in the first 100s:

$$\mathbf{r} = t^2\hat{\mathbf{i}} + 0{\cdot}01t^3\hat{\mathbf{j}}.$$

8. What is the angular displacement of two points on the surface of the earth, assumed spherical, for which a straight tunnel between them would only be two-thirds as long as the distance along the surface? (Find an equation for the angle and give an approximate solution.)

9. Find the length of the curve $(x/a)^{2/3} + (y/a)^{2/3} = 1$.

10. Estimate the length of the perimeter of the ellipse $4x^2 + y^2 = 4$.

4. POLAR COORDINATES

You may have already attempted to find an expression for the motion of a windscreen wiper. (Exercise A, Question 10.) As with most *rotational* motion, this can be cumbersome using cartesian coordinates and is best done using polar representation.

$$r = c, \qquad \theta = k \sin bt, \qquad \text{where } b, c, k \text{ are constants.}$$

Suggest some suitable values for these constants.

The area swept out by the blade depends on the arc length, while the reaction between blade and wiper arm depends on the acceleration $\ddot{\mathbf{r}}$. How are these to be worked out using polar coordinates?

A possible line of approach is to express $\mathbf{r}$ in terms of its cartesian components and make use of our previous results.

$$\mathbf{r} = r\cos\theta\,\hat{\mathbf{i}} + r\sin\theta\,\hat{\mathbf{j}}.$$

This is already rather daunting to differentiate even once. The brave reader may care to try. We shall first consider a unit vector $\hat{\mathbf{r}}$ in the direction of $\mathbf{r}$.

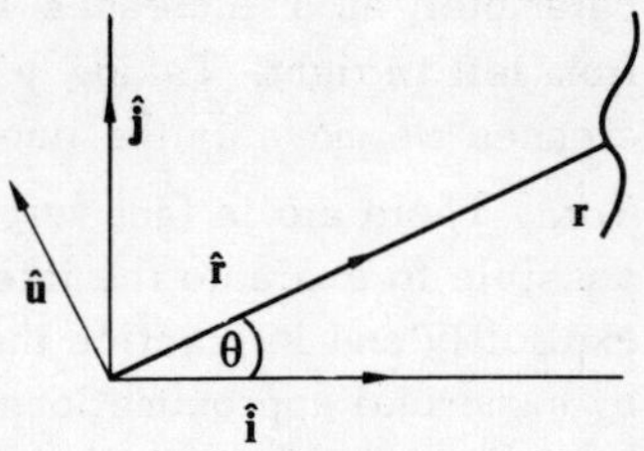

Fig. 11.

4.1 Derivative of unit vector

Since $r = 1$,

$$\hat{\mathbf{r}} = \cos\theta\,\hat{\mathbf{i}} + \sin\theta\,\hat{\mathbf{j}} = \begin{pmatrix}\cos\theta\\ \sin\theta\end{pmatrix},$$

$$\dot{\hat{\mathbf{r}}} = -\sin\theta\cdot\dot{\theta}\,\hat{\mathbf{i}} + \cos\theta\cdot\dot{\theta}\,\hat{\mathbf{j}} = \begin{pmatrix}-\sin\theta\\ \cos\theta\end{pmatrix}\dot{\theta} = \dot{\theta}\,\hat{\mathbf{u}}.$$

So $\dot{\hat{\mathbf{r}}} = \dot{\theta}\,\hat{\mathbf{u}}$, where $\hat{\mathbf{u}}$ is a unit vector, called the *transverse* unit vector, obtained from $\hat{\mathbf{r}}$ by a positive (anticlockwise) quarter-turn

$$\begin{pmatrix}0 & -1\\ 1 & 0\end{pmatrix}\begin{pmatrix}\cos\theta\\ \sin\theta\end{pmatrix} = \begin{pmatrix}-\sin\theta\\ \cos\theta\end{pmatrix}$$

and $\dot{\theta}$ measures the rate of change of direction of $\hat{\mathbf{r}}$.

Geometrically, the unit vector $\hat{\mathbf{r}}$ moves to a new position $\hat{\mathbf{r}}_N$. The change $\mathbf{c}$ in $\hat{\mathbf{r}}$ is found from a vector triangle.

We have established that the initial direction of change is perpendicular to $\hat{\mathbf{r}}$ and that the magnitude of the rate of change is $\dot{\theta}$, thus depending only on how the direction of $\hat{\mathbf{r}}$ changes. If the direction of $\hat{\mathbf{r}}$ does not change, then $\dot{\theta} = 0$, which implies that $\dot{\hat{\mathbf{r}}} = 0$ and thus $\hat{\mathbf{r}}$ is unaltered. This is the case with the base vectors $\hat{\mathbf{i}}$ and $\hat{\mathbf{j}}$.

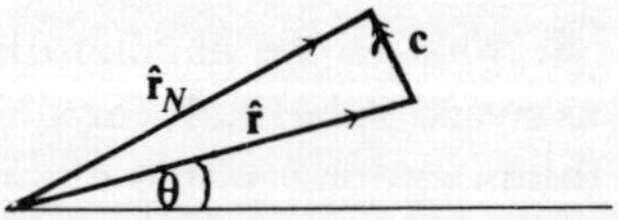

Fig. 12.

4.2 Derivative of non-unit vector

If $\mathbf{r}$ is of constant, but not unit, length, it is very convenient to exhibit its magnitude r and direction $\hat{\mathbf{r}}$ by writing it as

$$\begin{aligned}\mathbf{r} &= r\hat{\mathbf{r}}\\ \Rightarrow \dot{\mathbf{r}} &= r\dot{\hat{\mathbf{r}}} \quad \text{(since } r \text{ is constant)}\\ &= r\dot{\theta}\,\hat{\mathbf{u}},\end{aligned}$$

showing that the rate of change of $\mathbf{r}$ is still perpendicular to $\mathbf{r}$ but is r times as great as for a unit vector $\hat{\mathbf{r}}$. In fact the situation is simply an enlargement of Figure 12 with scale factor r.

If $\mathbf{r}$ changes in magnitude as well as direction we have

$$\begin{aligned}\mathbf{r} &= r\hat{\mathbf{r}}\\ \Rightarrow \dot{\mathbf{r}} &= r\dot{\hat{\mathbf{r}}} + \dot{r}\hat{\mathbf{r}} \quad \text{(since } r \text{ now varies with time)}\\ &= r\dot{\theta}\hat{\mathbf{u}} + \dot{r}\hat{\mathbf{r}},\end{aligned}$$

giving a change of $\dot{r}$ in the direction of $\mathbf{r}$, as well as the change of $r\dot{\theta}$ perpendicular to $\mathbf{r}$ as before.

So, in general, the velocity $\dot{\mathbf{r}}$ has two components, $\dot{r}$ *radially* and $r\dot{\theta}$ *transversely*.

Thus
$$\begin{aligned} v &= \sqrt{(\dot{r}^2 + r^2\dot{\theta}^2)} \\ &= \sqrt{(\dot{r}^2 + r^2\omega^2)}, \end{aligned}$$

where ω is frequently used to denote the magnitude $\dot{\theta}$ of the angular velocity.

Example 6.
$$\begin{aligned} r &= 0{\cdot}3, \qquad \theta = \sin 2t \\ \Rightarrow \dot{\mathbf{r}} &= 0{\cdot}3\dot{\theta}\hat{\mathbf{u}} \end{aligned}$$

$\Rightarrow$ velocity $= 0{\cdot}6 \cos 2t$ perpendicular to $\mathbf{r}$ (i.e. tangentially, since the path is circular).

Example 7.
$$r = 10 + \sin t, \qquad \theta = 2t,$$
this is oscillatory motion about a circle.
$$\begin{aligned} \dot{\mathbf{r}} &= \dot{r}\hat{\mathbf{r}} + r\dot{\theta}\hat{\mathbf{u}} \\ &= (\cos t)\hat{\mathbf{r}} + (20 + 2\sin t)\hat{\mathbf{u}}. \end{aligned}$$

4.3 Arc length

With parameter p we get:
$$\begin{aligned} \mathbf{r} &= r\hat{\mathbf{r}} \\ \Rightarrow \mathbf{r}' &= r'\hat{\mathbf{r}} + r\theta'\hat{\mathbf{u}} \\ \Rightarrow s'\hat{\mathbf{t}} &= r'\hat{\mathbf{r}} + r\theta'\hat{\mathbf{u}} \\ \Rightarrow s'^2 &= r'^2 + (r\theta')^2, \text{ since } \hat{\mathbf{t}} \text{ is a unit vector,} \\ \Rightarrow s &= \int \sqrt{[(r')^2 + (r\theta')^2]}\,dp. \end{aligned}$$

Note: With time as the parameter this becomes $v^2 = \dot{r}^2 + (r\dot{\theta})^2$. With θ as parameter we get:
$$s = \int \sqrt{\left[\left(\frac{dr}{d\theta}\right)^2 + r^2\right]}\,d\theta.$$

Example 8.
$$\begin{aligned} r &= \cos^2 p, \quad \theta = 2p \\ \Rightarrow r' &= -2\sin p\cos p, \quad \theta' = 2 \\ \Rightarrow s &= \int \sqrt{[4\sin^2 p\cos^2 p + 4\cos^4 p]}\,dp \\ &= \int 2|\cos p|\sqrt{[\sin^2 p + \cos^2 p]}\,dp \\ &= [2|\sin p|]. \end{aligned}$$

Alternatively: $r = \cos^2\tfrac{1}{2}\theta \Rightarrow \dfrac{dr}{d\theta} = -\sin\tfrac{1}{2}\theta\cos\tfrac{1}{2}\theta$

$$\Rightarrow \quad s = \int\sqrt{[\sin^2\tfrac{1}{2}\theta\cos^2\tfrac{1}{2}\theta + \cos^4\tfrac{1}{2}\theta]}\,d\theta$$

$$= \int|\cos\tfrac{1}{2}\theta|\sqrt{[\sin^2\tfrac{1}{2}\theta + \cos^2\tfrac{1}{2}\theta]}\,d\theta$$

$$= [2|\sin\tfrac{1}{2}\theta|].$$

4.4 Acceleration

$$\begin{aligned} \mathbf{r} &= r\hat{\mathbf{r}}, \\ \mathbf{v} = \dot{\mathbf{r}} &= \dot{r}\hat{\mathbf{r}} + r\dot{\theta}\hat{\mathbf{u}}, \\ \mathbf{a} = \dot{\mathbf{v}} &= \ddot{r}\hat{\mathbf{r}} + \dot{r}\dot{\hat{\mathbf{r}}} + (\dot{r}\dot{\theta} + r\ddot{\theta})\hat{\mathbf{u}} + r\dot{\theta}\dot{\hat{\mathbf{u}}}, \\ &= \ddot{r}\hat{\mathbf{r}} + \dot{r}\dot{\theta}\hat{\mathbf{u}} + (\dot{r}\dot{\theta} + r\ddot{\theta})\hat{\mathbf{u}} - r\dot{\theta}\dot{\theta}\hat{\mathbf{r}}, \end{aligned}$$

since $-\hat{\mathbf{r}}$ is obtained from $\hat{\mathbf{u}}$ by a quarter turn

$$\Rightarrow \mathbf{a} = (\ddot{r} - r\dot{\theta}^2)\hat{\mathbf{r}} + (2\dot{r}\dot{\theta} + r\ddot{\theta})\hat{\mathbf{u}}.$$

So, in the most general situation, the acceleration has components $(\ddot{r} - r\dot{\theta}^2)$ radially and $(2\dot{r}\dot{\theta} + r\ddot{\theta})$ transversely.

Special cases

(1) θ constant: the motion is in a straight line through the origin. $\dot{\theta} = \ddot{\theta} = 0$ and the acceleration reduces to $\ddot{r}$ radially, i.e. in the direction of the motion.

(2) r and $\dot{\theta}$ constant: the motion is with constant speed $v(= r\dot{\theta})$ round a circle. The acceleration reduces to $-r\omega^2$ radially, i.e. $r\omega^2$ towards the centre of the circle, which may also be written as v^2/r.

(3) r only is constant: the motion is circular but the speed is not constant. There is an acceleration $r\ddot{\theta}$ $(= \dot{v})$, transversely, i.e. tangential to the circle, as well as $-r\omega^2$ $(= -v^2/r)$ radially.

Example 9 (see Example 6). $r = 0{\cdot}3,\ \theta = \sin 2t.$

Here r is constant so

$$\begin{aligned} \mathbf{a} &= r\dot{\theta}^2\hat{\mathbf{r}} + r\ddot{\theta}\hat{\mathbf{u}} \\ &= -1{\cdot}2\cos^2 2t\hat{\mathbf{r}} - 1{\cdot}2\sin 2t\,\hat{\mathbf{u}}. \end{aligned}$$

This is a reasonable model of the motion of the blade of a windscreen wiper (mentioned at the start of this section). To give the blade this acceleration, assuming no resistance to motion, the interaction between wiper arm and blade must be at an angle α to the arm, where at any instant $\tan\alpha = \sin 2t/\cos^2 2t$.

EXERCISE D

1. Sketch the curve $r = \sin p,\ \theta = 2p$. Calculate the unit tangent vector for $p = \tfrac{3}{2}\pi$

and for $p = \frac{7}{6}\pi$ and show them clearly on your sketch.

2. The position of a point after t seconds is given by $r = \cos t$, $\theta = t$. Show that the point traces out a circle with constant speed, but that the speed is not equal to $r\dot{\theta}$. Show that the acceleration is of constant magnitude and is always directed towards the centre of the circle, but is not equal to v^2/r.

Find the general expressions for the lengths of the curves in Questions 3 to 6.

3. $r = 3$, $\theta = p$.

4. $r = 3p$, $\theta = \log p$.

5. $r = 2\cos p$, $\theta = p$.

6. $r = 2e^{\theta}$.

7. Use polar coordinates to obtain an expression for the length of a portion of the circumference of a circle of radius c.

8. The position of a particle at time t is given by

$$r = 10 + \sin t, \qquad \theta = 2t \text{ (see Example 7).}$$

Sketch the path. Calculate the velocity and acceleration when $t = \frac{1}{3}\pi$ and when $t = \frac{2}{3}\pi$, indicating the components and resultant clearly on your sketch.

9. Show that for a particle which moves so that $r = \sqrt{(at + b)}$ its radial acceleration is $-v^2/r$, whatever the function for θ.

5. CURVATURE

Anyone who has driven along a winding country lane should already have a good feeling for motion on a curve. The amount by which the direction changes, and how suddenly this occurs, is particularly significant. This we now investigate, but it would be valuable for you to decide how you would set about this, before reading on.

With every position $\mathbf{r}$ of a point P on a curve is associated a unit *tangent* $\hat{\mathbf{t}}$, in the direction of the curve at P, making an angle ψ with the x-axis. So the rate of change of $\hat{\mathbf{t}}$ with respect to the parameter p is given (see Section 4.1) by:

$$\hat{\mathbf{t}}' = \psi'\hat{\mathbf{n}}$$

where ψ' is the rate of change of direction of the curve as the parameter changes and the *normal* unit vector $\hat{\mathbf{n}}$ is obtained from $\hat{\mathbf{t}}$ by a positive quarter turn. If $\psi' > 0$, $\hat{\mathbf{n}}$ is directed to the concave side of the curve.

To calculate the rate of change ψ' we shall need to express ψ in terms of cartesian or polar coordinates.

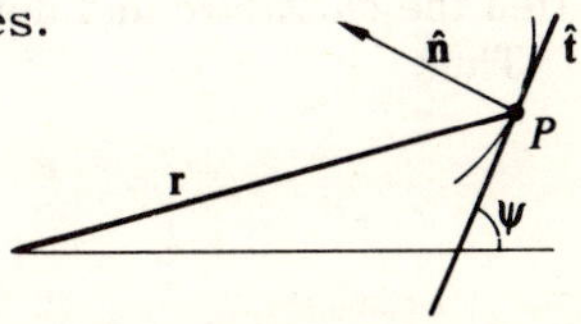

Fig. 13.

Now

$$
\begin{aligned}
s'\hat{\mathbf{t}} &= \mathbf{r}' \\
&= x'\hat{\mathbf{i}} + y'\hat{\mathbf{j}} \\
\Rightarrow \quad \hat{\mathbf{t}} &= x'/s'\hat{\mathbf{i}} + y'/s'\hat{\mathbf{j}} \\
\Rightarrow \quad \cos\psi\hat{\mathbf{i}} + \sin\psi\hat{\mathbf{j}} &= x'/s'\,\hat{\mathbf{i}} + y'/s'\,\hat{\mathbf{j}} \\
\Rightarrow \quad \cos\psi &= x'/s', \ \sin\psi = y'/s' \\
\Rightarrow \quad \tan\psi &= y'/x'
\end{aligned}
$$

(this is merely proving, from our definitions, that $\tan\psi$ is the gradient of the curve).

$$\psi = \tan^{-1}(y'/x')$$

$$\Longrightarrow \psi' = \frac{1}{1+z^2}\cdot\frac{dz}{dp} \quad \text{where } z = y'/x'$$

$$\psi' = [(x'y'' - y'x'')/x'^2]/[1 + (y'/x')^2]$$
$$= (x'y'' - y'x'')/(x'^2 + y'^2).$$

This tells us how the direction of the curve changes with the parameter p.

Example 10. Consider the locus $x = 2p$, $y = 6p + 1$.

Here $x' = 2$, $y' = 6$, $x'' = 0$, $y'' = 0$, and $\psi' = 0$. ψ is thus a constant. In fact $\tan\psi = y'/x' = 3$, and the locus is the straight line $y = 3x + 1$.

Example 11. For the circle

$$x = a\cos p, \qquad y = a\sin p,$$
$$x' = -a\sin p, \qquad y' = a\cos p.$$
$$x'' = -a\cos p, \qquad y'' = -a\sin p,$$

and

$$\psi' = \frac{a^2\sin^2 p + a^2\cos^2 p}{a^2\sin^2 p + a^2\cos^2 p} = 1.$$

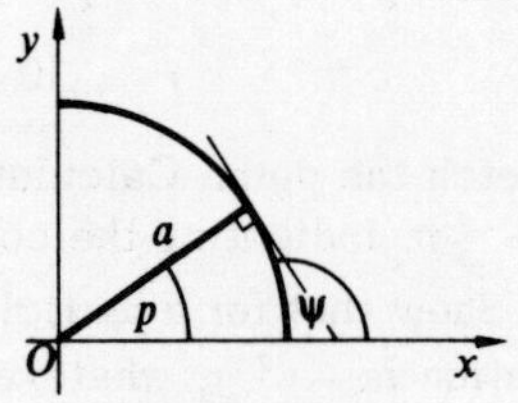

Fig. 14.

Integrating, $\psi = p + c$. Figure 14 shows that $c = \frac{1}{2}\pi$. This could have been obtained directly:

$$x' = -a\sin p,$$
$$y' = a\cos p$$
$$\Longrightarrow \cos\psi = -\sin p \text{ and } \sin\psi = \cos p,$$
$$\Longrightarrow \psi = p + \tfrac{1}{2}\pi \pmod{2\pi}.$$

5.1 Kappa

The acceleration, and thus the forces, depend on the change in direction since:

$$\mathbf{v} = v\hat{\mathbf{t}}$$
$$\Longrightarrow \mathbf{a} = \dot{v}\hat{\mathbf{t}} + v\dot{\psi}\hat{\mathbf{n}},$$

where time is the parameter.

However the sharpness of a bend depends on the change of direction as the position of P varies. The rate of change of ψ with respect to the arc length s is called the *curvature* and denoted by κ (kappa).

Thus

$$\kappa = \frac{d\psi}{ds} = \frac{\psi'}{s'} = \frac{x'y'' - y'x''}{[x'^2 + y'^2]^{3/2}}.$$

Clearly, the greater the value of κ the more sharply the curve turns.

Example 12. Continuing with the circle $x^2 + y^2 = a^2$ of Example 9:

$$\kappa = \frac{1}{[a^2\sin^2 p + a^2\cos^2 p]^{1/2}} = \frac{1}{a}.$$

The smaller the radius a of the circle, the larger κ becomes, and the tighter the circle is. Note that the curvature $1/a$ is the same for every point P of the circle.

5.2 Special parameter

If x is taken as the parameter: $x' = 1$, $x'' = 0$

$$\Rightarrow \kappa = \frac{d^2y}{dx^2} \bigg/ \left[1 + \left(\frac{dy}{dx}\right)^2\right]^{3/2}.$$

Example 13. Find the curvature at (1, 4) for the curve: $4y = x^3$.

$$\frac{dy}{dx} = \frac{3}{4}x^2,$$

$$\frac{d^2y}{dx^2} = \frac{3}{2}x,$$

$$\kappa = \frac{3}{2}x \bigg/ \left[1 + \frac{9}{16}x^4\right]^{3/2}$$

$$= \frac{96}{125}, \text{ when } x = 1.$$

In most cases it is best not to use any formula for curvature, but to proceed from first principles.

Example 14. Find the curvature at any point of the curve

$$x = a\cos 3p + 3a\cos p,$$
$$y = a\sin 3p + 3a\sin p.$$

Here $x' = -3a\sin 3p - 3a\sin p = -6a\sin 2p\cos p$

$y' = 3a\cos 3p + 3a\cos p = +6a\cos 2p\cos p.$

Thus $$s'\hat{t} = \begin{pmatrix} x' \\ y' \end{pmatrix} = 6a\cos p \begin{pmatrix} -\sin 2p \\ \cos 2p \end{pmatrix}.$$

Since $\begin{pmatrix} -\sin 2p \\ \cos 2p \end{pmatrix}$ is a unit vector, it is now clear that $\hat{t} = \begin{pmatrix} -\sin 2p \\ \cos 2p \end{pmatrix}$ and

$s' = 6a\cos p.$

Hence $\cos\psi = -\sin 2p$, $\sin\psi = \cos 2p$, and $\psi = \frac{1}{2}\pi + 2p.$

Finally, $\kappa = \psi'/s' = 2/(6a\cos p) = 1/(3a\cos p).$

5.3 Polar coordinates

The expression for curvature in polar coordinates is so cumbersome that it is rarely used. Instead, it is best to use θ as a parameter for cartesian coordinates:

$$r = f(\theta) \Rightarrow \begin{cases} x = f(\theta)\cos\theta \\ y = f(\theta)\sin\theta \end{cases}.$$

EXERCISE E

Find the curvature at a general point for each of the curves in the first 8 questions.

1. $y = 4x + 3$ **2.** $x = 2p^3,\ y = 3p^2$.

3. $x = 3\sin p,\ y = 3\cos p$. **4.** $x = 5p,\ y = 12p$.

5. $r = 3,\ \theta = p$. **6.** $r = 3p,\ \theta = \log p$.

7. $r = 2\cos p,\ \theta = p$. **8.** $r = 2e^{\theta}$.

9. A car drives along the curve $4y^3 = 27x^2$, starting at the origin, at a constant speed of 13 units/s. Find its speed in the x and y directions after 4s.

10. A car travels along the curve $r = p^2,\ \theta = 3p$ at a steady speed of 25 units/s, starting at the origin. What is its position after 5s?

11. A Z-bend is in the shape of the curve $y = (x+1)x(x-1)$. Find where the curve is sharpest (curvature greatest) and show your result on a sketch.

12. Find the arc length and the curvature at a general point for the curve

$$x = 4a\cos\theta + a\cos 4\theta,$$
$$y = 4a\sin\theta + a\sin 4\theta.$$

Sketch the curve and find its total length. It is a three-cusped epicycloid.

13. Find the curvature at any point of the curve

$$x = a\cos^3 t, \qquad y = a\sin^3 t.$$

Sketch the curve and find its total length.

6. CIRCLE OF CURVATURE

We know from Example 10 that the curvature for a circle of radius a is $1/a$. This gives us a standard of comparison for the curvature of a curve at any point.

The fact itself is fairly obvious – if the radius turns through an angle α, the point on the circumference moves a distance $a\alpha$ along the curve, while its tangent turns through an angle β, which clearly equals α. (Figure 15.)

$$\Rightarrow \kappa = \frac{\beta}{a\alpha} = \frac{1}{a}$$

$$\Rightarrow a = \frac{1}{\kappa}.$$

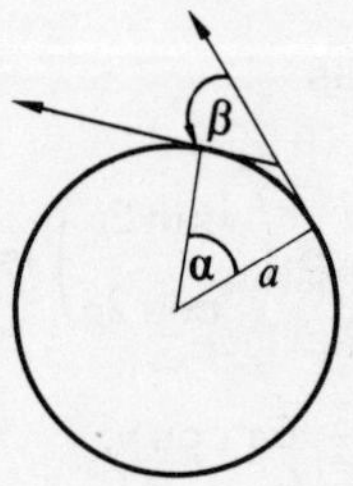

Fig. 15.

Thus a circle of curvature κ has radius $1/\kappa$. $1/\kappa$ is usually denoted by ρ, and is called the *radius of curvature.*

ρ is the radius of the circle with the same curvature as that at the point P of the curve we are considering.

The circle with radius ρ, touching the curve internally at P, is called the *circle of curvature* at P.

Thus any curve can be considered as being composed of a series of arcs of different circles.

6.1 Centre of curvature

The centre of the circle of curvature is called the *centre of curvature* at the point of the curve being considered.

It is evidently on the concave side of the curve (see Figure 16) and $PK = \rho$. Its position vector is therefore

$$OK = \mathbf{r} + \rho\hat{\mathbf{n}} = \begin{pmatrix} x \\ y \end{pmatrix} + \frac{ds}{d\psi}\begin{pmatrix} -\sin\psi \\ \cos\psi \end{pmatrix},$$

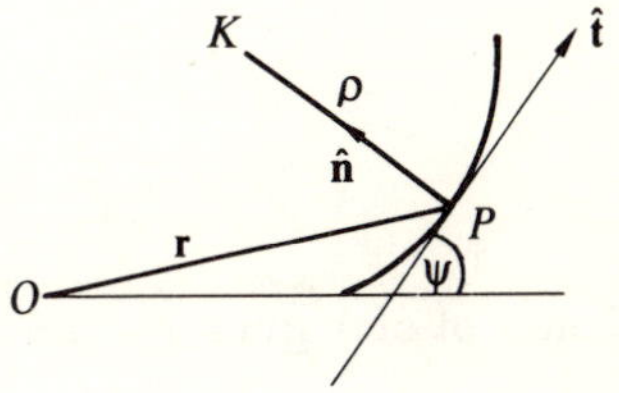

Fig. 16.

where we have chosen to measure s so that it increases with ψ.

Now
$$\frac{d\mathbf{r}}{ds} = \begin{pmatrix} dx/ds \\ dy/ds \end{pmatrix} = \hat{\mathbf{t}} = \begin{pmatrix} \cos\psi \\ \sin\psi \end{pmatrix},$$

so that

$$\cos\psi = dx/ds \qquad \text{and} \qquad \sin\psi = dy/ds.$$

Hence
$$\mathbf{OK} = \begin{pmatrix} x \\ y \end{pmatrix} + \frac{ds}{d\psi}\begin{pmatrix} -dy/ds \\ dx/ds \end{pmatrix}$$

$$= \begin{pmatrix} x - dy/d\psi \\ y + dx/d\psi \end{pmatrix}.$$

The centre of curvature at a point (x, y) of a curve is therefore the point

$$\left(x - \frac{dy}{d\psi}, y + \frac{dx}{d\psi}\right),$$

with position vector $\mathbf{r} + \rho\hat{\mathbf{n}}$.

If two curves meet at P, x, y must have the same value at P. If they touch at P, they must also have the same gradient dy/dx at P. If they have the same curvature at P, they must also have the same second derivative d^2y/dx^2 at P. (See Question 7 in Exercise F.)

As the tangent is the best linear approximation to a curve at a point, so the circle of curvature may be thought of as the best circular approximation to a curve.

Example 15. Find the radius and centre of curvature at $P(1, 4)$ for the curve:

$$4y = x^3$$

$$\kappa = \frac{96}{125} \quad \text{(see Example 13)}$$

$$\Rightarrow \rho = \frac{125}{96}.$$

Now
$$\frac{dy}{dx} = \frac{3}{4}x^2.$$

At P:
$$\Rightarrow \mathbf{t} = \begin{pmatrix} 4 \\ 3 \end{pmatrix}$$

$$\Rightarrow \hat{\mathbf{n}} = \frac{1}{5}\begin{pmatrix} -3 \\ 4 \end{pmatrix}.$$

Centre of curvature $\mathbf{r} + \rho\hat{\mathbf{n}} = \begin{pmatrix} 1 \\ 4 \end{pmatrix} + \frac{25}{96}\begin{pmatrix} -3 \\ 4 \end{pmatrix}.$

Giving the point:
$$\left(\frac{7}{32}, \frac{121}{24}\right).$$

6.2 Acceleration

We saw (Section 5.1) that the acceleration depended on the rate of change of direction $\dot{\psi}$.

Now
$$\dot{\psi} = \frac{d\psi}{ds} \times \frac{ds}{dt} = \kappa v = v/\rho.$$

Thus
$$\mathbf{a} = \dot{v}\hat{\mathbf{t}} + v\dot{\psi}\hat{\mathbf{n}}$$
$$= \dot{v}\hat{\mathbf{t}} + v^2/\rho\,\hat{\mathbf{n}},$$

showing that the components of acceleration for an object moving along a curve with speed v (not necessarily constant) are $\dot{v}$ *tangentially* and v^2/ρ *normally* which are, of course, the same as if the object had at this moment been moving along a circle of radius ρ (see Section 4.4).

Example 16. A car travels at constant speed 12 m/s along the horizontal road given by $4y = x^3$. What is the greatest horizontal force between the wheels and the road?

Here $\dot{v} = 0$, so to remain on the road the car must be accelerated normally at v^2/ρ $(= \kappa v^2)$ m/s.

This is greatest when κ is greatest.

Now
$$\kappa = \frac{3}{2}x\left[1 + \frac{9}{16}x^4\right]^{-3/2} \quad \text{(see Example 13).}$$

Differentiating we find
$$\frac{d\kappa}{dx} = 0 \Rightarrow x = (16/45)^{1/4}$$

$$\Rightarrow \kappa = 2^{-3/2} \cdot 3^{-1} \cdot 5^{5/4}.$$

Thus a force of $48.2^{-3/2} \cdot 5^{5/4} M$ (= $127M$) newtons is needed, where M is the mass of the car.

EXERCISE F

1. Find the radius and centre of curvature at a general point on the curve $x = 4a\cos\theta + a\cos 4\theta,\ y = 4a\sin\theta + a\sin 4\theta$.

2. Find the radius and centre of curvature at a general point on the curve $x = a\cos^3 t,\ y = a\sin^3 t$.

3. Prove that the centre of curvature at a point (x, y) of a curve is at the point

$$\left(x - \frac{y'(x'^2 + y'^2)}{x'y'' - y'x''},\qquad y + \frac{x'(x'^2 + y'^2)}{x'y'' - y'x''}\right),$$

where dashes denote differentiation with respect to a parameter p.

4. Sketch the *equiangular spiral* $\mathbf{r} = ae^{k\theta}$. Prove that $\hat{\mathbf{t}}$ is a scalar multiple of $k\hat{\mathbf{r}} + \hat{\mathbf{u}}$ and hence that the curve makes a fixed angle ϕ with $\mathbf{r}$ at every point. Use this to express ψ in terms of θ. Show that the radius of curvature is proportional to r.

5. When cornering, a vehicle is liable to skid if the force normal to the wheels reaches a certain (fixed) limit. Show that for most rapid cornering the speed should be kept proportional to the square root of the radius of curvature.

6. Find the radius and centre of curvature at the point P of the curve $x = 2p^3$, $y = 3p^2$, with parameter p.

7. Repeat Question 6, using the following method:

Let the equation of the circle of curvature be

$$(x - a)^2 + (y - b)^2 = \rho^2.$$

The circle and the curve must both pass through P. They must have the same gradient at P.

They must have the same value of d^2y/dx^2 at P.

These three conditions determine the values of a, b, p.

(This method can be used for any curve.)

*7. INVOLUTE AND EVOLUTE

Throughout this section we shall take the arc length s as our parameter, so that:

$$\mathbf{r}' = \hat{\mathbf{t}},\qquad \hat{\mathbf{t}}' = \kappa\hat{\mathbf{n}},\qquad \hat{\mathbf{n}}' = -\kappa\hat{\mathbf{t}}.$$

7.1 Involute

With any curve there is associated another curve, its *involute*, such that the normal at any point on the involute is a tangent to the original curve.

Consider any point P_1, with position vector $\mathbf{r}_1$, on the involute, and let the normal at P_1 touch the curve at P. (Figure 17.) Thus P_1 lies on the tangent at P. $\Rightarrow \mathbf{r}_1 = \mathbf{r} + \lambda\hat{\mathbf{t}}$, where λ depends on the position of P. Differentiating with respect to s_1, the arc length of the involute

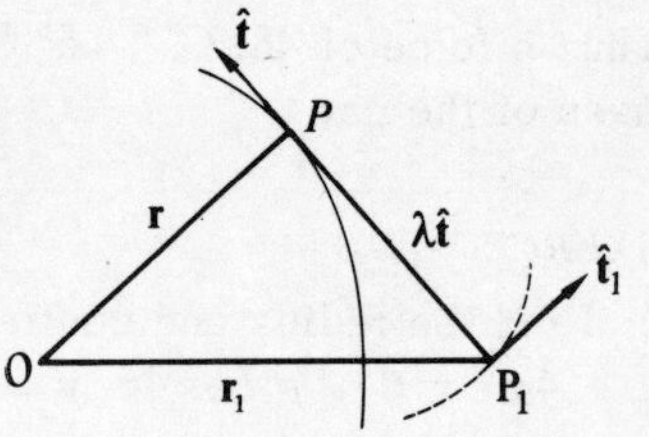

Fig. 17.

$$\Rightarrow \hat{\mathbf{t}}_1 = [\hat{\mathbf{t}} + \lambda'\hat{\mathbf{t}} + \lambda\kappa\hat{\mathbf{n}}]\frac{ds}{ds_1},$$

where $\hat{\mathbf{t}}_1$ is the unit tangent at P_1; but since PP_1 is normal to the involute

$$\begin{aligned} \hat{\mathbf{t}}\cdot\hat{\mathbf{t}}_1 &= 0 \\ \Rightarrow \quad \hat{\mathbf{t}}\cdot\hat{\mathbf{t}} + \lambda'\hat{\mathbf{t}}\cdot\hat{\mathbf{t}} + \lambda\kappa\hat{\mathbf{t}}\cdot\hat{\mathbf{n}} &= 0 \\ \Rightarrow 1 + \lambda' &= 0 \\ \Rightarrow \quad \lambda &= -s + c \\ \Rightarrow \quad \mathbf{r}_1 &= \mathbf{r} - (s - c)\hat{\mathbf{t}}. \end{aligned}$$

Thus there is a family of involutes, given by different values of the constant c. Furthermore, since $PP_1 = s - c$, each involute is the locus of a point on a length of string which is placed along the original curve and then unwrapped.

Example 17. To find the involutes of a circle $\mathbf{r} = a\hat{\mathbf{r}}$.

Here

$$\begin{aligned} \mathbf{r}_1 &= a\hat{\mathbf{r}} - (a\theta - c)\hat{\mathbf{t}} \\ \Rightarrow \quad x_1 &= a\cos\theta + (a\theta - c)\sin\theta, \\ \text{and} \quad y_1 &= a\sin\theta - (a\theta - c)\cos\theta. \end{aligned}$$

Draw some of these curves by unwrapping string from round a tin.

7.2 Evolute

With any curve there is also associated another curve, its *evolute*, such that a tangent to the evolute is a normal to the original curve. Let P_2, with position vector $\mathbf{r}_2$, be the point of the evolute lying on the normal to the curve at P. (Figure 18.)

Then $\mathbf{r}_2 = \mathbf{r} + \mu\hat{\mathbf{n}}$, where μ depends on P. Differentiating with respect to s_2, the arc length of the evolute

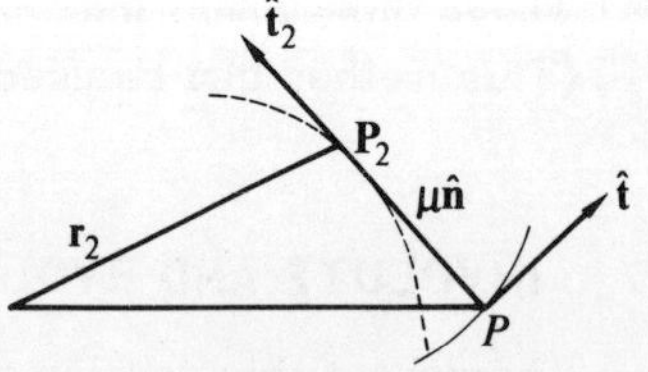

Fig. 18.

$$\Rightarrow \hat{\mathbf{t}}_2 = [\hat{\mathbf{t}} - \mu\kappa\hat{\mathbf{t}} + \mu'\hat{\mathbf{n}}]\frac{ds}{ds_2}.$$

But $\hat{\mathbf{t}}_2 = \hat{\mathbf{n}}$, if the normal at P is to be the tangent at P_2.

Hence $\quad 1 - \mu\kappa = 0 \quad$ and $\quad \mu'\dfrac{ds}{ds_2} = 1,$

since $\hat{\mathbf{t}}_2$ is in the direction of $\hat{\mathbf{n}}$ and has unit length,

$$\Rightarrow \mu = 1/\kappa = \rho, \quad \text{and} \quad \frac{d\rho}{ds}\cdot\frac{ds}{ds_2} = 1$$

$$\Rightarrow \mathbf{r}_2 = \mathbf{r} + \rho\hat{\mathbf{n}} \quad \text{and} \quad s_2 = \rho + c.$$

Hence there is a unique evolute associated with a curve and it is the locus of its centre of curvature, since $PP_2 = \rho$.

Further, since its arc-length, measured from a suitable zero-point, is equal to the radius of curvature, the original curve is one of its involutes, with $P_2P = s_2 - c$. (Compare with Section 7.1.) 'Involution' and 'Evolution' may therefore be thought of as inverse operations; the evolute of an involute of any curve is the curve itself.

7.3 Parametric functions

We have frequently assumed that we may take the arc length s as our parameter and that it is then possible to find suitable parametric functions for the position vector $\mathbf{r}$. With this assumption, we may use Taylor's approximation to obtain

$$\mathbf{r} \approx \mathbf{r}_0 + s\dot{\mathbf{r}}_0 + \frac{s^2}{2}\ddot{\mathbf{r}}_0 + \frac{s^3}{6}\cdot\dddot{\mathbf{r}}_0,$$

where $\mathbf{r}_0$ is the position vector of the point A from which s is measured.

Hence $$\mathbf{r} \approx \mathbf{r}_0 + s\hat{\mathbf{t}}_0 + \frac{s^2}{2}\kappa\hat{\mathbf{n}}_0 + \frac{s^3}{6}[\dot{\kappa}\hat{\mathbf{n}}_0 - \kappa^2\hat{\mathbf{t}}_0],$$

and $$\mathbf{r} - \mathbf{r}_0 \approx \left[s - \frac{\kappa^2 s^3}{6}\right]\hat{\mathbf{t}}_0 + \left[\frac{\kappa s^2}{2} + \frac{\dot{\kappa}s^3}{6}\right]\hat{\mathbf{n}}_0.$$

If we take axes through A in directions of $\hat{\mathbf{t}}_0$ and $\hat{\mathbf{n}}_0$, we get:

$$x \approx s - \frac{\kappa^2 s^3}{6}, \qquad y \approx \frac{\kappa s^2}{2} + \frac{\dot{\kappa}s^3}{6},$$

which give approximate parametric functions for $\mathbf{r}$. Note that, near the origin, approximately

$$x = s, \qquad y = \frac{\kappa s^2}{2};$$

so that the curve approximates to the parabola $y = \frac{1}{2}\kappa x^2$ and the curvature at the origin is the limit of $2y/x^2$, as x and y tend to zero.

EXERCISE G

1. Find the curvature at the origin of the curve $x = 2ap$, $y = ap^2$

(i) using the formula of Section 4,

(ii) by finding the limit of $2y/x^2$ as $x, y \to 0$.

2. Find the curvature of the curve $x = 2at/(1 + t^2)$, $y = b(1 - t^2)/(1 + t^2)$ at the point $(0, b)$ by making a suitable transformation and then finding a limit.

3. Show that the evolute of the cycloid $x = p + \sin p$, $y = 1 + \cos p$ is an equal cycloid.

4. Sketch an involute of an equilateral triangle.

5. What is the involute of a cycloid?

6. Find which of the conic sections has the curve $x = 2p^3$, $y = 3p^2$ as its evolute.

7. Find the evolute of the curve $r = 3p$, $\theta = \log p$.

8. A see-saw consists of a straight plank on a fixed cylindrical barrel. Find the equation of the locus of an end of the plank.

9. Find out how involutes are used in the design of gear teeth. (For example, see *Mathematical Models* by Cundy & Rollett.)

8. CURVES

We conclude by looking at some of the properties of a few curves of interest.

8.1 Cycloids

We have already considered the case of a circle rolling along a straight line. Here we investigate a circle rolling along the circumference of a fixed circle.

For convenience, we take the rolling circle to have radius a and the fixed circle radius $(m - 1)a$, with axes along and perpendicular to the initial line of centres. (Figure 19.) Consider P' the position of the original point P of contact, when the circle has rolled along to Q, where $P\hat{O}Q = \alpha$.

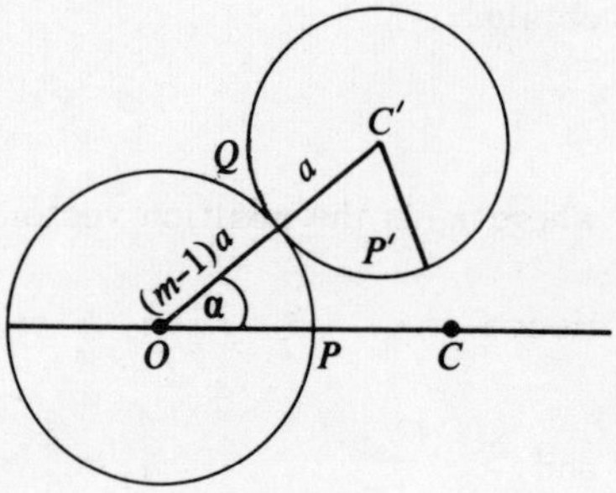

Fig. 19.

$$\text{Arc } QP' = \text{arc } QP = (m-1)\alpha$$
$$\Rightarrow A\hat{C}'P = (m-1)\alpha$$
$$\Rightarrow P'C' \text{ makes an angle } m\alpha \text{ with the } x\text{-axis.}$$

Hence for P':

$$x = ma\cos\alpha - a\cos m\alpha,$$
$$y = ma\sin\alpha - a\sin m\alpha.$$

Such a curve is called an *epicycloid*.

Similarly, if a circle of radius a rolls on the inside of a fixed circle of radius $(n + 1)a$, we obtain the *hypocycloid*:

$$x = na\cos\alpha + a\cos n\alpha,$$
$$y = na\sin\alpha - a\sin n\alpha.$$

Different values of m and n give rise to some fascinating curves, from the romantic cardioid ($m = 2$) to the complex interlaced designs which can be obtained with the 'Spirograph' toy.

8.2 Spiral

It is well known that multiplication by a complex number gives a transformation of the Argand diagram which is a spiral similarity.* But why does it get this name?

Multiplication by $a(\cos\alpha + j\sin\alpha)$ gives enlargement a and rotation α. Repeated multiplication gives enlargement a^N with rotation $N\alpha$. Thus with a rotation θ we get an enlargement $a^{\theta/\alpha}$. If this is applied to a point B, modulus b,

* See S.M.P. Further Mathematics IV, *Extensions of Calculus*.

on the positive real axis then B is transformed to the point with modulus $ba^{\theta/\alpha}$ and argument θ. Thus for any rotation θ it is transformed to a point on the curve whose polar equation is $r = ba^{\theta/\alpha}$ which is a spiral as shown in Figure 20. Furthermore, if ϕ is the angle between the tangent at any point and the radius vector, then

$$\tan\phi = r\frac{d\theta}{dr} \quad \text{(See Miscellaneous Exercise, Question 14)}$$

$$= r \div \frac{dr}{d\theta}$$

$$= ba^{\theta/\alpha} \div (1/\alpha \cdot \ln a \cdot ba^{\theta/\alpha})$$

$$= \alpha/\ln a$$

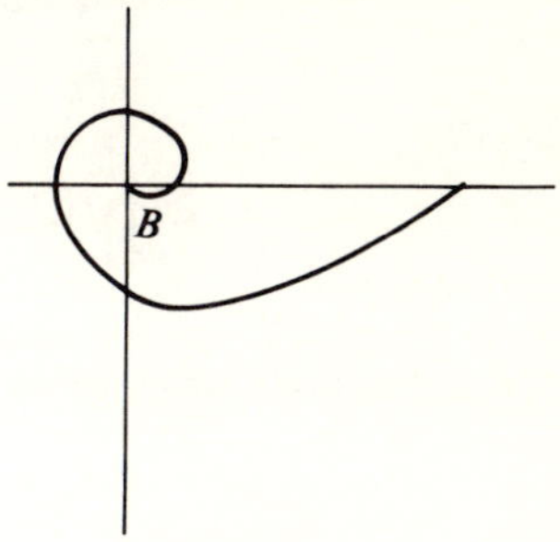

Fig. 20.

which is independent of b and θ, and the curve is an equiangular spiral. (See also Exercise F, Question 4.) Thus multiplication by a complex number can be thought of as a transformation of each point along an equiangular spiral.

8.3 Catenary

A heavy cable hangs between two supports B and C (Figure 21). Consider a portion of the cable from the bottom A to a point P. It is in equilibrium under the action of three forces: a constant tension $\mathbf{F}$ at A, a variable tension $\mathbf{T}$ at P and the gravitational attraction ws, where w is the weight per unit length of cable.

Hence $-F\hat{\mathbf{i}} - ws\hat{\mathbf{j}} + T\hat{\mathbf{t}} = \mathbf{0}$, with axes as shown.

$\Rightarrow F\sin\psi - ws\cos\psi = 0$,

taking the component perpendicular to $\hat{\mathbf{t}}$, with ψ the angle between $\hat{\mathbf{t}}$ and $\hat{\mathbf{i}}$.

$\Rightarrow s = a\tan\psi$, where $a = F/w$.

This is called the *Intrinsic* equation of the curve (in terms of s, ψ). It indicates how the inclination changes along the curve, and leads ultimately to the cartesian form for this curve, a *catenary*; in fact, $x = ap$, $y = a\cosh p$, where $OA = a = F/w$.

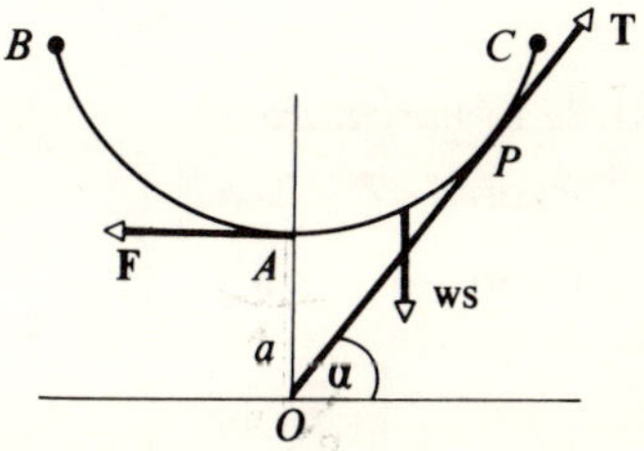

Fig. 21.

SUMMARY

Notation. Throughout, our attention is restricted to the plane, and ψ denotes the angle between the tangent to a curve and the x-axis. 'Hats' are used to emphasise unit vectors. Dashes denote differentiation with respect to the parameter p; i.e. $x' = dx/dp$, $\mathbf{r}' = d\mathbf{r}/dp$, etc. Dots are used when time is specifically the parameter: $\dot{x}$ = speed in direction Ox, etc.

Velocity and Acceleration

	Cartesian.	Polar (Radial, Transverse).	Intrinsic (Tangent, Normal).
$\mathbf{v}$	$= \dot{x}\hat{\mathbf{i}} + \dot{y}\hat{\mathbf{j}}$	$= \dot{r}\hat{\mathbf{r}} + r\dot{\theta}\hat{\mathbf{u}}$	$= v\hat{\mathbf{t}}$,
$\mathbf{a}$	$= \ddot{x}\hat{\mathbf{i}} + \ddot{y}\hat{\mathbf{j}}$	$= (\ddot{r} - r\dot{\theta}^2)\hat{\mathbf{r}} + (2\dot{r}\dot{\theta} + r\ddot{\theta})\hat{\mathbf{u}}$	$= \dot{v}\hat{\mathbf{t}} + (v^2/\rho)\hat{\mathbf{n}}$.

Length of curve s

$$s = \int \sqrt{[x'^2 + y'^2]}\,dp = \int \sqrt{\left[1 + \left(\frac{dy}{dx}\right)^2\right]}\,dx$$

$$= \int \sqrt{[r'^2 + (r\theta')^2]}\,dp = \int \sqrt{\left[\left(\frac{dr}{d\theta}\right)^2 + r^2\right]}\,d\theta .$$

Special results when parameter is s

$$\mathbf{r}' = \hat{\mathbf{t}}, \qquad \hat{\mathbf{t}}' = \kappa\hat{\mathbf{n}}, \qquad \hat{\mathbf{n}}' = -\kappa\hat{\mathbf{t}},$$

$$\begin{pmatrix} x' \\ y' \end{pmatrix} = \begin{pmatrix} \cos\psi \\ \sin\psi \end{pmatrix}, \qquad \tan\psi = y'/x' = dy/dx.$$

Curvature κ

$$\hat{\mathbf{t}}' = \psi'\hat{\mathbf{n}},$$

$$\psi' = \frac{x'y'' - y'x''}{x'^2 + y'^2},$$

$$\kappa = \frac{\psi'}{s'} = \frac{d\psi}{ds} = \frac{x'y'' - y'x''}{[x'^2 + y'^2]^{3/2}} = \frac{d^2y/dx^2}{\left[1 + \left(\frac{dy}{dx}\right)^2\right]^{3/2}}.$$

At origin: $\kappa = \lim_{x \to 0} 2y/x^2$, for curve touching x-axis.

Circle of curvature

Radius $\rho = 1/\kappa$.

Centre $\mathbf{r} + \rho\hat{\mathbf{n}} = \left(x - \frac{dy}{d\psi}\right)\hat{\mathbf{i}} + \left(y + \frac{dx}{d\psi}\right)\hat{\mathbf{j}}$

$$= \left[x - \frac{y'(x'^2 + y'^2)}{x'y'' - y'x''}\right]\hat{\mathbf{i}} + \left[y + \frac{x'(x'^2 + y'^2)}{x'y'' - y'x''}\right]\hat{\mathbf{j}}.$$

Involute (unwrapping of string)

$$\mathbf{r}_1 = \mathbf{r} - (s - c)\,\hat{\mathbf{t}}.$$

Evolute (envelope of normals, locus of centre of curvature)

$$\mathbf{r}_2 = \mathbf{r} + \rho\hat{\mathbf{n}}.$$

MISCELLANEOUS EXERCISE

1. Verify for the catenary $x = ap$, $y = a \cosh p$, that the arc length is given by $s = a \tan\psi$, where ψ is the angle between the tangent and the x-axis.

2. Obtain parametric functions for the involute of a catenary, unwinding from its lowest point A. Show that this is the same curve, the tractrix, as is the path of an object, initially at A, and dragged along by a string of length a, the other end of which is moved along the x-axis.

3. Sketch the hypocycloids for which $n = 2$ and $n = 3$. [See Section 8.1].

4. Sketch the epicycloids for which (a) $m = 1$, (b) $m = 2$, (c) $m = 3$. [See Section 8.1].

5. A fixed wheel rotates with constant angular velocity while an object starting from the centre moves along one of the spokes at a constant speed. Show that the path of the object is the curve $r = a\theta$. Sketch this curve and suggest how it might be used as a linkage to convert a constant angular velocity into a constant linear velocity.

6. Sketch the curve $r = a/\theta$.

7. Find the length of arc of the equiangular spiral $r = e^{\theta}$. Show that the curvature is inversely proportional to r and that the evolute is an equal spiral.

8. On the same diagram, sketch the curves

(a) $r = a\cos\theta$, and $r = a/\cos\theta$, and $r = a$;

(b) $r^2 = a^2\cos 2\theta$, and $r^2 = a^2/\cos 2\theta$, and $r = a$;

and comment on the results.

9. Sketch the curve $x = e^p \sin p$, $y = e^p \cos p$ and obtain an expression for the length of arc.

10. Show that the length of a complete undulation of the trochoid

$$x = a\alpha + b\sin\alpha, \qquad y = a - b\cos\alpha$$

is equal to the perimeter of an ellipse with semi-axes $a + b$ and $a - b$.

11. For the lemniscate $r^2 = a^2\cos 2\theta$, show that the curvature is proportional to r. Sketch the curve and explain how, and why, it is used in the construction of motorways.

12. Describe the curve $x = 1 + 2p$, $y = 5 - 3p$, $z = 4 + p$.

13. Find suitable equations for the hand-rail of a spiral staircase.

14. Prove that $\tan\phi = r(d\theta/dr)$ (see Section 8.2).

$$\left[\textit{Hint}: \phi = \psi - \theta,\ \tan\psi = \frac{dy}{dr}\bigg/\frac{dx}{dr},\ x = r\cos\theta\ \ y = r\sin\theta.\right]$$

15. If we remove the restriction that the curve must lie in a plane, then we need to introduce a further vector $\hat{\mathbf{b}}$ in order to specify the 'twist' of a curve. $\hat{\mathbf{n}}$ is still taken as the direction of change in $\hat{\mathbf{t}}$ so, with arc length as parameter, $\hat{\mathbf{t}}' = \kappa\hat{\mathbf{n}}$. (Curvature κ.) It is then convenient to take $\mathbf{b}$ perpendicular to $\mathbf{t}$ and $\mathbf{n}$ as shown in Figure 22. Thus $\hat{\mathbf{b}}\cdot\hat{\mathbf{t}} = 0$, $\hat{\mathbf{b}}\cdot\hat{\mathbf{n}} = 0$, $\hat{\mathbf{n}}\cdot\hat{\mathbf{t}} = 0$. Hence $\hat{\mathbf{b}}'\cdot\hat{\mathbf{t}} + \hat{\mathbf{b}}\cdot\hat{\mathbf{t}}' = 0 \Rightarrow \hat{\mathbf{b}}'\cdot\hat{\mathbf{t}} = 0$ (Why?) $\Rightarrow \hat{\mathbf{b}}'$ perpendicular to $\hat{\mathbf{t}}$. But $\hat{\mathbf{b}}'$ is perpendicular to $\hat{\mathbf{b}}$ (true for every unit vector). Hence $\hat{\mathbf{b}}'$ has the same direction as $\hat{\mathbf{n}}$, and we write $\hat{\mathbf{b}}' = -\tau\hat{\mathbf{n}}$. ($\tau$ is the *torsion*, the rate of twist of a corkscrew along the curve.) Also $\hat{\mathbf{n}}' \perp \hat{\mathbf{n}} \Rightarrow \hat{\mathbf{n}}'$ is parallel to the plane of $(\hat{\mathbf{t}}, \hat{\mathbf{b}}) \Rightarrow \hat{\mathbf{n}}' = \lambda\hat{\mathbf{t}} + \mu\hat{\mathbf{b}}$.

Using $\hat{\mathbf{n}} \cdot \hat{\mathbf{t}} = 0$, prove that $\lambda = -\kappa$. Using $\hat{\mathbf{n}} \cdot \hat{\mathbf{b}} = 0$, prove that $\mu = \tau$. Hence obtain the *Serret–Frenet formulae*:

$$\hat{\mathbf{t}}' = \kappa\hat{\mathbf{n}}, \quad \hat{\mathbf{b}}' = -\tau\hat{\mathbf{n}}, \quad \hat{\mathbf{n}}' = \tau\hat{\mathbf{b}} - \mathbf{k}\hat{t}.$$

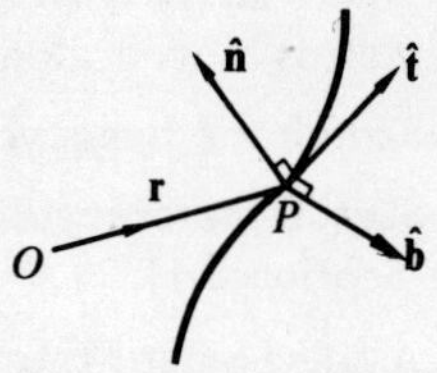

Fig. 22.

2. Polar Kinematics and Conics

1. CENTRAL FORCE AND ORBIT

In the previous chapter, the radial and transverse velocities and accelerations were established for a particle moving along a curve given by its polar equation. We now propose to investigate the relationship between such curves and the forces acting on a particle moving along them.

The work that follows will deal with central forces – that is, forces directed towards a fixed point, which will be taken as the origin of polar coordinates – and a subsequent section will look at properties of some important curves associated with central forces.

Practical illustrations of this type of work are much in evidence with the launching of satellites and moon probes. Relative to earth, the force of attraction between a satellite and earth is a central force.

As the force under such circumstances cannot be altered, it is speed which plays an important part in determining the course of satellites. For instance, the moon flight *Apollo 10* started by orbiting the earth at 27 900 km/h and an increase to 38 850 km/h put it on a lunar trajectory. Similarly it reached the vicinity of the moon at 9100 km/h and a reduction in speed to 6000 km/h brought it into circular orbit around the moon. The various problems included in this chapter, although often simplified, should serve to show how the theory is applied in this context.

1.1 Central force and acceleration

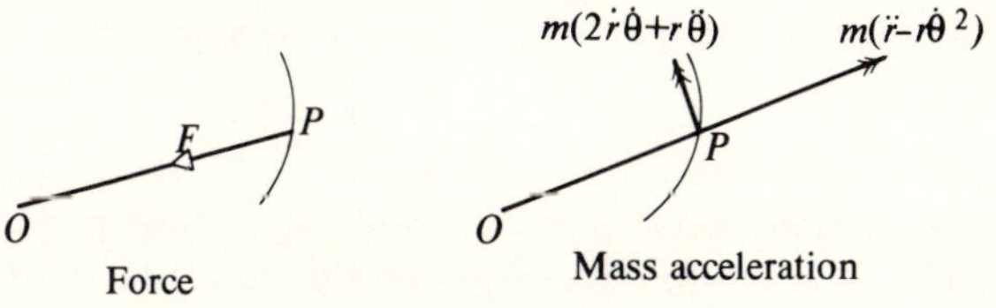

Fig. 1

Equating force to mass acceleration

Radially: $$F = -m(\ddot{r} - r\dot{\theta}^2) \tag{1}$$

Transversely: $$0 = m(2\dot{r}\dot{\theta} + r\ddot{\theta}). \tag{2}$$

Integrating the second equation it follows that $r^2\dot{\theta}$ = a constant, which we shall denote by h.

$$r^2\dot{\theta} = h. \tag{3}$$

This useful result holds for all motion under a central force whatever the nature of that force may be.

1.2 Area

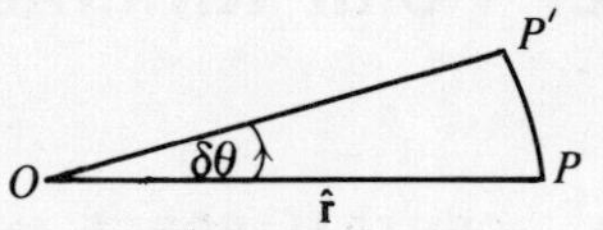

Fig. 2.

The area described by OP in time δt is $\frac{1}{2}r^2\delta\theta$. The rate of description of area by the line OP is therefore $\frac{1}{2}r^2\dot{\theta}$. This quantity is termed *areal speed.* It follows that, for all motion under a central force, the rate at which area is swept out is constant, the areal speed being equal to $\frac{1}{2}h$.

1.3 Force and orbit

Equations (1) and (3) are of the utmost importance since they enable a relationship to be found between force and orbit, as is illustrated in the following examples:

Example 1. A satellite of mass 1000 kg is moving in a circular orbit 480 km above the earth. Initially its speed is 27 300 km/h. Taking the radius of the earth to be 6400 km, show that the speed of the satellite remains constant and find its areal speed. Find also the force acting on the satellite in newtons.

The polar equation of the orbit is $r = 6880$.

Now
$$r^2\dot{\theta} = h \ (= \text{constant})$$
$$\Rightarrow rv = \text{constant, since } v = r\dot{\theta} \text{ for circle}$$
$$\Rightarrow v = \text{constant.}$$

The speed of the satellite therefore remains constant.

$$h = rv$$
$$= 6880 \times 27\,300$$
$$\Rightarrow \text{areal speed}$$
$$= \tfrac{1}{2} \times 6880 \times 27\,300$$
$$= 9{\cdot}39 \times 10^7 \text{ km}^2/\text{h}.$$

For uniform circular motion, force $= mv^2/r$ centrally. The speed of the satellite is $7{\cdot}58 \times 10^3$ m/s and hence the force exerted on the satellite is of magnitude

$$\frac{1000 \times 7{\cdot}58^2 \times 10^6}{6880 \times 10^3} \text{ N} = 8{\cdot}35 \times 10^3 \text{ N}.$$

Example 2. A particle of unit mass is describing the curve $r = 2 + \cos\theta$ under a central force acting towards O. Sketch the orbit. If it is initially at $\theta = 0$ with speed 5 units, find the magnitude of the velocity and the angle it makes with the radius vector when $\theta = \frac{1}{3}\pi$. Find also the force acting on the particle when $\theta = \frac{2}{3}\pi$.

$$r = 2 + \cos\theta,$$
$$\Rightarrow \dot{r} = -\sin\theta \cdot \dot{\theta} \qquad \text{(A)}$$
$$\Rightarrow \dot{r} = -h/r^2 \sin\theta,$$

since $r^2\dot{\theta} = h$.

Now $$v^2 = \dot{r}^2 + (r\dot{\theta})^2 = \left(\frac{-h}{r^2}\cdot\sin\theta\right)^2 + \left(\frac{h}{r}\right)^2. \qquad \text{(B)}$$

For any value of θ we can calculate the value of r, from (A). Thus, if we knew the value of h, we could calculate v from (B). h is a constant for a particular orbit, which it should be possible to calculate from the initial conditions. Initially

$$\theta = 0 \quad \text{and} \quad v = 5$$

$$\Rightarrow r = 3 \text{ from (A)} \quad \text{and} \quad h = 15, \text{ from (B)}.$$

Hence, from (B), when $\theta = \frac{1}{3}\pi$,

$$v^2 = \left(-\frac{15}{2\frac{1}{2}^2}\cdot\frac{\sqrt{3}}{2}\right)^2 + \left(\frac{15}{2\frac{1}{2}}\right)^2 = 36.\frac{28}{25}$$

$$v = \frac{12}{5}\sqrt{7}.$$

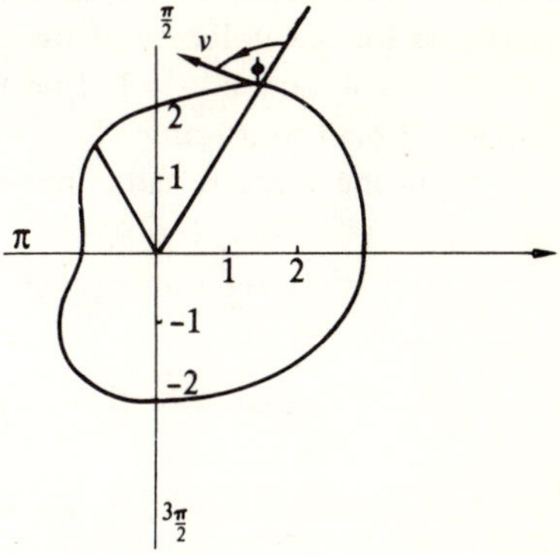

Fig. 3.

If direction of motion makes an angle ϕ with the radius vector, then

$$\tan\phi = \frac{h/r}{-h\sin\theta/r^2} = \frac{-r}{\sin\theta} = \frac{-5}{2}\times\frac{2}{\sqrt{3}}$$

$$\Longrightarrow \phi = \tan^{-1}\left(\frac{-5}{\sqrt{3}}\right).$$

The central force acting on the particle has magnitude $-\ddot{r} + r\dot{\theta}^2$ since the particle has unit mass.

Now, from (A), $$\ddot{r} = \frac{2h}{r^3}\sin\theta\cdot\dot{r} - \frac{h}{r^2}\cos\theta\,\dot{\theta}$$

$$= \frac{-2h^2}{r^5}\sin^2\theta - \frac{h^2}{r^4}\cos\theta,$$

and $$r\dot{\theta}^2 = \frac{h^2}{r^3}.$$

Thus, when $\theta = \frac{2}{3}\pi$, $r = \frac{3}{2}$,

$$\text{Force} = \frac{h^2}{r^5}\left[2\sin^2\theta + r\cos\theta + r^2\right]$$

$$= \frac{15^2}{\left(\frac{3}{5}\right)^5}\left(\frac{3}{2} - \frac{3}{4} + 2\tfrac{1}{4}\right) = \frac{800}{9} \text{ units, centrally.}$$

Example 3. A particle is moving under a central force towards the origin equal to $5/r^2$ per unit mass. Prove that

$$\ddot{r} = \frac{h^2}{r^3} - \frac{5}{r^2}, \text{ where } h \text{ is constant,}$$

and that

$$\dot{r}^2 = c - \frac{h^2}{r^2} + \frac{10}{r},$$

where c is a constant which depends on the initial conditions. Hence find an expression for the velocity of the particle.

If $h = 4$ and $c = -1$, find the maximum and minimum distances of the particle from the origin.

Equating force to mass acceleration in radial and transverse directions

$$\frac{-5}{r^2}\cdot m = m(\ddot{r} - r\dot{\theta}^2) \quad \text{and} \quad r^2\dot{\theta} = h, \text{ a constant,}$$

$$\Rightarrow \quad \frac{-5}{r^2} = \ddot{r} - r\cdot\frac{h^2}{r^4},$$

$$\Rightarrow \quad \ddot{r} = \frac{h^2}{r^3} - \frac{5}{r^2}. \tag{A}$$

Multiply both sides of (A) by $2\dot{r}$ and integrate

$$\Rightarrow \quad \dot{r}^2 = \frac{-h^2}{r^2} + \frac{10}{r} + \text{constant,}$$

i.e.

$$\dot{r}^2 = c - \frac{h^2}{r^2} + \frac{10}{r}. \tag{B}$$

Now

$$v^2 = \dot{r}^2 + r^2\dot{\theta}^2,$$

$$= \dot{r}^2 + \frac{h^2}{r^2}.$$

Thus

$$v^2 = \frac{10}{r} + c \quad \text{and} \quad v = \sqrt{\left(\frac{10}{r} + c\right)}. \tag{C}$$

Maximum and minimum values of r occur when $\dot{r} = 0$, i.e. when

$$c - \frac{h^2}{r^2} + \frac{10}{r} = 0.$$

Putting in values of c and h

$$\Rightarrow \quad -r^2 + 10r - 16 = 0, \qquad \text{since } r \neq 0.$$

$$\Rightarrow \quad r^2 - 10r + 16 = 0,$$

$$\Rightarrow \quad (r-2)(r-8) = 0,$$

$$\Rightarrow \quad r = 2 \text{ or } 8.$$

From (A)

$$\ddot{r} = \frac{16}{r^3} - \frac{10}{r^2},$$

which is positive for $r = 2$, and negative for $r = 8$, which confirms that the minimum and maximum distances of the particle from the origin are 2 units and 8 units respectively.

Note: When r is a maximum or a minimum the particle is travelling at right angles to the radius vector and $h = rv$. As a check, from (C),

when $r = 2, \quad v = 2,$

when $r = 8, \quad v = \frac{1}{2},$

which both give $h = 4$.

1.4 Apses

A point P on an orbit where OP is normal to the curve is called an *apse*, and the length OP is the *apsidal distance*.

If the central force is a function of the distance, then the orbit will be symmetrical about the line joining the centre of force to an apse.

At an apse, therefore,

$$\dot{r} = 0 \quad \text{and} \quad v = r\dot{\theta}, \qquad \Rightarrow h = \text{speed} \times \text{apsidal distance.} \tag{4}$$

This is a useful result since it often provides a simple means of calculating the very important constant h.

EXERCISE A

1. Sketch the curves

(a) $r = 2a\cos\theta$, (b) $r = a\sec\theta$,

(c) $r = \dfrac{2}{1 - \cos\theta}$, (d) $r = \dfrac{3}{2 + \cos\theta}$,

(e) $r = \dfrac{3}{1 + 2\cos\theta}$.

2. Equation (2) states that $2\dot{r}\dot{\theta} + r\ddot{\theta} = 0$. Prove that this implies $r^2\dot{\theta} = $ constant.

3. v is the speed of a particle at a point P moving on a curve under a central force. p is the length of the perpendicular from the pole onto the tangent at P. Prove that $pv = h$.

4. A satellite is moving in a circular orbit around the earth. If the time for one orbit is 96 minutes and the height of the satellite above the earth is 500 km, find its speed and the force acting on it if its mass is 800 kg. (Take radius of earth as 6400 km.)

5. Find the time for one orbit of the satellite in Example 1, on page 28.

6. The path of a particle of unit mass is given parametrically by the equations $r = t$, $\theta = 6\pi/t$. Sketch the curve for the values of t from 1 to 12. Find the velocity and acceleration vectors in terms of their radial and transverse components and show that this motion is consistent with motion under a central force. Find this force when $t = 2$ and $t = 3$.

7. A particle describes the curve $r = 1/\sqrt{t}$, $\theta = kt^2$. Show that this motion is consistent with motion under a central force. If the areal speed is 10 units find the value of k.

8. The force acting on a space capsule orbiting the earth is inversely proportional to the square of its distance from the centre of the earth. Show that in circular orbit its distance from the centre of the earth is inversely proportional to the square of its speed.

Two space capsules of equal mass are in circular orbit around the earth at heights of 490 km and 320 km. The speed of the latter is 27 700 km/h, find the speed of the former. (Take the radius of the earth as 6400 km.)

9. If in Example 3 on page 29, the data had been the same except that $c = 0$, what could be deduced about the motion in this case?

10. A particle of mass 2 units is describing the curve $r = 2a \cos\theta$ under the action of a force directed towards the pole. Find the magnitude and direction of the velocity and the force acting when $\theta = \frac{1}{4}\pi$, if the speed is $a/2$ units when $\theta = 0$.

11. A particle of unit mass is describing the curve $r = 2/(1 - \cos\theta)$ under the action of a central force. Show that $\dot{r} = \frac{1}{2}\, h \sin\theta$ and $r\dot{\theta} = h/r$ and hence find the ratio of the speeds when $\theta = \frac{1}{2}\pi$ and $\theta = \pi$.

Obtain an expression for the force in terms of h, r, and θ and by eliminating θ show that it is inversely proportional to r^2.

12. Show that if $u = 1/r$, then $\ddot{r} - r\dot{\theta}^2$ can be written as $-h^2u^2\,[(\mathrm{d}^2u/\mathrm{d}\theta^2) + u]$, where $h = r^2\dot{\theta}$.

13. Show that if $u = 1/r$, then $v^2 = h^2\,[(\mathrm{d}u/\mathrm{d}\theta)^2 + u^2]$.

14. A particle of unit mass is describing the curve $r = 3/(2 + \cos\theta)$ under the action of a central force towards the pole, so that when $\theta = 0$, its speed is 2 units. Express this curve in u, θ form, where $u = 1/r$, and use the expressions derived in Questions 12 and 13 to find the speed and the force acting when (a) $\theta = \frac{1}{2}\pi$ and (b) $\theta = \pi$.

15. A particle is moving along the curve $r = a \sec\theta$ under a central force towards the pole. Use the u, θ form to show that the force is zero. Comment on this situation.

16. A particle is moving under a central force along the curve $r = Ae^{-2\theta}$. Use the u, θ form to show that this force is proportional to $1/r^3$.

17. In Example 2 on page 28, eliminate θ to express the force as a function of r.

18. A particle is moving under a central force towards the origin equal to r per unit mass. Prove that

$$\ddot{r} = \frac{h^2}{r^3} - r, \text{ where } h \text{ is constant,}$$

and

$$\dot{r}^2 = c - \frac{h^2}{r^2} - r^2, \text{ where } c \text{ is constant.}$$

If $h = 6$ and $c = 13$ find the maximum and minimum distances of the particle from the origin and the speeds of the particle at these points. If $c = 0$, what is the nature of the motion?

2. THE INVERSE SQUARE LAW OF ATTRACTION

Newton's Law of Gravitation states that any two particles masses m and M

in the universe, are attracted to each other by a force $\gamma(Mm/r^2)$, where r is the distance between them and γ is known as the *gravitational constant*.

Planets therefore can be regarded as moving in space under the action of a central force inversely proportional to their distance from the sun. Satellites and space capsules will also move in a similar manner around the earth or sun. Orbits under this law of force are thus particularly important.

2.1 Motion under the inverse square law

If the force per unit mass on a particle is equal to μ/r^2, then

Radially: $$\ddot{r} - r\dot{\theta}^2 = -\mu/r^2. \tag{5}$$

Transversely: $$r^2\dot{\theta} = h. \tag{6}$$

The time can be eliminated by making use of the result:

$$\frac{\mathrm{d}}{\mathrm{d}t} = \frac{\mathrm{d}}{\mathrm{d}\theta} \times \frac{\mathrm{d}\theta}{\mathrm{d}t},$$

which from (6) $$= \frac{h}{r^2} \cdot \frac{\mathrm{d}}{\mathrm{d}\theta}. \tag{7}$$

The first equation then becomes a differential equation in r and θ only, which can be integrated to give the polar equation of the orbit.

This direct approach is followed up in Exercise B and also in Section 6, but is not as straightforward as it would seem.

We shall consider the motion in the x and y direction, which gives a simpler method for obtaining the equation of the orbit.

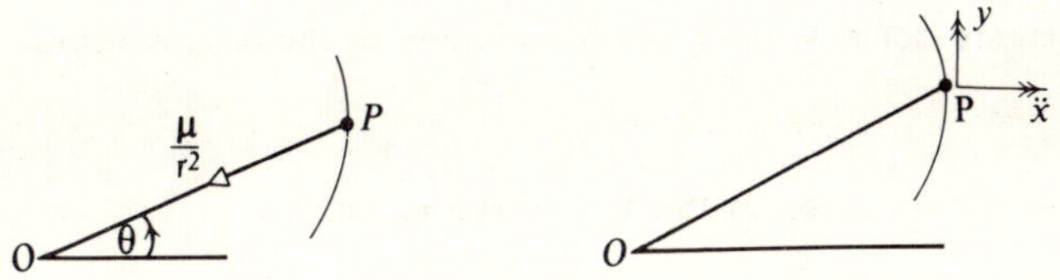

Fig. 1.

x direction: $$\frac{\mathrm{d}}{\mathrm{d}t}\dot{x} = \frac{-\mu}{r^2}\cos\theta$$

y direction: $$\frac{\mathrm{d}}{\mathrm{d}t}\dot{y} = \frac{-\mu}{r^2}\sin\theta$$

From (7) $$\Longrightarrow \frac{h}{r^2}\frac{\mathrm{d}}{\mathrm{d}\theta}\dot{x} = \frac{-\mu}{r^2}\cos\theta, \qquad \frac{h}{r^2}\frac{\mathrm{d}}{\mathrm{d}\theta}\dot{y} = \frac{-\mu}{r^2}\sin\theta.$$

Integrating $$\Longrightarrow \dot{x} = \frac{-\mu}{h}\sin\theta + A, \qquad \dot{y} = \frac{\mu}{h}\cos\theta + B,$$ where A, B are arbitrary constants.

We now change back into polar coordinates.

$$\left.\begin{aligned} \Longrightarrow \quad \dot{r}\cos\theta - r\dot{\theta}\sin\theta &= \frac{-\mu}{h}\sin\theta + A \\ \dot{r}\sin\theta + r\dot{\theta}\cos\theta &= \frac{\mu}{h}\cos\theta + B \end{aligned}\right\}.$$

Eliminating $\dot{r}$ between these equations

$$\Longrightarrow \quad r\dot{\theta}\,[\cos^2\theta + \sin^2\theta] = \frac{\mu}{h}[\cos^2\theta + \sin^2\theta] + B\cos\theta - A\sin\theta$$

$$\Longrightarrow \quad \frac{h}{r} = \frac{\mu}{h} + B\cos\theta - A\sin\theta,$$

which may be written $\dfrac{1}{r} = \dfrac{\mu}{h^2} + k\cos(\theta + \alpha)$, where k, α are arbitrary constants.

By suitable choice of the direction from which θ is measured α can be taken as zero:

$$\Longrightarrow \quad \frac{1}{r} = \frac{\mu}{h^2} + k\cos\theta. \tag{8}$$

So this is the polar equation of the path of any particle moving under a central, inverse square law, force.

The initial position and velocity determine the values of μ/h^2 and k, which in their turn completely determine the shape of the orbit.

We investigate some of the possible shapes in the next exercise.

EXERCISE B

Sketch the curves given in the first three questions.

1. $\dfrac{1}{r} = 2 + \cos\theta$; $\quad \dfrac{1}{r} = 1 + \cos\theta$; $\quad \dfrac{1}{r} = 1 + 2\cos\theta$.

2. $\dfrac{1}{r} = \dfrac{1}{2} + \cos\theta$; $\quad \dfrac{1}{r} = \dfrac{1}{2} + \dfrac{1}{2}\cos\theta$; $\quad \dfrac{1}{r} = 1 + \dfrac{1}{2}\cos\theta$.

3. $\dfrac{1}{r} = 3 + 2\cos\theta$; $\quad \dfrac{1}{r} = 2 + 2\cos\theta$; $\quad \dfrac{1}{r} = 2 + 3\cos\theta$.

4. How is the shape of the curve $1/r = a + b\cos\theta$ related to the relative magnitude of a and b?

5. Verify that

$$\frac{1}{r} = \frac{\mu}{h^2} + k\cos\theta \quad \text{and} \quad r^2\dot{\theta} = h$$

together imply that $\ddot{r} - r\dot{\theta}^2 = -(\mu/r^2)$.

6. Motion under a central force μ/r^2 per unit mass

$$\Longrightarrow \quad h^2u^2\left(\frac{d^2u}{d\theta^2} + u\right) = \mu u^2 \quad \text{(See Exercise A, Question 12)}$$

$$\Rightarrow \quad \frac{d^2u}{d\theta^2} + u = \mu/h^2.$$

Verify that $u = (\mu/h^2) + k \cos(\theta + \alpha)$ is a solution of this differential equation whatever the values of the constants k and α.

7. Fill in the missing steps in the following chain of reasoning:

Motion under a central force μ/r^2 per unit mass

$$\Rightarrow \quad \ddot{r} - \frac{h^2}{r^3} = \frac{-\mu}{r^2}$$

$$\Rightarrow \quad \frac{d}{d\theta}(\dot{r}) - \frac{h}{r} = \frac{-\mu}{h}$$

$$\Rightarrow \quad \frac{d}{d\theta}\left(-\frac{1}{r^2}\frac{dr}{d\theta}\right) + \frac{1}{r} - \frac{\mu}{h^2} = 0$$

$$\Rightarrow \quad \frac{d^2}{d\theta^2}\left(\frac{1}{r} - \frac{\mu}{h^2}\right) + \left(\frac{1}{r} - \frac{\mu}{h^2}\right) = 0$$

$$\Rightarrow \quad \frac{1}{r} - \frac{\mu}{h^2} = k \cos(\theta + \alpha).$$

3. FOCUS-DIRECTRIX DEFINITION OF A CONIC

The curves given by the orbit equation

$$\frac{1}{r} = \frac{\mu}{h^2} + k \cos\theta$$

are known as conics (or conic sections). We found in Exercise B that there were certainly three distinct shapes, ellipse, hyperbola, parabola, depending on the values of the constants, that is, on the initial conditions. We shall now investigate these curves more fully, but from a somewhat different standpoint.

A *conic* can be defined as the locus of a point which moves in a plane so that its distance from a fixed point S is a constant multiple of its distance from a fixed line d, both S and d being in the plane.

The fixed point is known as the *focus* and the line as the *directrix*. The constant multiple is called the *eccentricity* of the conic and is denoted by e.

3.1 Polar equation of a conic

Choose the focus S to be the origin and the perpendicular from S to the directrix d to be the initial line

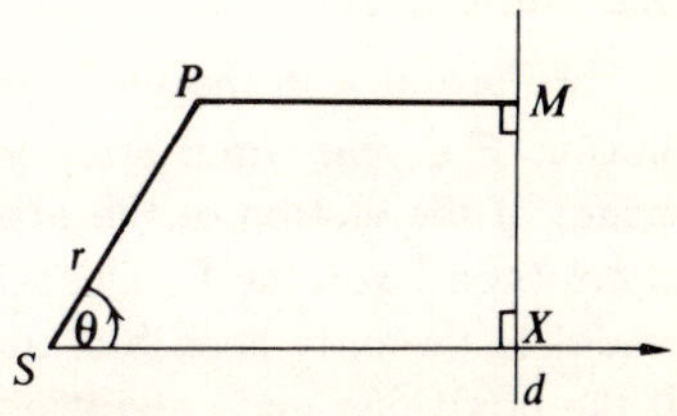

Fig. 5.

$$SP = ePM$$

$$\Rightarrow \quad r = e(SX - r\cos\theta)$$

$$\Rightarrow \quad r(1 + e\cos\theta) = eSX$$

$$= \text{constant } (= l \text{ say})$$

$$\Rightarrow \quad l/r = 1 + e\cos\theta, \tag{9}$$

which is the polar equation of a conic with the focus as pole.

Note: when $\theta = \frac{1}{2}\pi$,

$$SP = ePM$$
$$= eSX$$
$$= l.$$

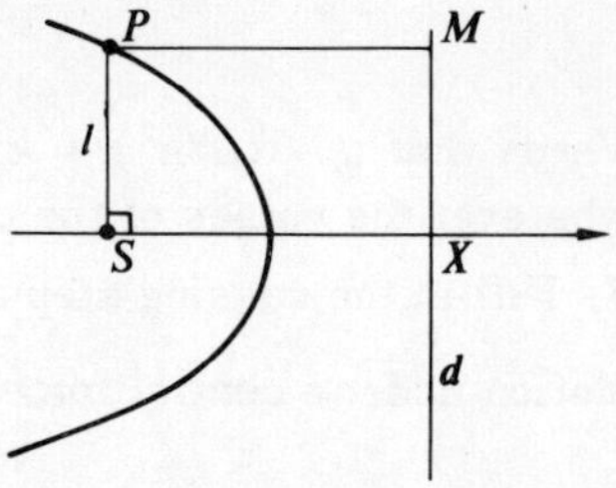

Fig. 6.

The chord of a conic through the focus and parallel to the directrix is known as the *latus rectum*. Hence it can be seen that the constant l is equal to half the length of the latus rectum. Also, comparing equations (8) and (9), we get the very useful relation

$$l = h^2/\mu \tag{10}$$

connecting the law of force and size of the corresponding conic.

The conic is an ellipse, parabola or hyperbola according as e is less than, equal to, or greater than 1. The diagrams below show the three types of conic.

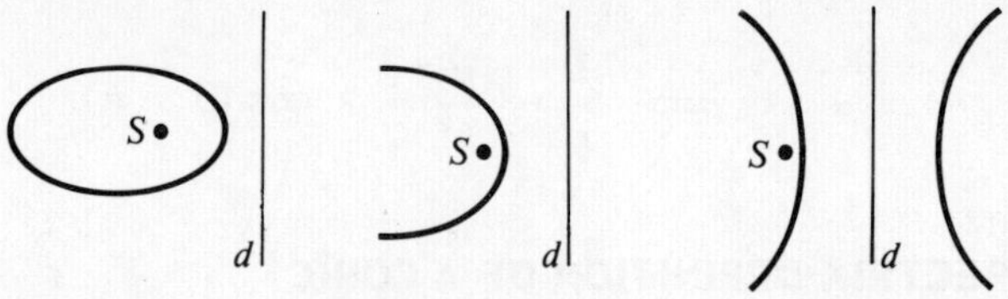

Fig. 7.

Thus, under gravitational attraction, there are only three possible types of orbit.

If an orbit is an ellipse, then there are two apses. This is the orbit made by the planets round the sun or satellites round the earth.

In parabolic orbit there is only one apse, the curve being similar in shape to that of free flight under gravity. The ultimate direction of the particle would approach a direction parallel to the apse line.

A hyperbola has two branches, as illustrated, and the direction of motion as r increases approaches a straight line. In practice, of course, a particle moving under a central force can traverse only one branch and the orbit would have only one apse.

3.2 Satellites

We are now in the very remarkable position that from Newton's Laws of Motion $\mathbf{F} = m\mathbf{a}$, Gravitation $F = \gamma(Mm/r^2)$ and Interaction, we can obtain a good model of the motion of the planets, and, in theory, of the whole universe. Furthermore (see Exercise C, Question 11), we are in a position to show that Newton's model is the only possible simple model for the observed motion of the heavens. If the positions and velocities of all the objects in the universe at one instant were known from observation, we should be able to determine them at any subsequent time merely by calculation.

In practice, even using computers, it is not possible to take many observations into account. Nevertheless, this model enables such events as eclipses to be forecast with considerable accuracy, and enables space travel to be achieved with the minimum use of fuel.

Such calculations, involving the interaction of two or more bodies, are beyond the scope of this book. Nor shall we consider Einstein's refinement of Newton's model to take account of relativistic effects.

However, we are now in a position to solve problems along the following lines: A satellite is orbiting earth in an ellipse, where the maximum and minimum heights from earth are known. (The position of greatest height is called the *apogee* and the position of least height the *perigee*.) The speed at the apogee is given, and it is desired to find details of the orbit and the velocity at the perigee. This latter velocity is increased by a certain amount so as to put the satellite into a hyperbolic orbit, what will be the ultimate direction of the satellite's motion

The example which follows is based on the above problem but in order not to confuse the theory with awkward calculations, simple numerical values have been chosen.

Example 4. (a) A particle is moving in an elliptical path under the inverse square law of attraction so that its maximum and minimum distances from O are 5 units and 4 units respectively. Its speed at maximum distance is 16 units/s. Find the orbit, and the speed when 4 units from O.

The centre of attraction O must be a focus of the ellipse. Thus, since the extreme distances from O occur when the particle is at an apse, with the apse line as initial line, the ellipse can be taken as $l/r = 1 + e\cos\theta$. Now $r = 4$ when $\theta = 0$ and $r = 5$ when $\theta = \pi$

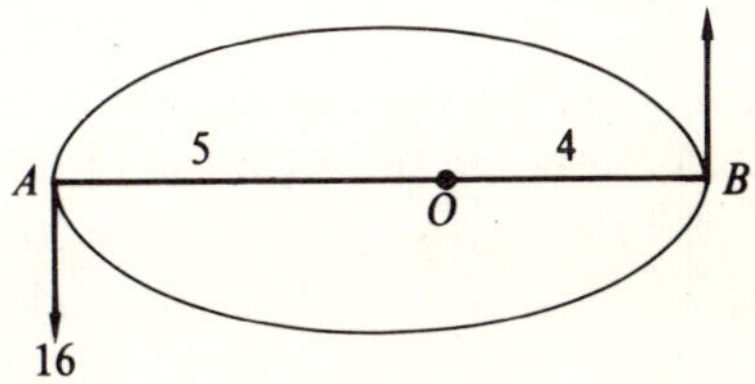

Fig. 8.

$$\Longrightarrow \tfrac{1}{4}l = 1 + e,$$

$$\tfrac{1}{5}l = 1 - e,$$

giving $l = 40/9$, $e = 1/9$, and the equation of the ellipse is

$$40 = r(9 + \cos\theta).$$

In the usual notation,

$$\begin{aligned} h &= 0A \times \text{speed at } A, \\ &= 80, \\ &= 0B \times \text{speed at } B, \end{aligned}$$

hence speed at B is 20 units/s.

(b) The speed of the particle at B is now increased instantaneously by 50%, determine the new orbit.

We now have the situation where the new orbit is another conic (since the inverse square law still holds) and where B is an apse. Suppose the conic is

$l_1/r = 1 + e_1 \cos\theta$ with the same initial line as before.

$$\text{From (10):} \quad l = h^2/\mu \text{ and } l_1 = h_1^2/\mu$$

$$\Rightarrow \quad \frac{l_1}{l} = \frac{h_1^2}{h^2}, \quad \text{using suffix 1 for new orbit.}$$

But $h_1 = \dfrac{3h}{2} = 120$, since speed is increased 50%.

Thus $$l_1 = \tfrac{9}{4} l, \Rightarrow l_1 = 10,$$

and since $OB = 4$, $\dfrac{l_1}{4} = 1 + e, \quad \Rightarrow \quad e_1 = \dfrac{3}{2}.$

Thus the new orbit is the hyperbola

$$10 = r(1 + \tfrac{3}{2}\cos\theta)$$

or

$$20 = r(2 + 3\cos\theta).$$

(c) Find the direction which this new orbit approaches and also the ultimate speed of the particle.

From the equation $20/r = 2 + 3\cos\theta$, $\cos\theta \to -\frac{2}{3}$ as $r \to \infty$, and the direction of motion will make an angle $\cos^{-1}(-\frac{2}{3})$ with initial line.

Now $$v^2 = \dot{r}^2 + (r\dot{\theta})^2$$

and so we try to express this in terms of the known angle θ.
Differentiating the equation of orbit:

$$\frac{-20}{r^2}\dot{r} = 3\sin\theta\,\dot{\theta}$$

$$\Rightarrow \quad \dot{r} = \frac{3}{20} h_1 \sin\theta,$$

since $$r^2\dot{\theta} = h_1 .$$

Thus $$v^2 = h_1^2\left[\frac{9}{20^2}\sin^2\theta\right] + \left[\frac{h_1}{r}\right]^2$$

$$\Rightarrow \quad v^2 = \frac{120^2}{20^2}\,[9(1 - \cos^2\theta) + (2 + 3\cos\theta)^2],$$

since $h_1 = 120$.

As $$\cos\theta \to \tfrac{-2}{3}$$

$$v^2 \to 36 \times 5,$$

$$v \to 6\sqrt{5},$$

$\Rightarrow$'velocity at infinity' $= 6\sqrt{5}$ units/s.

EXERCISE C

In this exercise, all questions involving central forces are such that the force is inversely proportional to r^2.

1. For motion along the curve $1/r = \frac{1}{2} + \frac{2}{5}\cos\theta$, find the apsidal distances and hence the ratio of maximum to minimum speeds.

2. A satellite is in orbit round the earth with speeds at apogee and perigee in the ratio 7 : 8. The distance between the apogee and perigee is 15 000 km. Find the distances of apogee and perigee from the centre of the earth and hence the equation of orbit when the line joining the centre of the earth to the perigee is taken as initial line.

3. Sketch the curves

(a) $\dfrac{1}{r} = \dfrac{1}{2}(1 - \sin\theta)$,

(b) $\dfrac{1}{r} = \dfrac{1}{3}(2 + \sin\theta)$,

(c) $\dfrac{1}{r} = \dfrac{1}{3}(1 + 2\sin\theta)$.

How are these related to curves in Exercise A, Question 1?

4. A particle is describing an ellipse of eccentricity $\frac{1}{2}$. When at the perigee the speed is doubled, find the new eccentricity of the orbit.

5. A particle is describing a hyperbola of eccentricity $\frac{3}{2}$. When at the apse the velocity is halved, find the new eccentricity of the orbit.

6. A particle is describing an ellipse of eccentricity $\frac{1}{2}$. It is desired to change its velocity at the apogee so as to make the orbit circular. In what way should the velocity be altered?

7. A particle is describing a hyperbola of eccentricity $\frac{3}{2}$ and it is desired to change the velocity at an apse so as to make the orbit parabolic. What change of speed is required?

8. Find the ratio of maximum to minimum forces acting on a particle moving in the orbit $10/r = 5 + \cos\theta$.

9. A particle moving along the hyperbola $1/r = \sqrt{(3)} - 2\cos\theta$ has speed $4/[\sqrt{(3)} + 2]$ units/s at the apse. Find the direction which the motion approaches and the ultimate speed of the particle.

10. A particle is attracted to a fixed point O with force μ/r^2 per unit mass. Initially it is projected from a point P with speed v at right angles to OP where $OP = a$. If the orbit takes the form $l/r = 1 + e\cos\theta$, use the u, θ form for acceleration to show that $h^2 = \mu l$. Write down expressions for l and h in terms of a and v and hence show that $v^2 = \mu(1 + e)/a$.

What conditions must be satisfied by v for the orbit to be

(a) an ellipse,

(b) a parabola,

(c) a hyperbola?

11. Kepler (1571–1630) from his observations concluded

(a) that the planets have elliptical orbits with the sun as focus,

(b) that the radius from the sun to a planet sweeps out equal areas in equal times.

Prove that these statements together with Newton's Laws of Motion imply that the motion of the planets is subject to a central inverse square law of force.

4. CARTESIAN EQUATION OF CONICS

The polar equation of a conic is

$$\frac{l}{r} = 1 + e\cos\theta$$

$$\Rightarrow \quad l = r + er\cos\theta$$

$$\Rightarrow \quad r = l - er\cos\theta$$

$$\Rightarrow \quad x^2 + y^2 = (l - ex)^2$$

$$\Rightarrow \quad (1 - e^2)x^2 + y^2 = l^2 - 2elx. \tag{11}$$

4.1 Ellipse

When $e < 1$, equation (11) becomes:

$$x^2 + \frac{2el}{1-e^2}x + \frac{y^2}{1-e^2} = \frac{l^2}{1-e^2}.$$

Completing the square:

$$\left(x + \frac{el}{1-e^2}\right)^2 + \frac{y^2}{1-e^2} = \frac{l^2}{(1-e^2)^2}.$$

Denoting the quantity $l/(1 - e^2)$ by a, this becomes:

$$(x + ae)^2 + \frac{y^2}{1 - e^2} = a^2$$

$$\Rightarrow \quad \frac{(x + ae)^2}{a^2} + \frac{y^2}{a^2(1 - e^2)} = 1,$$

where $l = a(1 - e^2)$.

$$\Rightarrow \quad \frac{(x + ae)^2}{a^2} + \frac{y^2}{b^2} = 1,$$

where $\quad b^2 = a^2(1 - e^2) = al.$

A translation of the ellipse through

$$\begin{pmatrix} ae \\ 0 \end{pmatrix}$$

gives $\quad \dfrac{x^2}{a^2} + \dfrac{y^2}{b^2} = 1,$

the standard equation of the ellipse in cartesian coordinates.

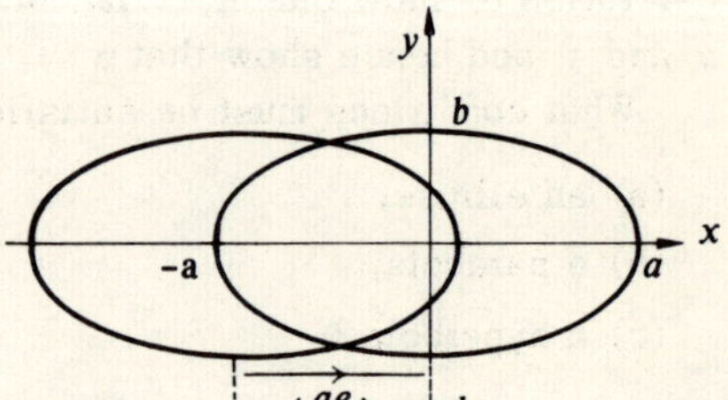

Fig. 9.

Note that this equation is expressed in terms of two constants a and b. These are more convenient to work with than e and l. All four constants are, of course, related as shown above and any two could be used.

4.2 Hyperbola

When $e > 1$, a similar approach leads to the cartesian equation

$$\frac{x^2}{a^2} - \frac{y^2}{b^2} = 1,$$

where $al = a^2(e^2 - 1) = b^2$.

4.3 Parabola

If $e = 1$, the equation (11) becomes

$$y^2 = l^2 - 2lx = l(l - 2x).$$

Reflection in the line $x = \frac{1}{4}l$, gives,

$$y^2 = 2lx,$$

or $$y^2 = 4ax, \text{ where } l = 2a.$$

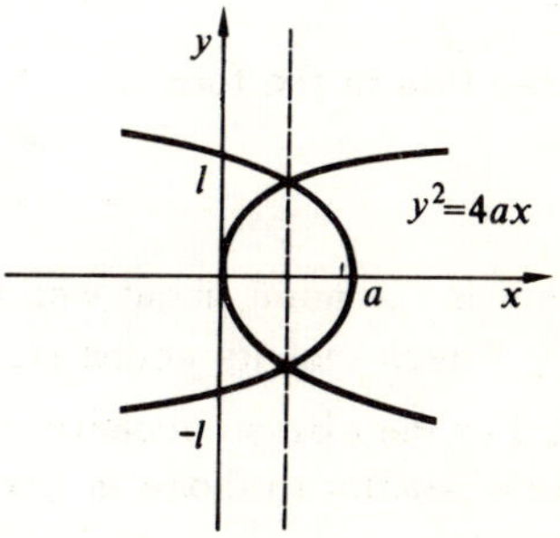

Fig. 10.

This is the standard cartesian equation of the parabola.

EXERCISE D

1. Carry out working similar to that in 4.1 to obtain the result for the hyperbola in 4.2.

2. Use $a^2(1 - e^2) = b^2$ to find the eccentricity of the ellipse

$$\frac{x^2}{25} + \frac{y^2}{16} = 1.$$

3. Show that the circle $x^2 + y^2 = 9$ transforms into the ellipse

$$\frac{x^2}{9} + \frac{y^2}{4} = 1,$$

under a stretch factor $\frac{2}{3}$ parallel to the y axis. What would be the area of the ellipse?

4. A transformation given by the matrix

$$\begin{pmatrix} 4 & 0 \\ 0 & 3 \end{pmatrix}$$

is applied to the circle $x^2 + y^2 = 1$. Show that the resulting curve is an ellipse and find its eccentricity.

5. Find the equation of the ellipse

$$\frac{x^2}{9} + \frac{y^2}{4} = 1$$

after a translation

$$\begin{pmatrix}-1\\ 2\end{pmatrix}$$

and show that it can be written in the form $4x^2 + 9y^2 + 8x - 36y + 4 = 0$.

6. A hyperbola has eccentricity 2, focus $S\,(1, 3)$ and directrix $x = 4$.

If P is the point (x, y) on the hyperbola, write down expressions for SP^2 and the square of the distance from P to the directrix.

Use the focus directrix property to show that the equation of the hyperbola is

$$3x^2 - y^2 - 30x + 6y + 54 = 0.$$

Write this in the form

$$\frac{(x - \lambda)^2}{a^2} - \frac{(y - \mu)^2}{b^2} = 1.$$

What is the point about which the hyperbola has point symmetry?

Check that its eccentricity is 2 using $b^2 = a^2(e^2 - 1)$.

7. For the ellipse eccentricity $\frac{1}{3}$, focus $(1, -2)$ and directrix $x = -3$, carry out steps similar to those in Question 6.

8. Use the focus directrix definition to show that the equation of the parabola focus $(2, 0)$ and directrix $x = -2$ is $y^2 = 8x$.

*5. GEOMETRICAL PROPERTIES OF CONICS

5.1 A tangent property of conics

It is necessary to establish a property concerning the tangent at a point on a conic in order that other simple properties may be derived. We shall first prove the following result.

If any chord PQ of a conic focus O meets the directrix in R, then OP and OQ are equally inclined to OR.

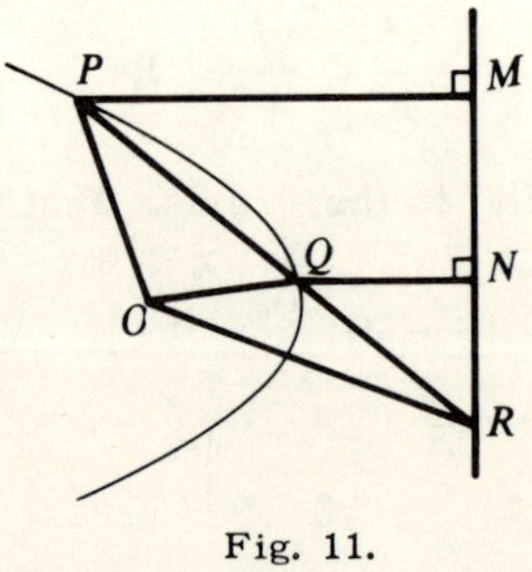

Fig. 11.

Now $\dfrac{PM}{QN} = \dfrac{PR}{QR}$ and $\dfrac{PM}{QN} = \dfrac{OP}{OQ}$ (Focus-directrix property)

$$\Rightarrow \quad \frac{PR}{RQ} = \frac{-p}{q}$$

in the usual notation, where $OP = p$, etc.

By the ratio theorem:

$$(p - q)\mathbf{r} = p\mathbf{q} - q\mathbf{p}$$

$$\Rightarrow (p - q)\mathbf{r}\cdot\mathbf{p} = p\mathbf{q}\cdot\mathbf{p} - qp^2$$

and

$$(p - q)\mathbf{r}\cdot\mathbf{q} = pq^2 - q\mathbf{p}\cdot\mathbf{q}.$$

Hence

$$\left(\frac{p - q}{p}\right)\mathbf{r}\cdot\mathbf{p} = \mathbf{q}\cdot\mathbf{p} - qp$$

and

$$\left(\frac{p - q}{q}\right)\mathbf{r}\cdot\mathbf{q} = pq - \mathbf{p}\cdot\mathbf{q}.$$

Thus

$$\frac{1}{p}\,\mathbf{r}\cdot\mathbf{p} = \frac{-1}{q}\mathbf{r}\cdot\mathbf{q}$$

$$\Rightarrow \cos\angle POR = -\cos\angle QOR \quad \text{(by definition of dot product)}$$

$\Rightarrow$ OP and OQ are equally inclined to OR.

If Q now moves along the curve towards P the chord PQ will approach the tangent at P and, since OR will always bisect $\angle POQ$ externally, in the limiting position $\angle ROP = 90°$.

Thus we have the following result. If the tangent at P to a conic meets the directrix in R, then PR subtends a right angle at the focus.

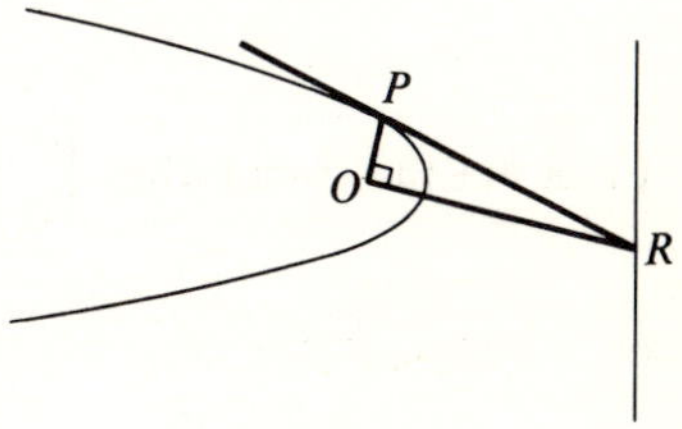

Fig. 12.

5.2 Focal properties and symmetry of central conics

From the standard cartesian equations of the ellipse and hyperbola it can be seen that these curves have line symmetry about both axes, and thus point symmetry about the origin. The position of point symmetry is known as the centre of the conic, and the ellipse and hyperbola are referred to as central conics.

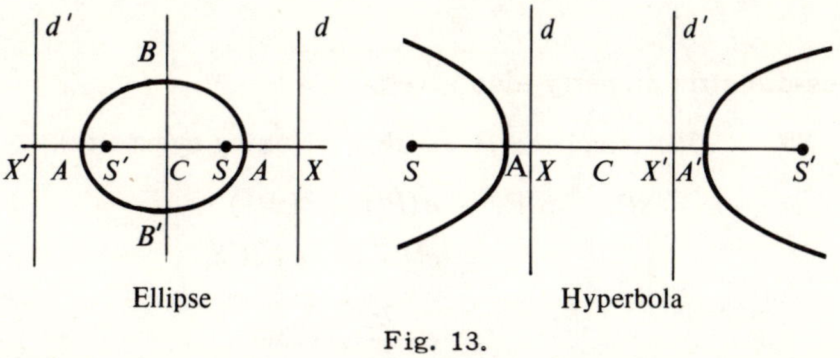

Fig. 13.

The length AA' is known as the major axis of the conic, and in the case of the ellipse BB' is the minor axis. In terms of the standard equations

$$AA' = 2a, \qquad BB' = 2b.$$

These conics were generated using the focus-directrix property with the point

S and line d. However, the existence of symmetry shows that the same curve would have been traced using the symmetrically placed point S' as focus and d' as directrix.

Consequently, any central conic has associated with it two foci and two directrices.

The notation of the above figure will apply throughout this section.

Example 5. Find the length of CX for the ellipse in terms of a and e. Show that if P is any point on the ellipse, then $SP + S'P = 2a$.

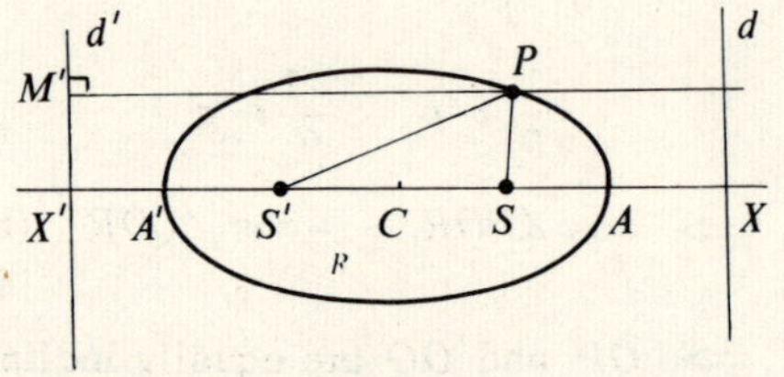

Fig. 14.

From 4.1 the translation $\begin{pmatrix} ae \\ 0 \end{pmatrix} = \mathbf{CS}$

$$\Rightarrow CS = ae$$

$$\Rightarrow SA = a - ae.$$

But $\qquad SA = eAX$ (Focus-directrix property)

$$\Rightarrow a - ae = eAX,$$

and

$$CX = CA + AX$$

$$= a + \frac{a - ae}{e}$$

$$= \frac{a}{e}.$$

The focus-directrix property also gives

$$SP = ePM \quad \text{and} \quad S'P = ePM' \quad \text{(using symmetry).}$$

Thus

$$SP + S'P = e(PM + PM')$$

$$= eMM' = e \cdot 2CX$$

$$= e \cdot \frac{2a}{e} = 2a.$$

How does this enable an ellipse to be drawn with the aid of a length of string?

Example 6. If P is any point on a hyperbola, show that the tangent at P bisects the angle SPS.

From 5.1 PR and PR' subtend right angles at S and S' respectively.

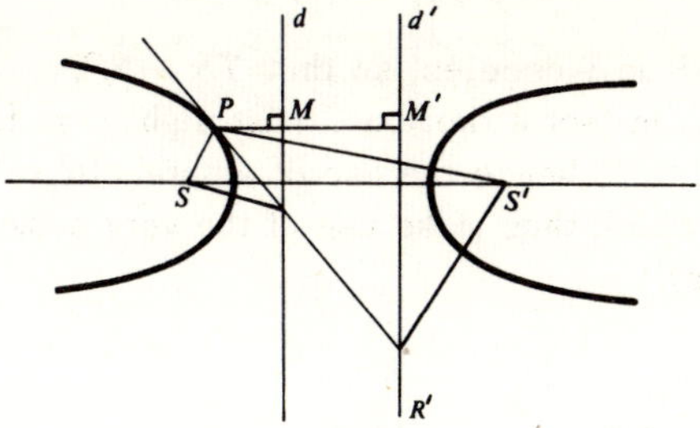

Fig. 15.

Now $\qquad SP = ePM \quad \text{and} \quad S'P = ePM'$

$$\Rightarrow \quad \frac{SP}{S'P} = \frac{PM}{PM'} = \frac{PR}{PR'}$$

or

$$\frac{SP}{PR} = \frac{S'P}{PR'}$$

$$\Rightarrow \quad \cos \angle SPR = \cos \angle S'PR'$$

$\Rightarrow$ tangent at P bisects the angle SPS'.

5.3 Properties of the parabola

A parabola has eccentricity equal to one and only one line of symmetry, the axis of the parabola. The single focus lies on this axis and the directrix is perpendicular to it.

Example 7. Show that the tangent at any point P on a parabola bisects the angle between the line joining P to the focus S and the perpendicular from P to the directrix. If the tangent at P meets the axis at T, show that $ST = SP$.

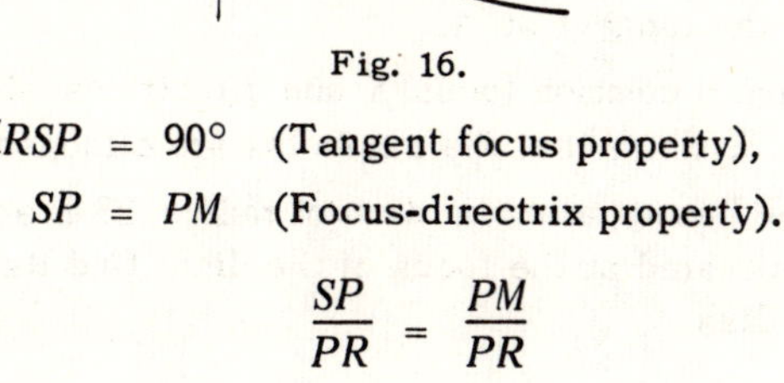

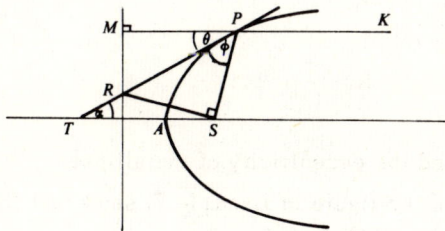

Fig. 16.

Now $\qquad \angle RSP = 90°$ (Tangent focus property),

and $\qquad SP = PM$ (Focus-directrix property).

Thus

$$\frac{SP}{PR} = \frac{PM}{PR}$$

$$\Rightarrow \quad \cos\phi = \cos\theta$$

$$\Rightarrow \quad \phi = \theta,$$

and PT bisects the angle SPM.

Since $$PM \parallel TS, \qquad \theta = \alpha.$$

Thus $\phi = \alpha$ and ΔTSP is isosceles, so that $TS = SP$.

Note that $TMPS$ is in fact a rhombus. Also light rays falling along the line KP would be reflected to S, hence the use of a parabolic reflector for headlamps, radar and telescopes (which thus make use of the very same curve (a conic) as the orbits they observe).

EXERCISE E

1. Find the length of CX for the hyperbola in terms of a and e, and show that if P is any point on the hyperbola, then $|SP - S'P| = 2a$.

2. If P is a point on the ellipse with foci S and S', show that SP and $S'P$ are equally inclined to the tangent at P.

3. Two tangents are drawn to a conic from a point on the directrix. Show that the chord joining the points of contact passes through the corresponding focus.

4. Show that the tangents at the end of a focal chord of a parabola meet at right angles on the directrix.

5.

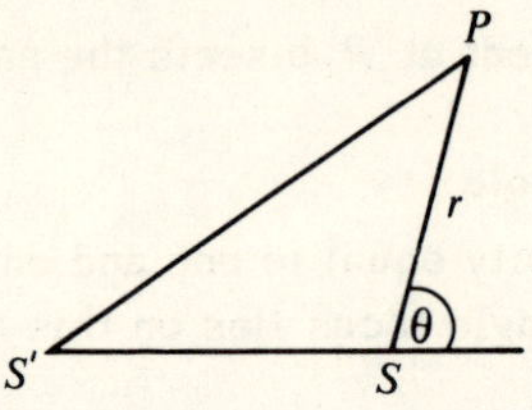

In the figure, P is any point on the ellipse in which S, S' are foci. $SS' = 2ae$, $SP + S'P = 2a$. Use the cosine formula to deduce the polar equation of the ellipse.

6. With the usual notation for the ellipse, show that

(a) $SB = a$

(b) $CS = e^2 CX$

(c) $CS \cdot SX = b^2$.

7. If $\angle SBS' = 90°$, find the eccentricity of the ellipse.

8. With the notation of the figure in Example 7, show that for the parabola SM and PT intersect on the tangent at A.

9. Two parabolas have a common focus S and directrices which are parallel and on opposite sides of S. Show that the parabolas are orthogonal.

10. A radio telescope has a parabolic dish of radius 25 m and its depth at the centre is 8m. An aerial is situated at the focus of the dish, find its distance from the deepest point in the dish.

*6. FURTHER EXAMPLES OF MOTION UNDER A CENTRAL FORCE

In this final section it is proposed to investigate the orbits which result from various laws of force with certain initial conditions.

For a central force which is a function of the distance, the motion is governed by the two equations first met in Section 1.1, namely

$$F(r) = -(\ddot{r} - r\dot{\theta}^2) \quad \text{and} \quad r^2\dot{\theta} = h,$$

where $F(r)$ is the force per unit mass.

Eliminating $\dot{\theta}$ gives
$$\ddot{r} - \frac{h^2}{r^3} = -F(r).$$

Multiply by $2\dot{r}$ and integrate with respect to t

$$\dot{r}^2 + \frac{h^2}{r^2} = -2\int F(r)\,\mathrm{d}r$$

$$\Rightarrow \left(\frac{h}{r^2}\cdot\frac{\mathrm{d}r}{\mathrm{d}\theta}\right)^2 = -\frac{h^2}{r^2} - 2\int F(r)\,\mathrm{d}r \quad \text{(see Section 2.1)}$$

$$\Rightarrow \left(\frac{\mathrm{d}r}{\mathrm{d}\theta}\right)^2 = -r^2 - \frac{2r^4}{h^2}\int F(r)\,\mathrm{d}r. \tag{12}$$

If the nature of $F(r)$ is known, then the equation (12) is a differential equation in r and θ whose solution is the polar equation of the orbit.

Example 8. Find the equation of the orbit of a particle if the central force is μ/r^5 per unit mass and the speed of the particle at an apse of distance 1 unit is $\sqrt{(\mu/2)}$.

The initial conditions give $h = 1\sqrt{(\mu/2)} = \sqrt{(\mu/2)}$.

Now
$$\ddot{r} - r\dot{\theta}^2 = \frac{-\mu}{r^5}$$

and proceeding as above we obtain

$$\left(\frac{\mathrm{d}r}{\mathrm{d}\theta}\right)^2 = -r^2 - \frac{2r^4}{h^2}\int\frac{\mu}{r^5}\,\mathrm{d}r$$

$$\Rightarrow \left(\frac{\mathrm{d}r}{\mathrm{d}\theta}\right)^2 = -r^2 - 4r^4\int\frac{\mathrm{d}r}{r^5}$$

$$\Rightarrow \left(\frac{\mathrm{d}r}{\mathrm{d}\theta}\right)^2 = -r^2 + 4r^4\left(\frac{1}{4r^4} + A\right).$$

But at an apse
$$\frac{\mathrm{d}r}{\mathrm{d}\theta} = 0 \quad \text{and} \quad r = 1$$

$$\Rightarrow 0 = -1 + 1 + 4A$$

$$\Rightarrow A = 0,$$

and hence
$$\left(\frac{\mathrm{d}r}{\mathrm{d}\theta}\right)^2 = 1 - r^2$$

$$\Rightarrow \quad \frac{dr}{d\theta} = \sqrt{(1 - r^2)} \tag{A}$$

$$\Rightarrow \quad \int_1^r \frac{dr}{\sqrt{(1 - r^2)}} = \int_0^\theta d\theta,$$

if we choose the initial line as the given apse line.

Thus
$$[\sin^{-1} r]_1^r = [\theta]_0^\theta$$

$$\Rightarrow \quad \sin^{-1} r - \tfrac{1}{2}\pi = \theta$$

$$\Rightarrow \quad r = \sin(\theta + \tfrac{1}{2}\pi)$$

$$\Rightarrow \quad r = \cos\theta.$$

It should be noted that if the negative root were chosen in equation (A) the same result would have been obtained.

Whilst the above method is applicable in theory to any function $F(r)$ it is helpful in some cases to make the substitution $r = 1/u$ in which case it has been shown (Exercise A, Question 12) that $-h^2u^2[(d^2u/d\theta^2) + u]$ is an alternative expression for the radial acceleration.

The following example illustrates the use of this method.

Example 9. A satellite is launched in such a way that when the rocket burns out, its speed is $\frac{1}{4}\sqrt{(21\mu)}$ units and its distance from the centre of the earth is $\frac{8}{9}$ units. If its direction at this instant makes an angle $\sin^{-1} 9/2\sqrt{21}$ with the line joining the centre of the earth O to the satellite P, and the force of attraction is μ/OP^2 per unit mass, show that the orbit is an ellipse. Find the distances of apogee and perigee and the maximum and minimum speeds of the satellite.

In the usual notation

$$h^2u^2\left(\frac{d^2u}{d\theta^2} + u\right) = \mu u^2$$

$$\Rightarrow \quad h^2\left(\frac{d^2u}{d\theta^2} + u\right) = \mu.$$

Multiply by $2\dfrac{du}{d\theta}$ and integrate

$$h^2\left[\left(\frac{du}{d\theta}\right)^2 + u^2\right] = 2\mu u + \text{constant.} \tag{A}$$

$$\Rightarrow v^2 = 2\mu u + \text{constant (See Exercise A Question 13.)}$$

Initially, $v = \frac{1}{4}\sqrt{(21\mu)}$ and $u = \frac{9}{8} \Rightarrow \text{constant} = \frac{-15}{16}\mu.$

Also initial conditions give

$$h = rv\sin\phi$$

$$\Rightarrow \quad h = \frac{8}{9}\cdot\frac{1}{4}\sqrt{(21\mu)}\cdot\frac{9}{2\sqrt{21}}$$

$$\Rightarrow \quad h = \sqrt{\mu}.$$

Thus equation (A) becomes

$$\mu\left[\left(\frac{du}{d\theta}\right)^2 + u^2\right] = 2\mu u - \tfrac{15}{16}\mu$$

$$\Rightarrow \left(\frac{du}{d\theta}\right)^2 = -u^2 + 2u - \frac{15}{16}$$

$$= \tfrac{1}{16} - (\mu - 1)^2.$$

At an apse

$$\frac{du}{d\theta} = 0 \Rightarrow u - 1 = \pm\tfrac{1}{4}$$

$$\Rightarrow \quad u = \tfrac{5}{4} \text{ or } \tfrac{3}{4}.$$

Now

$$\int_{\frac{5}{4}}^{u} \frac{du}{\sqrt{[\frac{1}{16} - (u-1)^2]}} = \int_0^{\theta} d\theta$$

choosing initial line $\theta = 0$, when $u = \frac{5}{4}$.

Thus

$$[\sin^{-1} 4(u-1)]_{5/4}^{u} = \theta$$

$$\Rightarrow \sin^{-1} 4(u-1) - \tfrac{1}{2}\pi = \theta$$

$$\Rightarrow \quad 4(u-1) = \sin(\theta + \tfrac{1}{2}\pi)$$

$$= \cos\theta$$

$$\Rightarrow \quad u = 1 + \tfrac{1}{4}\cos\theta,$$

or

$$\frac{1}{r} = 1 + \frac{1}{4}\cos\theta,$$

which is the equation of an ellipse.

At the apogee $r = \frac{4}{3}$, and at the perigee $r = \frac{4}{5}$.

The maximum speed occurs when $r = \frac{4}{5}$ and equals

$$\frac{h}{\frac{4}{5}} = \frac{5\sqrt{\mu}}{4}.$$

The minimum speed occurs when $r = \frac{4}{3}$ and equals

$$\frac{h}{\frac{4}{3}} = \frac{3\sqrt{\mu}}{4}.$$

Example 10. A particle describes the orbit $1/r^2 = 2 + \cos 2\theta$ under a central force towards the origin. Show that this force is proportional to r.

Equation of orbit is

$$u^2 = 2 + \cos 2\theta \qquad \text{(A)}$$

$$\Rightarrow \quad 2u\frac{du}{d\theta} = -2\sin 2\theta$$

$$\Rightarrow \quad u\frac{du}{d\theta} = -\sin 2\theta$$

$$\Rightarrow \quad u\frac{d^2u}{d\theta^2} + \left(\frac{du}{d\theta}\right)^2 = -2\cos 2\theta.$$

Thus $u^3\dfrac{d^2u}{d\theta^2} + \sin^2 2\theta = -2u^2\cos 2\theta \quad \left(\text{substituting for } u\dfrac{du}{d\theta}\right).$

Eliminating θ from (A) gives

$$u^3\frac{d^2u}{d\theta^2} + [1-(u^2-2)^2] = 2u^2(2-u^2)$$

$$\Rightarrow \quad u^3\frac{d^2u}{d\theta^2} - 3 + 4u^2 - u^4 = 4u^2 - 2u^4$$

$$\Rightarrow \quad u^3\frac{d^2u}{d\theta^2} + u^4 = 3$$

$$\Rightarrow \quad u^2\left(\frac{d^2u}{d\theta^2} + u\right) = \frac{3}{u}.$$

In the usual notation, this implies $F = 3h^2/u$, a force proportional to r.

EXERCISE F

1. Show that if the negative root is taken in equation (A) of Example 8, the same orbit is obtained.

2. A particle moving under a central force per unit mass of μr, is projected from an apse, distance $\frac{1}{4}\sqrt{2}$ units with speed $\sqrt{(\mu/2)}$ units/s. Show that, with suitable choice of initial line, the equation of the orbit is $1/r^2 = 5 + 3\cos 2\theta$.

3. A particle describes the curve $r = 2a\sin\theta$ under the action of a central force, show that this force is proportional to $1/r^5$.

4. O is a fixed point and a particle of unit mass is projected from a point A at right angles to the line OA with velocity V. The particle is attracted to O with a force $\mu u^3(1+u^2)$. If OA is 2 units and $V^2 = 9\mu/32$, show that the orbit is $r = 2\cos\frac{1}{3}\theta$.

5. A particle describes the curve $1/r = \cos n\theta$ under a central force; show that this force is inversely proportional to r^3.

6. A particle describes the curve $r = a(1+\cos\theta)$ under a central force, show that this force is proportional to $1/r^4$.

7. A particle moves under a force equal to μ/r^3 per unit mass. Initially it is moving with speed V at an angle $\frac{3}{4}\pi$ with the direction of the radius vector length a. Show that if $V^2 = 2\mu/a^2$, then initially $du/d\theta = 1/a$ and determine the polar equation of the orbit, where the initial line is chosen as the direction of the radius vector at the start.

8. A particle mass m moves under a central force

$$m\left[\frac{9}{r^4} - \frac{10}{r^5}\right]$$

and is projected from an apse, distance 5 units, with a speed $\frac{1}{5}$ unit/s. Show that the orbit can be written in the form

$$r = 3 + 2\cos\theta.$$

SUMMARY

For motion under a central force

$$r^2\dot{\theta} = h \quad \text{(a constant).}$$

The rate of description of area (areal speed) $= \frac{1}{2}h$.

Also h = speed × apsidal distance.

For an inverse square law force of μ/r^2 per unit mass the orbit is

$$\frac{1}{r} = \frac{\mu}{h^2} + k\cos\theta,$$

which is a conic. A conic is the locus of a point whose distance from a fixed point (the focus) is a constant multiple (e, the eccentricity) of its distance from a fixed line (the directrix).

The polar equation of any conic is

$$\frac{l}{r} = 1 + e\cos\theta$$

where l (the semi latus rectum) is the distance from the focus to the conic in a direction parallel to the directrix. Also $l = k^2/\mu$.

For $e < 1$ the conic is an ellipse with 'standard' cartesian equation

$$\frac{x^2}{a^2} + \frac{y^2}{b^2} = 1, \text{ where } al = a^2(1 - e^2) = b^2.$$

For $e = 1$ the conic is a parabola with 'standard' cartesian equation

$$y^2 = 4ax,$$

where $1 = 2a$.

For $e > 1$ the conic is a hyperbola with 'standard' cartesian equation

$$\frac{x^2}{a^2} - \frac{y^2}{b^2} = 1, \text{ where } al = a^2(e^2 - 1) = b^2.$$

The ellipse and hyperbola (by their symmetry) have two foci.

The sum (for the ellipse) or difference (for the hyperbola) of the distances of any point on the conic from the foci is constant ($= 2a$).

The parabola has the special property, as a reflector, that rays parallel to its axis of symmetry will be reflected to the focus.

3. Vector Products

1. MOMENTS

1.1 Rotation

In previous discussions of the forces applied to bodies we have restricted our attention to the translational effect of the forces. It is obvious from everyday life that when we apply forces to objects they often move with rotational as well as translational motion. Pushing a clock pendulum or a child's swing causes it to rotate, and jerking the string of a yo-yo (i.e. giving it an impulse) causes it to rotate rapidly, at the same time moving it up and down.

A good example of this occurs with a space vehicle when one of the rockets fails to fire on take-off. The space vehicle does not move in a straight upward path but moves in a tight curve back towards the ground. Thus the firing of all but one of the rockets produces rotational motion. Similarly when a space craft is far enough from the earth not to be strongly affected by gravity, it can control its movements by small propulsive forces. The firing of one of its rockets usually causes rotation, so in order to navigate the craft and manoeuvre it successfully we must be able to anticipate and calculate the rotational effect of forces.

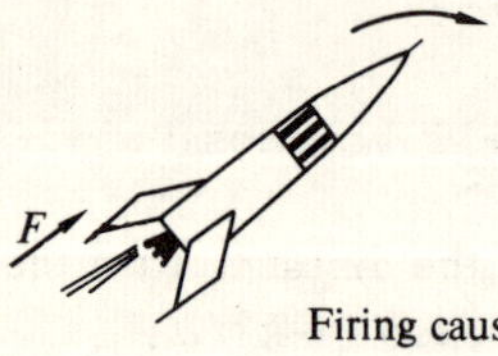

Firing causes rotation

Fig. 1.

This chapter will be concerned with the solution of the basic problem – what is the rotational effect of forces? We will develop a mathematical convention for describing rotation that will eventually lead to a general formula for the rotational effect of any system of forces.

1.2 Examples

Consider the following particular cases of rotation:

Example 1. A model helicopter has rotating rotors powered by solid fuel 'jets' fixed at the end of each rotor.

If the jets are fixed to fire along (parallel to) the rotors, then there is no rotation, and by experiment the fastest rotation is produced by jets aligned at right angles to the line PB. (See Figure 2).

If the jet is fixed at an angle θ to the rotor (Figure 3), then we can replace **F** by its components $F \cos\theta$ acting along the rotor and $F \sin\theta$ perpendicular to it.

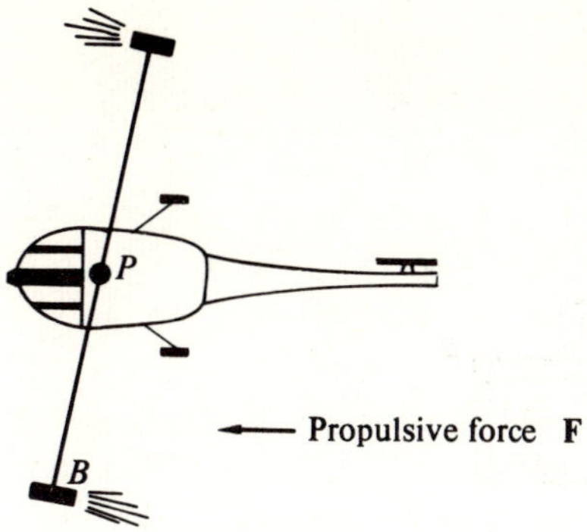

Fig. 2.

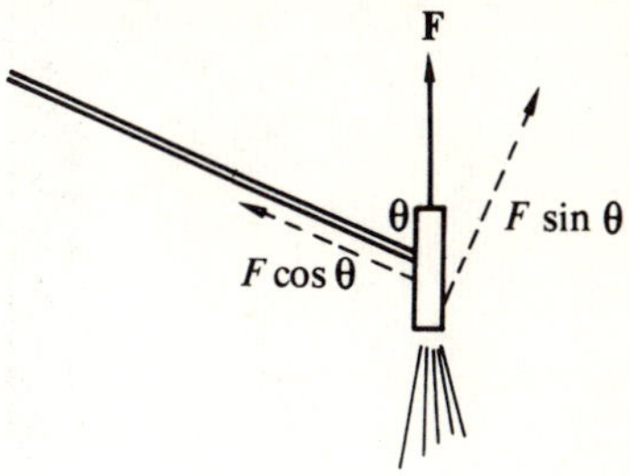

Fig. 3.

The former cannot cause rotation about the pivot as it acts through it, while the whole of $F \sin\theta$ is used to push the rotor around. So the turning effect of the force **F** is $F \sin\theta$ where θ is the angle between the force and the rotor. (Note that there is no rotation when $\theta = 0°$ and the maximum rotational effect is when $\theta = 90°$. What happens if $\theta > 90°$?)

Example 2. A crane supports a fixed load of weight **W**. Discuss the positioning of the load along the horizontal jib of the crane.

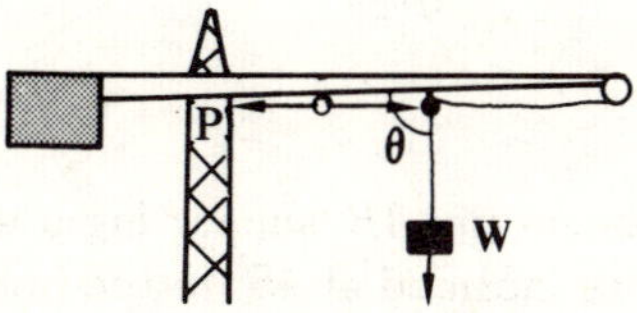

Fig. 4.

In this situation **W** is fixed and θ is 90° so the 'turning effect', i.e. the strain on P, is caused by **W**. Does this effect change for different values of a, the distance of **W** from P? Clearly it does, and experiment shows that it varies directly with the distance a. So if the distance is doubled, then the turning effect of **W** is twice as much as before (when $a = 0$ there is no turning effect). In this situation the turning effect (or moment) of **W** is measured by the *product* $W \times a$. Moments of forces measured in this way are useful because they can be added and equated, as in the examples below.

Example 3. An inn sign is supported by a rigid iron framework ABC attached to a vertical wall at A and C such that $\angle ABC = 30°$. The sign of mass 10 kg is supported equally at B and D, where $BD = 20$ cm and $DA = 10$ cm (see Figure 5).

Find the tension in BC.

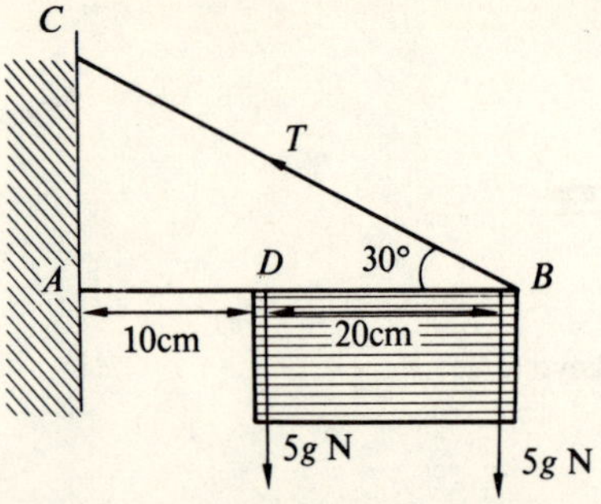

Fig. 5.

We can solve this problem by considering the rod AB. It is not rotating about A, so the total rotational effect of the three forces acting on it must be zero. We therefore 'take moments' about A:

(i) Moment of **T** about A is $(T \sin 30°) \times 0{\cdot}3$ newton m.

(ii) Moment of force at B about A is $(5g \sin 90°) \times 0{\cdot}3$ Nm.

(iii) Moment of force at D about A is $(5g \sin 90°) \times 0{\cdot}1$ Nm.

The effect of **T** is to rotate in the opposite direction to the forces at B and D, so for equilibrium:

$$(T \sin 30° \times 0{\cdot}3) = (5g \times 0{\cdot}3) + (5g \times 0{\cdot}1) = 2g.$$

Therefore $$T = \frac{2g}{0{\cdot}15} = 13\tfrac{1}{3}g \text{ newtons.}$$

EXERCISE A

1. Figure 6 represents a crane jib AB supporting a weight **W** and held in position by a stay BC. Given AB is inclined at 45° to the horizontal and $\angle ABC = 30°$ find the tension in BC in terms of **W**. (Take moments about A.)

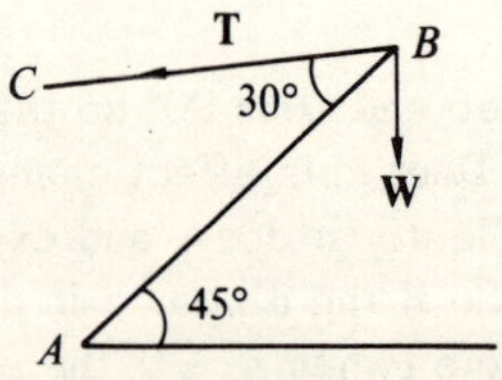

Fig. 6.

2. In Examples 1, 2 and 3 the rotation is said to be about a point. Is this strictly true? Check that the point concerned lies in the *plane* of rotation and that the rotation in each case can be thought of as about an axis perpendicular to the plane of rotation. Suggest how the problems would be altered if all the forces did not act in the same plane, while rotation was only possible in the original plane of rotation.

3. The distance between the back wheels of a coach is 2 metres. The coach must be able to rest on a slope of 45° without toppling. Find the maximum height of the centre of gravity (assumed to be symmetrically positioned).

4. A uniform ladder of length 3 metres and mass 15 kg rests on rough horizontal ground against a smooth vertical wall. By taking moments about the lower end find the reaction at the wall, given that the lower end of the ladder is 1 metre from the wall.

5. A bolt of diameter 0·5 cm is tightened by a spanner of 'effective' length 15 cm. A force of 5 newtons is applied to the spanner, what is the force produced on the shaft of the bolt?

6. A uniform solid cube of wood rests on a horizontal surface. The coefficient of friction between the two is 0·7. A horizontal force is applied halfway along a top edge of the cube and perpendicular to the edge. If this force is gradually increased from zero, will the cube slide or topple over?

7. A force **F** acts at one end of a rod of length l. The acute angle between the force and the rod is θ. By resolving **F** find its turning effect about the other end of the rod, B. Would you get the same result if you used the obtuse angle $(\pi - \theta)$? Show that the formula is the product of the magnitude of **F** and the perpendicular distance of its line of action from B.

2. THE VECTOR PRODUCT

2.1 Moments as vectors

The examples of the previous section illustrate that if we wish to calculate the moment of a force **F** about a point O then this is given by $rF \sin\theta$ (where **r** is the vector joining O to the point of application of **F**). $rF \sin\theta = |\mathbf{r}| \times |\mathbf{F}| \times \sin\theta$ where θ is the angle between **r** and **F**.

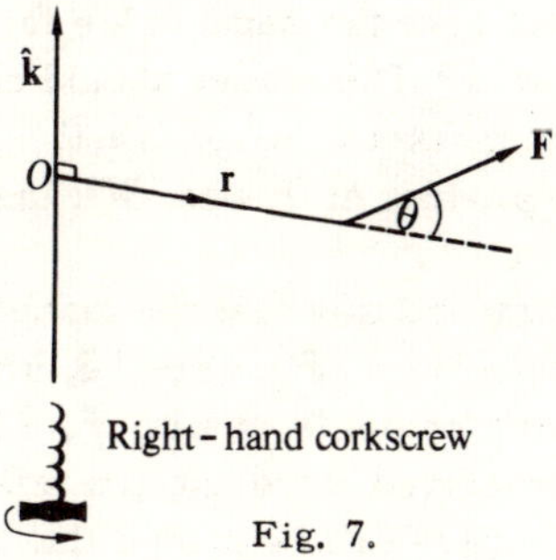

Fig. 7.

The axis of rotation is perpendicular to the plane of **r** and **F** (that is, in the direction of the unit vector $\hat{\mathbf{e}}$). In fact the moment of a force about O really means the moment of the force *about an axis through O perpendicular to the force*. The possibility of a non-perpendicular axis is investigated in Section 4.

Thus knowing **r** and **F** we can describe the rotational effect of **F** about O as being of magnitude $|\mathbf{r}| \times |\mathbf{F}| \times \sin\theta$ about an axis of direction $\hat{\mathbf{e}}$. Suppose we were to go one stage further and 'represent' this turning effect completely by *one vector* whose magnitude is the moment and whose direction is that of the axis of rotation: the vector $|\mathbf{r}| \times |\mathbf{F}| \times \sin\theta\,\hat{\mathbf{e}}$. (Remember $\hat{\mathbf{e}}$ is a unit vector.)

This vector sums up all we want to know about the turning effect of **F** and we will find it is not just an artificial creation but is extremely useful and in many ways can be treated as an ordinary vector.

2.2 Vector product

This representation is called the *vector product* of **r** and **F** and is denoted by $\mathbf{r}\wedge\mathbf{F}$.†

$$\mathbf{r}\wedge\mathbf{F} = |\mathbf{r}| \times |\mathbf{F}| \times \sin\theta\,\hat{\mathbf{e}} = rF\sin\theta\,\hat{\mathbf{e}}. \tag{1}$$

Strictly speaking there are two (opposite) directions perpendicular to the plane of **r** and **F**. We choose $\hat{\mathbf{e}}$ by a Right-Hand Corkscrew Rule: a right-hand corkscrew would move in the direction of $\hat{\mathbf{e}}$ if it were rotated under the action of **F**. (See Figure 7.)

2.3 Point of application

An iron framework $OABCP$ is free to rotate about O and is acted on by a force **F** applied to the point P in the direction of ABP. (See Figure 8.)

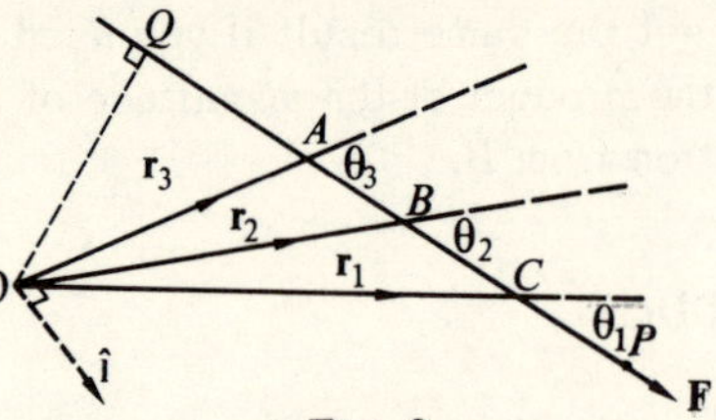

Fig. 8.

Intuitively we see that the moment of **F** about O must be unique, it has only *one* turning effect of a certain magnitude. We have a choice, however, in calculating this magnitude, depending on where we take the *point of application* of **F**. If we take it to be C then we use $\mathbf{r}_1$ and θ_1 to calculate the vector product $|\mathbf{r}_1| \times |\mathbf{F}| \times \sin\theta_1\,\hat{\mathbf{e}}$. Will this give the same value for the moment as taking the point of application at B, or at A? The reader should check that in fact the three results are identical, that is: $r_1F\sin\theta_1 = r_2F\sin\theta_2 = r_3F\sin\theta_3$ (show that each of these is equal to the product of F and OQ, the perpendicular from O to the line of action of **F**.)

We can therefore generalise and say that the moment of any force F about a point O is given by the formula $|\mathbf{r}| \times |\mathbf{F}| \times \sin\theta\,\hat{\mathbf{e}}$, where **r** is *any* position vector from O to the line of **F** making an angle θ with **F**. The reader should check that this formula still holds if (for a fixed **r**) we use the reflex angle $(2\pi - \theta)$ instead of θ. This very important principle can be stated thus: *The turning effect (or moment) of a force* **F** *about a point* O *is unique and is given by* $|\mathbf{r}| \times |\mathbf{F}| \times \sin\theta\,\hat{\mathbf{e}}$ *where* **r** *is any vector from* O *to the line of* **F** *and* θ *can be the acute or obtuse angle between* **r** *and* **F**. This is the vector product $\mathbf{r}\wedge\mathbf{F}$.

Example 4. A force is represented in magnitude (newtons) and direction by the vector

$$\begin{pmatrix}1\\4\\2\end{pmatrix}.$$

† Sometimes denoted by $\mathbf{r}\times\mathbf{F}$ and called the 'cross product' to distinguish it from the 'dot product' or scalar product.

This force acts on a body which is fixed at the origin (0, 0, 0) but is free to rotate about that point. The vector product $\mathbf{r} \wedge \mathbf{F}$ is

$$\begin{pmatrix} 8 \\ -1 \\ -2 \end{pmatrix} \text{Nm.}$$

What is the magnitude of the moment of $\mathbf{F}$ about the origin? Find the perpendicular distance of the line of $\mathbf{F}$ from the origin.

The magnitude of the moment of the force is $|\mathbf{r} \wedge \mathbf{F}|$, i.e. $\sqrt{[8^2 + (-1)^2 + (-2)^2]}$. Therefore $|\mathbf{r} \wedge \mathbf{F}| = \sqrt{69}\,\text{Nm}$.

As $$\mathbf{F} = \begin{pmatrix} 1 \\ 4 \\ 2 \end{pmatrix} \text{ then } F = \sqrt{(1^2 + 4^2 + 2^2)} = \sqrt{21}\,\text{N}.$$

But the moment $= pF$ where p is the perpendicular distance from the origin to the line of $\mathbf{F}$.

So $\sqrt{69} = p\sqrt{21}$. Therefore $p = \sqrt{\frac{69}{21}} = \sqrt{\frac{23}{7}}$ m.

2.4 Addition of vector products

Are we justified in adding vector products as though they were 'ordinary' vectors? If we can do this then clearly vector products are a very useful representation of turning moments.

Generally speaking, suppose two forces $\mathbf{F}_1$ and $\mathbf{F}_2$ are acting on a rigid body at P and we wish to calculate their turning effect about the point O.

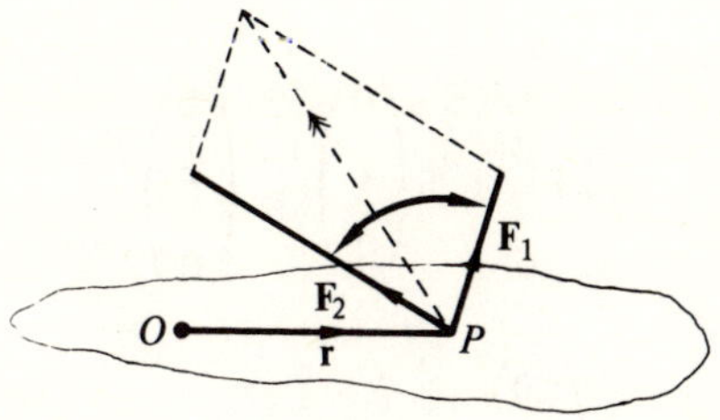

Fig. 9.

We would expect that the turning effect of $\mathbf{F}_1$ alone and of $\mathbf{F}_2$ alone, when *combined*, would be the same as the turning effect of the resultant $(\mathbf{F}_1 + \mathbf{F}_2)$. That is:

$$\mathbf{r} \wedge \mathbf{F}_1 + \mathbf{r} \wedge \mathbf{F}_2 = \mathbf{r} \wedge (\mathbf{F}_1 + \mathbf{F}_2).$$

This would follow immediately if $\mathbf{r}$, $\mathbf{F}_1$ and $\mathbf{F}_2$ were in the same plane (why?), but the result is in fact true for all possible vectors $\mathbf{r}$, $\mathbf{F}_1$ and $\mathbf{F}_2$. A proof of this result is outlined in Exercise C, Question 9; note that we are proving that the vector product is distributive over addition.

We can generalise this result and say that vector products can be added even if the forces act at different points on a body. This result is not obvious; if we have forces $\mathbf{F}_1$, $\mathbf{F}_2$, $\mathbf{F}_3$, with corresponding position vectors $\mathbf{r}_1$, $\mathbf{r}_2$, $\mathbf{r}_3$, ... then the vector sum $(\mathbf{r}_1 \wedge \mathbf{F}_1 + \mathbf{r}_2 \wedge \mathbf{F}_2 + \mathbf{r}_3 \wedge \mathbf{F}_3 + \dots)$ is the resultant moment of the force system applied to the body. This result is discussed in Section 7 but will be assumed throughout the chapter.

Example 5. A cube *ABCDEFGH* of side 1 m is acted on by three forces 5*N* at *A*, 3*N* at *C*, and 2*N* at *E* in the directions shown in Figure 10. Calculate the resultant vector and scalar moments of these forces about *D*.

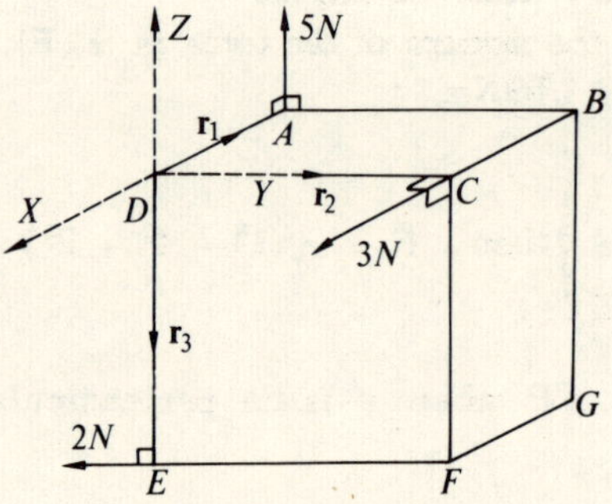

Fig. 10.

Take *D* as origin and the axes parallel to the sides of the cube as in Figure 10. (Thus *A* is (–1, 0, 0), *B* is (–1, 1, 0), etc.)

The vector product of the force at *A* is $\mathbf{r}_1 \wedge \mathbf{F}_1 = r_1 F_1 \sin\theta\, \hat{\mathbf{e}}$. Here $r_1 = 1$, $F_1 = 5$, and $\theta = 90°$.

Therefore $\mathbf{r}_1 \wedge \mathbf{F}_1 = 5\,\hat{\mathbf{e}}$, where by the Right-Hand Corkscrew Rule $\hat{\mathbf{e}}$ is in the direction *AB*, that is $\begin{pmatrix}0\\1\\0\end{pmatrix}$.

So
$$\mathbf{r}_1 \wedge \mathbf{F}_1 = 5\begin{pmatrix}0\\1\\0\end{pmatrix} = \begin{pmatrix}0\\5\\0\end{pmatrix}.$$

Similarly at *C* $\quad \mathbf{r}_2 \wedge \mathbf{F}_2 = \begin{pmatrix}0\\0\\-3\end{pmatrix}$ and $\mathbf{r}_3 \wedge \mathbf{F}_3 = \begin{pmatrix}-2\\0\\0\end{pmatrix}$.

So the resultant turning effect at *D* is

$$\begin{pmatrix}0\\5\\0\end{pmatrix} + \begin{pmatrix}0\\0\\-3\end{pmatrix} + \begin{pmatrix}-2\\0\\0\end{pmatrix} = \begin{pmatrix}-2\\5\\-3\end{pmatrix} \text{Nm},$$

i.e. the combined moment has magnitude $\sqrt{\{(-2)^2 + (5)^2 + (-3)^2\}} = \sqrt{38}$ Nm and

the axis of rotation is through the origin, and in the direction $\begin{pmatrix} -2 \\ 5 \\ -3 \end{pmatrix}$.

2.5 Couples

When a door-handle is turned it is rotated but not translated. Similarly when we unscrew nuts or bolts we apply a turning force only. A set of forces that causes rotation but no translation is equivalent to a *couple* – which is two equal and opposite forces situated at a distance d apart. Thus a couple is the simplest system of forces producing rotation only.

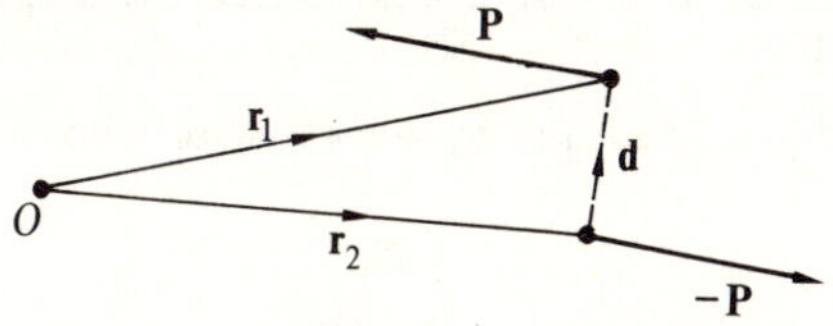

Fig. 11.

Suppose $\mathbf{P}$ and $-\mathbf{P}$ act as in Figure 11 and we wish to find their effect about the point O (which can be any point in space). Their translational effect is zero since $\Sigma \mathbf{F}_i = \mathbf{P} + -\mathbf{P} = \mathbf{0}$. The sum of the moments of the forces is $\mathbf{r}_1 \wedge \mathbf{P} + \mathbf{r}_2 \wedge -\mathbf{P} = (\mathbf{r}_1 - \mathbf{r}_2) \wedge \mathbf{P} = \mathbf{d} \wedge \mathbf{P}$ which is independent of the position of O. Although a couple is a special case, it should be treated as any other force system.

Note: In general a system of forces has a translational effect as well as a rotational effect. Its rotational effect about a point O is sometimes called its *couple* (*or moment*) *about* O. We have shown that, if its translational effect happens to be zero, then its couple about O is independent of the position of O, and the system is equivalent to *a couple*, no point needing to be specified.

EXERCISE B

1. The centre control room of a space craft is taken to be the origin, the coordinates of one of its rockets are (0, 7, 0) and the direction of the rocket is

$$\begin{pmatrix} 0 \\ 0 \\ 1 \end{pmatrix}.$$

The rocket fires, giving a thrust of 10N. Find $\mathbf{r} \wedge \mathbf{F}$ about the origin in this case, and calculate the combined moment about the origin of this thrust and another of 50N from a rocket at (5, 0, 0) inclined in the direction

$$\begin{pmatrix} 0 \\ 1/\sqrt{2} \\ 1/\sqrt{2} \end{pmatrix}.$$

2. Given that a force **F** acts on the space craft in Question 1 so that

$$\mathbf{r} \wedge \mathbf{F} = \begin{pmatrix} 2 \\ 3 \\ 1 \end{pmatrix}$$

and the perpendicular distance from the line of **F** to the control room is 30 m, find the scalar moment of **F** about O and hence the magnitude of **F**. Can you find the direction of **F**?

3. The space craft above is struck by a meteorite whose effect is that of a force

$$\begin{pmatrix} 2 \\ 2 \\ 0 \end{pmatrix} \text{N}$$

acting at the point (0, 0, 40). Draw a diagram and deduce the vector moment of this force about the origin (assumed fixed). Is it possible to nullify the rotational effect of the collision by firing one or both of the rockets in Question 1?

4. Calculate the turning moment about the origin of a force

$$\begin{pmatrix} 3 \\ 0 \\ 0 \end{pmatrix} \text{N},$$

whose line of action passes through (0, 1, 2). Suppose its line of action had passed through (10, 1, 2)? Does this suggest a simplification of three-dimensional problems?

5. A cube of side 1 m has a corner at the origin and three sides as $\hat{\mathbf{i}}$, $\hat{\mathbf{j}}$, $\hat{\mathbf{k}}$. It is acted on by forces

(a) $$\begin{pmatrix} 0 \\ 9 \\ 9 \end{pmatrix} \text{N at } (1, 1, 0),$$

(b) $$\begin{pmatrix} 7 \\ 0 \\ 0 \end{pmatrix} \text{N at } (1, 0, 1),$$

(c) $\begin{pmatrix} 0 \\ 0 \\ 5 \end{pmatrix}$ N at (0, 1, 0).

Find the resultant moment tending to rotate the cube about (0, 0, 0). What is the resultant moment tending to rotate it about (1, 1, 0)?

6. From the definition, calculate the vector products $\mathbf{r} \wedge \mathbf{F}$ where

(a) $\mathbf{r} = \begin{pmatrix} 7 \\ 0 \\ 0 \end{pmatrix}, \quad \mathbf{F} = \begin{pmatrix} 0 \\ 2 \\ 2 \end{pmatrix},$

(b) $\mathbf{r} = \begin{pmatrix} 1 \\ 1 \\ 0 \end{pmatrix}, \quad \mathbf{F} = \begin{pmatrix} 1 \\ 1 \\ \sqrt{\frac{2}{3}} \end{pmatrix},$

(c) $\mathbf{r} = \begin{pmatrix} 1 \\ 1 \\ 2 \end{pmatrix}, \quad \mathbf{F} = \begin{pmatrix} 2 \\ -2 \\ 0 \end{pmatrix}.$

(*Hint*: use a diagram to find θ and $\hat{\mathbf{e}}$.)

7. From the definition, what happens to $\mathbf{r} \wedge \mathbf{F}$ when:

(a) $\mathbf{r}$ and $\mathbf{F}$ are perpendicular;

(b) $\mathbf{r}$ and $\mathbf{F}$ are in the same direction;

(c) $\mathbf{r}$ and $\mathbf{F}$ *as vectors* are transposed, i.e. $\mathbf{F} \wedge \mathbf{r}$ is calculated?

Illustrate your answers with diagrams.

8. In general a force **F** acting some distance from Q (see Figure 12) has both a turning and translational effect on Q (Q is not fixed). By introducing two equal and opposite forces **F** and $-$**F** at Q show that the effect of **F** is equivalent to a couple and a translational force. If Q is fixed, what is the effect of **F**?

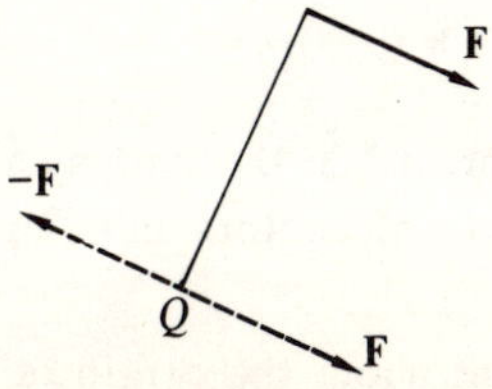

Fig. 12.

3. GENERAL PROPERTIES OF THE VECTOR PRODUCT

We shall find that the idea of a vector product has important applications in geometry, kinematics and mechanics. In this section we shall summarise the properties discovered so far and set out a formal definition of the vector product. We can define the vector product $\mathbf{a} \wedge \mathbf{b}$ for *any* two shift vectors without necessarily thinking of $\mathbf{a}$ as a position vector and $\mathbf{b}$ as a force.

3.1 Definition of vector product

Let $\mathbf{a}$ and $\mathbf{b}$ be two non-zero vectors and θ the angle between them (either angle will suffice as shown in 2.3). The *vector product,* $\mathbf{a} \wedge \mathbf{b}$ is defined as a vector of magnitude $|\mathbf{a}| \cdot |\mathbf{b}| \sin\theta$ in a direction perpendicular to $\mathbf{a}$ and $\mathbf{b}$ taken to be in the direction of a right-hand corkscrew rotating from $\mathbf{a}$ to $\mathbf{b}$.

Localise $\mathbf{a}$ and $\mathbf{b}$ at the origin then $\mathbf{a} \wedge \mathbf{b} = (ab \sin\theta)$, where $\hat{\mathbf{e}}$ is a unit vector perpendicular to the plane of $\mathbf{a}$ and $\mathbf{b}$.

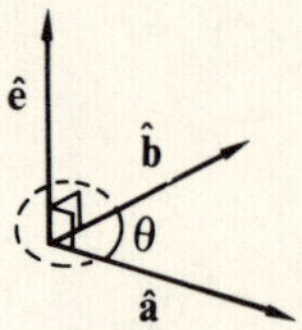

Fig. 13.

3.2 Properties of the vector product

(a) Scalars can be multiplied through the vector product

$$(k\mathbf{a}) \wedge (l\mathbf{b}) = kl(\mathbf{a} \wedge \mathbf{b}) = (kl\mathbf{a}) \wedge \mathbf{b}, \text{ etc.}$$

(b) The vector product is not commutative. In fact $\mathbf{a} \wedge \mathbf{b} = -\mathbf{b} \wedge \mathbf{a}$ (The reader should check this from the definition, see Exercise B, Question 7).

(c) The vector product is distributive over addition

$$\mathbf{a} \wedge (\mathbf{b} + \mathbf{c}) = \mathbf{a} \wedge \mathbf{b} + \mathbf{a} \wedge \mathbf{c}$$

(A proof is outlined in Exercise C, Question 9).

3.3 Components

The vector product of any vector with itself is zero, and if $\mathbf{a}$ and $\mathbf{b}$ are perpendicular then $\mathbf{a} \wedge \mathbf{b} = ab\hat{\mathbf{e}}$. It follows that if $\hat{\mathbf{i}}, \hat{\mathbf{j}}$, and $\hat{\mathbf{k}}$ are unit vectors along the x, y, z axes respectively then:

$$\hat{\mathbf{i}} \wedge \hat{\mathbf{i}} = \hat{\mathbf{j}} \wedge \hat{\mathbf{j}} = \hat{\mathbf{k}} \wedge \hat{\mathbf{k}} = \mathbf{0}$$
$$\hat{\mathbf{i}} \wedge \hat{\mathbf{j}} = \hat{\mathbf{k}} = -\hat{\mathbf{j}} \wedge \hat{\mathbf{i}}$$
$$\hat{\mathbf{j}} \wedge \hat{\mathbf{k}} = \hat{\mathbf{i}} = -\hat{\mathbf{k}} \wedge \hat{\mathbf{j}}$$
$$\hat{\mathbf{k}} \wedge \hat{\mathbf{i}} = \hat{\mathbf{j}} = -\hat{\mathbf{i}} \wedge \hat{\mathbf{k}}$$

First \ Second	$\hat{\mathbf{i}}$	$\hat{\mathbf{j}}$	$\hat{\mathbf{k}}$
$\hat{\mathbf{i}}$	$\mathbf{0}$	$\hat{\mathbf{k}}$	$-\hat{\mathbf{j}}$
$\hat{\mathbf{j}}$	$-\hat{\mathbf{k}}$	$\mathbf{0}$	$\hat{\mathbf{i}}$
$\hat{\mathbf{k}}$	$\hat{\mathbf{j}}$	$-\hat{\mathbf{i}}$	$\mathbf{0}$

These results are summarised in the anti-symmetric array above. They enable us to calculate vector products of vectors in component form without laborious working.

Example 6. Find the moment about the origin of a force, acting at the point (1, 1, 1), which is represented in magnitude and direction by the vector

$$\begin{pmatrix} 1 \\ 0 \\ 1 \end{pmatrix}.$$

In this case $\mathbf{F} = \hat{\mathbf{i}} + \hat{\mathbf{k}}$ and $\mathbf{r} = \hat{\mathbf{i}} + \hat{\mathbf{j}} + \hat{\mathbf{k}}$.
Therefore $\mathbf{r} \wedge \mathbf{F} = (\hat{\mathbf{i}} + \hat{\mathbf{j}} + \hat{\mathbf{k}}) \wedge (\hat{\mathbf{i}} + \hat{\mathbf{k}})$.
By the Distributive Law:

$$\begin{aligned} \mathbf{r} \wedge \mathbf{F} &= (\hat{\mathbf{i}} \wedge \hat{\mathbf{i}}) + (\hat{\mathbf{i}} \wedge \hat{\mathbf{k}}) + (\hat{\mathbf{j}} \wedge \hat{\mathbf{i}}) + (\hat{\mathbf{j}} \wedge \hat{\mathbf{k}}) + (\hat{\mathbf{k}} \wedge \hat{\mathbf{i}}) + (\hat{\mathbf{k}} \wedge \hat{\mathbf{k}}) \\ &= (\hat{\mathbf{i}} \wedge \hat{\mathbf{k}}) + (\hat{\mathbf{j}} \wedge \hat{\mathbf{i}}) + (\hat{\mathbf{j}} \wedge \hat{\mathbf{k}}) + (\hat{\mathbf{k}} \wedge \hat{\mathbf{i}}) \\ &= -\hat{\mathbf{j}} + -\hat{\mathbf{k}} + \hat{\mathbf{i}} + \hat{\mathbf{j}} \\ &= \hat{\mathbf{i}} - \hat{\mathbf{k}}. \end{aligned}$$

Thus the moment is represented by the vector

$$\begin{pmatrix} 1 \\ 0 \\ -1 \end{pmatrix},$$

that is, it has a magnitude of $\sqrt{2}$ about an axis in the direction

$$\begin{pmatrix} 1 \\ 0 \\ -1 \end{pmatrix}.$$

(If the working is correct then the direction of the axis is perpendicular to both $\mathbf{F}$ and $\mathbf{r}$, i.e.

$$\begin{pmatrix} 1 \\ 0 \\ -1 \end{pmatrix} \cdot \begin{pmatrix} 1 \\ 0 \\ 1 \end{pmatrix} = 0 \quad \text{and} \quad \begin{pmatrix} 1 \\ 0 \\ -1 \end{pmatrix} \cdot \begin{pmatrix} 1 \\ 1 \\ 1 \end{pmatrix} = 0.)$$

Suppose we wish to calculate, in general, the moment about the origin of a force

$$\mathbf{F} = \begin{pmatrix} P \\ Q \\ R \end{pmatrix} \text{ acting at } (a, b, c).$$

Then working out $\quad (a\hat{\mathbf{i}} + b\hat{\mathbf{j}} + c\hat{\mathbf{k}}) \wedge (P\hat{\mathbf{i}} + Q\hat{\mathbf{j}} + R\hat{\mathbf{k}})$,

gives $\quad (bR - cQ)\,\hat{\mathbf{i}} + (cP - aR)\,\hat{\mathbf{j}} + (aQ - bP)\,\hat{\mathbf{k}}$.

This result can more conveniently be thought of as the expansion of the determinant

$$\begin{vmatrix} \hat{\mathbf{i}} & \hat{\mathbf{j}} & \hat{\mathbf{k}} \\ a & b & c \\ P & Q & R \end{vmatrix} = \mathbf{r} \wedge \mathbf{F}.$$

This determinant form is often a quick way of working out vector products.

Example 7. A vertical television mast is held in place by three stays joined to the mast 12 m above the ground. Taking the base of the mast as the origin and the mast as the z-axis, the coordinates of the bottom of the stays are (0, –5, 0), (–3, 1, 0) and (3, 1, 0). If there is a tension of 20 N in the first stay, find the tensions (assumed equal) in the other two stays.

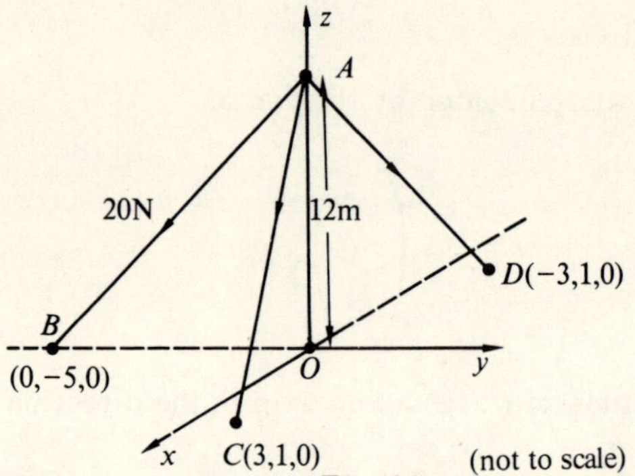

Fig. 14.

The forces acting on the mast are its weight, the reaction of the ground and the three tensions in the stays.

Taking moments about O does not involve the weight of the mast or the reaction at O. The directions **AB, AC, AD** are calculated as

$$\begin{pmatrix} 0 \\ -5 \\ -12 \end{pmatrix}, \begin{pmatrix} -3 \\ 1 \\ -12 \end{pmatrix} \text{ and } \begin{pmatrix} 3 \\ 1 \\ -12 \end{pmatrix}$$

respectively. So the *unit vectors* in these directions are

$$\frac{1}{\sqrt{169}}\begin{pmatrix} 0 \\ -5 \\ -12 \end{pmatrix}, \frac{1}{\sqrt{154}}\begin{pmatrix} -3 \\ 1 \\ -12 \end{pmatrix}, \frac{1}{\sqrt{154}}\begin{pmatrix} 3 \\ 1 \\ -12 \end{pmatrix}$$

Therefore the tensions in AB, AC, AD, are represented by the vectors

$$\frac{20}{13}\begin{pmatrix} 0 \\ -5 \\ -12 \end{pmatrix}, \frac{S}{\sqrt{154}}\begin{pmatrix} -3 \\ 1 \\ -12 \end{pmatrix} \text{ and } \frac{S}{\sqrt{154}}\begin{pmatrix} 3 \\ 1 \\ -12 \end{pmatrix}$$

As there is no resultant rotation about O the sum of the vector products of the above three tensions with $\begin{pmatrix} 0 \\ 0 \\ 12 \end{pmatrix}$ must be zero,

$$\text{i.e. } \frac{20}{13}\begin{vmatrix} \hat{\mathbf{i}} & \hat{\mathbf{j}} & \hat{\mathbf{k}} \\ 0 & 0 & 12 \\ 0 & -5 & -12 \end{vmatrix} + \frac{S}{\sqrt{154}}\begin{vmatrix} \hat{\mathbf{i}} & \hat{\mathbf{j}} & \hat{\mathbf{k}} \\ 0 & 0 & 12 \\ -3 & 1 & -12 \end{vmatrix} + \frac{S}{\sqrt{154}}\begin{vmatrix} \hat{\mathbf{i}} & \hat{\mathbf{j}} & \hat{\mathbf{k}} \\ 0 & 0 & 12 \\ 3 & 1 & -12 \end{vmatrix} = \mathbf{0},$$

which reduces to
$$\left(\frac{1200}{13} - \frac{24S}{\sqrt{154}}\right)\hat{\mathbf{i}} = \mathbf{0}.$$

Therefore
$$24S = \frac{1200\sqrt{154}}{13}, \qquad \text{i.e. } S = \frac{50\sqrt{154}}{13}\ \text{N}.$$

3.4 Angular velocity

Think of a space station rotating at a fixed rate about its central axis (see Figure 15). How would we measure the rotation of this craft? Clearly by the number of revolutions it completes in a unit of time or in radians per second, a scalar value for its *angular velocity*. Can we extend this idea to produce a useful *vector* quantity to measure rotational velocity? By analogy with previous work it would seem sensible to take the fixed direction of the axis of rotation as the unique direction characterising this rotation, so we can define *vector angular velocity* to be a vector in the direction of the axis of rotation with magnitude equal to the rate of rotation.

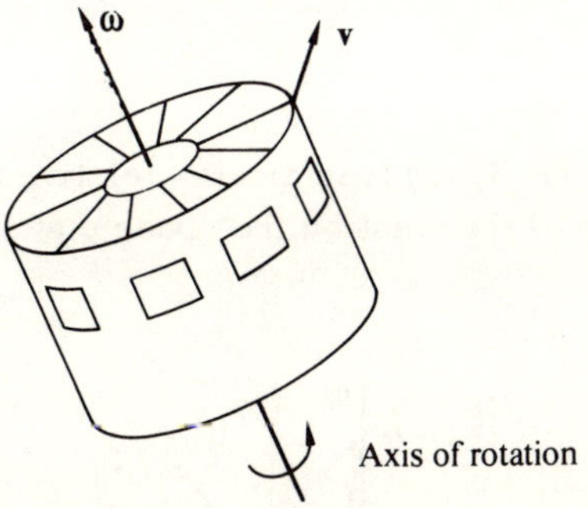

Fig. 15

In the case of the space craft rotating say at a rate of 12 rad/s about an axis in the direction

$$\begin{pmatrix} 1 \\ 7 \\ 3 \end{pmatrix}$$

its vector angular velocity $\boldsymbol{\omega}$ is given by

$$\boldsymbol{\omega} = 12 \times \frac{1}{\sqrt{59}}\begin{pmatrix} 1 \\ 7 \\ 3 \end{pmatrix}.$$

(Check that this has magnitude 12, i.e. we must calculate a *unit* vector in the direction of

$$\begin{pmatrix} 1 \\ 7 \\ 3 \end{pmatrix}).$$

What can we say of the instantaneous linear velocity, **v**, of any point on the space station relative to the centre? It must be in a direction perpendicular to $\boldsymbol{\omega}$ and also perpendicular to **r**, the position vector from the centre to the point with velocity **v** (why?). So **v** must be in the direction $\boldsymbol{\omega} \wedge \mathbf{r}$, and as **v** is directly proportional to ω and to the distance of the point from the axis then, with appropriate units, we can write:

$$\mathbf{v} = \boldsymbol{\omega} \wedge \mathbf{r}.$$

This important result shows that the vector product can be applied not only to forces but to the velocities of particles and bodies. We therefore have a strong mathematical link between the rotational effect of forces and the rotation of bodies, both can be expressed using vector products. This is a step nearer solving the main problem of relating forces to the rotational motion of bodies.

Example 8. A space platform is spinning with angular velocity 4 rad/s about an axis with direction

$$\begin{pmatrix} 0 \\ 2 \\ 1 \end{pmatrix}$$

passing through the point (1, 3, –2) (coordinates relative to some fixed point in space). Find the velocity of the point on the space platform with coordinates (4, –2, 1).

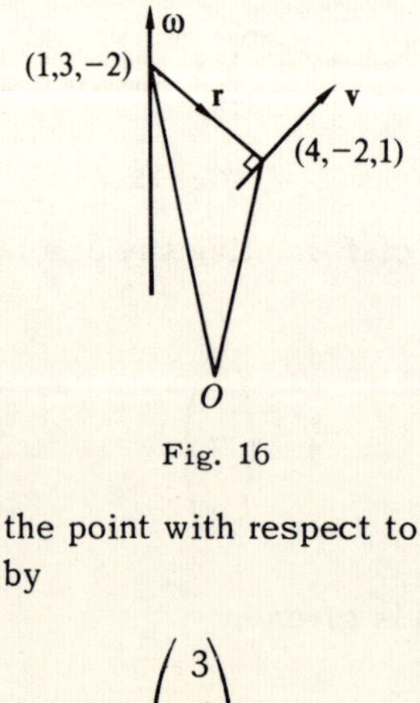

Fig. 16

The position vector **r** of the point with respect to the fixed point (1, 3, –2) on the axis of rotation is given by

$$\begin{pmatrix} 3 \\ -5 \\ 3 \end{pmatrix}.$$

So the velocity $\quad \mathbf{v} = \boldsymbol{\omega} \wedge \mathbf{r} = \dfrac{4}{\sqrt{5}}\begin{pmatrix}0\\2\\1\end{pmatrix} \wedge \begin{pmatrix}3\\-5\\3\end{pmatrix} = \dfrac{4}{\sqrt{5}}\begin{pmatrix}11\\3\\-6\end{pmatrix}.$

The reader should check this result.

Suppose we worked out $\mathbf{v}$ using some other point on the axis of rotation, would the answer be the same? As the axis has direction

$$\begin{pmatrix}0\\2\\1\end{pmatrix}$$

then any other point on it is given by $(1, 3, -2) + \lambda(0, 2, 1)$ (why?). Try the point $(1, 5, -1)$ so that

$$\mathbf{r} = \begin{pmatrix}4\\-2\\1\end{pmatrix} - \begin{pmatrix}1\\5\\-1\end{pmatrix} = \begin{pmatrix}3\\-7\\2\end{pmatrix}.$$

Check that the value of $\mathbf{v}$ is the same, can you see why this is so? (See Question 8 of Exercise C.)

The above example should confirm the intuitive idea that at any instant the velocity of any point of a spinning body can be found using the formula $\mathbf{v} = \boldsymbol{\omega} \wedge \mathbf{r}$, where $\mathbf{r}$ is the position vector of the point from any point on the axis of rotation. (Can you see the connection with the result of Section 2.3?)

EXERCISE C

1. Find the moment about the origin of:

(a) a force $\begin{pmatrix}2\\0\\-1\end{pmatrix}$ acting at the point $(1, 1, 0)$;

(b) a force $7\hat{\mathbf{i}} + 4\hat{\mathbf{j}} + 2\hat{\mathbf{k}}$ acting at the point $(2, -1, 6)$.

2. An unknown force $\begin{pmatrix}F_1\\F_2\\0\end{pmatrix}$ has a vector moment of $\begin{pmatrix}4\\1\\-1\end{pmatrix}$ about the origin and acts on a body on a point $(1, 3, 7)$.

Find F_1 and F_2.

3. A space craft is spinning about an axis fixed in space. A point on the craft 50 m from this axis has a linear velocity of magnitude 20 m/s. Find the (scalar) angular speed of the space craft and the (scalar) linear speed of a point 100 m from the axis of rotation.

4. A vertical flagpole is held in place by three taut cables. Taking the base of the pole as the origin, the cables are fastened to the ground at $(1, 3, 0)$, $(-2, 0, 0)$ and

(1, −3, 0) and they are fastened 5 m up the flagpole. The tensions in the cables are T N and 5 N respectively, find T.

5. Find T in Question 4 if:

(a) the cables are attached 3 m up the flagpole;

(b) the middle cable is fixed 3 m up and the other two 5 m up the flagpole.

6. Show that if a body is rotating with angular velocity $\boldsymbol{\omega}$ and the velocity of a point A of it is $\mathbf{V}$ then the velocity of any other point B of the body is $\mathbf{V} + \boldsymbol{\omega} \wedge \mathbf{AB}$.

7. The axis of rotation of a body is the line $\mathbf{r} = \mathbf{a} + t\mathbf{b}$. Thus the vector angular velocity of the body is some multiple of $\mathbf{b}$, say $p\mathbf{b}$. Let $\mathbf{r}'$ be the position vector of any other point on the body, show, by expanding, that:

$$p\mathbf{b} \wedge (\mathbf{r}' - \mathbf{a}) = p\mathbf{b} \wedge (\mathbf{r}' - (\mathbf{a} + t\mathbf{b}))$$

for all values of t. What is the significance of this result?

8. Given two forces $\mathbf{F}_1$ and $\mathbf{F}_2$ acting on a body such that their turning effect about a point is the same (i.e. $\mathbf{r}_1 \wedge \mathbf{F}_1 = \mathbf{r}_2 \wedge \mathbf{F}_2$). Does this mean that $\mathbf{F}_1 = \mathbf{F}_2$? If not, state the general connection between $\mathbf{F}_1$ and $\mathbf{F}_2$.

9. *Proof of Distributive Law*

(i) Use Question 8 to show that $\mathbf{a} \wedge \mathbf{c} = \mathbf{a} \wedge \mathbf{c}'$ where $\mathbf{c}'$ is the projection of $\mathbf{c}$ onto the plane perpendicular to $\mathbf{a}$.

(ii) Deduce that to prove the distributive law

$$\mathbf{a} \wedge (\mathbf{b} + \mathbf{c}) = \mathbf{a} \wedge \mathbf{b} + \mathbf{a} \wedge \mathbf{c}$$

we need only consider the special case when $\mathbf{a}$ is perpendicular to the plane of $\mathbf{b}$ and $\mathbf{c}$.

(iii) *In this case* show that $\mathbf{a} \wedge \mathbf{b}$ is obtained from $\mathbf{b}$, by rotating $\mathbf{b}$ through 90° in a plane perpendicular to $\mathbf{a}$, enlarging at the same time by a factor $|\mathbf{a}|$. (i.e. $\mathbf{b}$ maps onto $\mathbf{a} \wedge \mathbf{b} = \mathbf{p}$ where $|\mathbf{p}| = |\mathbf{a}| \times |\mathbf{b}|$)
Similarly $\mathbf{a} \wedge \mathbf{c}$ is obtained from $\mathbf{c}$ by rotating through 90° *in the same plane* (remember $\mathbf{b}$, $\mathbf{c}$ are perpendicular to $\mathbf{a}$) and enlargement by a factor $|\mathbf{a}|$.

(iv) Show that $\mathbf{a} \wedge \mathbf{b} + \mathbf{a} \wedge \mathbf{c} = \mathbf{a} \wedge (\mathbf{b} + \mathbf{c})$ by drawing a parallelogram with sides $\mathbf{b}$, and $\mathbf{c}$ and considering the effect of taking the vector product of $\mathbf{a}$ with $\mathbf{b}$, $\mathbf{c}$ and $(\mathbf{b} + \mathbf{c})$.

4. ROTATION ABOUT A FIXED AXIS

4.1 Scalar triple product

Until now we have been investigating the turning effect of a force on a body when the body is free to rotate about any axis. Suppose we apply forces to a body with a fixed axis, such as a flywheel or bicycle wheel? If we push the rim of a bicycle wheel parallel to the spindle or in towards the spindle the wheel will not rotate. The only part of the push that causes rotation is the tangential component, i.e. that part of the force perpendicular to the axis of rotation (the spindle) and also perpendicular to the line to the spindle from that point of the rim.

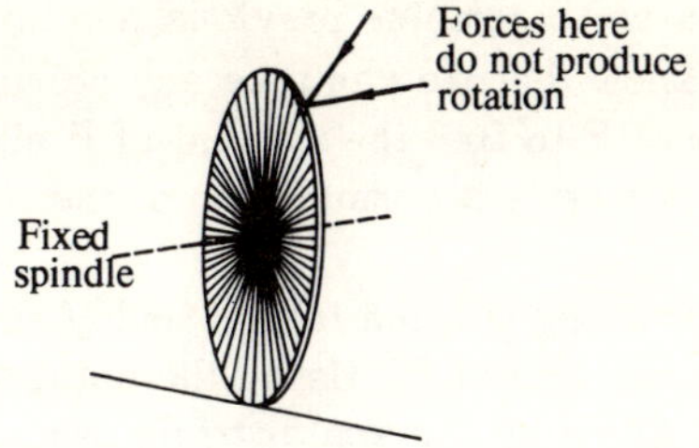

Fig. 17

Example 9. The flywheel in Figure 18 is free to rotate about a fixed axis AB. Suppose a force $\mathbf{F}$ is applied to the edge of the flywheel at a point whose position vector from the origin (which we take on the axis AB) is $\mathbf{r}$. Discuss the effect of $\mathbf{F}$.

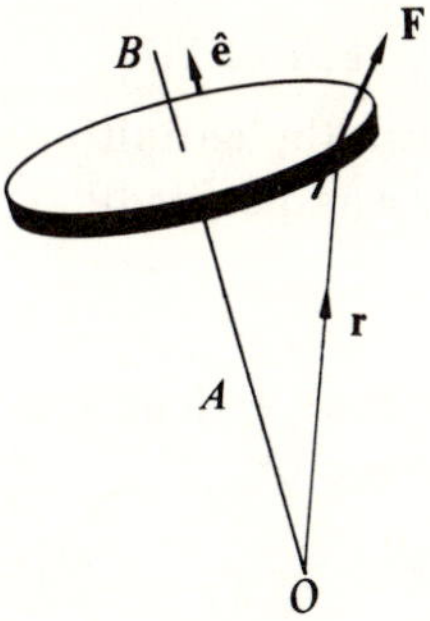

Fig. 18

Firstly $\mathbf{r} \wedge \mathbf{F}$ does not give the turning effect of $\mathbf{F}$ *about* AB, this would only be true if $\mathbf{F}$ happened to be a tangential force to the flywheel. Nevertheless $\mathbf{r} \wedge \mathbf{F}$ is the vector representing the turning effect of $\mathbf{F}$ so we really wish to know the *component* of this vector in the direction of AB. Thus if $\hat{\mathbf{e}}$ is a unit vector in the direction AB then the required component of $\mathbf{r} \wedge \mathbf{F}$ is $\hat{\mathbf{e}} \cdot (\mathbf{r} \wedge \mathbf{F})$. Such a quantity is called a *scalar triple product* and gives the scalar moment of the force $\mathbf{F}$ about the axis AB. Scalar triple products have many interesting and useful properties which are discussed in Exercise D.

4.2 Non-perpendicular axis

A force $\mathbf{F}$ is applied to a body along the line PB and the body is free to rotate about a fixed axis AQ which is not perpendicular to $\mathbf{F}$ (see Figure 19). What is the turning effect of $\mathbf{F}$ about the axis AQ?

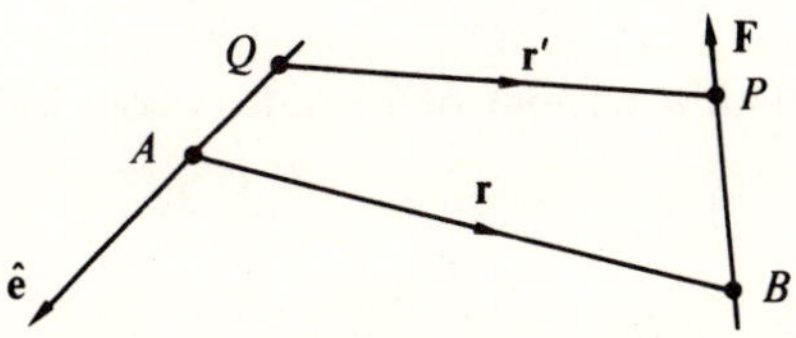

Fig. 19

This problem enables us to combine previous results into a neat general formulation. We wish to show that we can take any point on the axis of rotation and any point on the line of **F** to find the moment of **F** about AQ. This may seem surprising at first but it is merely a combination of the results already proved in Sections 2.3 and 4.1.

Let $\hat{\mathbf{e}}$ be a unit vector along QA and take A and Q as two general points on the axis, and P and B on the line of **F**. Using the notation of Figure 19, the moment of **F** about AQ is given by the scalar triple product $\hat{\mathbf{e}}.(\mathbf{r} \wedge \mathbf{F})$ but it is also given by $\hat{\mathbf{e}}.(\mathbf{r}' \wedge \mathbf{F})$. Hence we must show that these two expressions are identical (i.e. we are free to choose any points on the two lines).

Proof.

$$\mathbf{r}' = \mathbf{QA} + \mathbf{r} + \mathbf{BP}$$

$$\begin{aligned} \hat{\mathbf{e}}.(\mathbf{r}' \wedge \mathbf{F}) &= \hat{\mathbf{e}}.((\mathbf{QA} + \mathbf{r} + \mathbf{BP}) \wedge \mathbf{F}) && \mathbf{BP} \text{ is parallel to } \mathbf{F}, \\ &= \hat{\mathbf{e}}.(\mathbf{QA} \wedge \mathbf{F}) + \hat{\mathbf{e}}.(\mathbf{r} \wedge \mathbf{F}) && \mathbf{BP} \wedge \mathbf{F} = \mathbf{0}. \\ &= \hat{\mathbf{e}}.(\mathbf{r} \wedge \mathbf{F}) \end{aligned}$$

The term $\hat{\mathbf{e}}.(\mathbf{QA} \wedge \mathbf{F})$ is zero because (by definition) $\mathbf{QA} \wedge \mathbf{F}$ is perpendicular to **QA** which is in the direction of $\hat{\mathbf{e}}$. So $\hat{\mathbf{e}}$ is perpendicular to $(\mathbf{QA} \wedge \mathbf{F})$.

EXERCISE D

1. A millstone fixed to rotate about a vertical axis is acted on by a force represented in magnitude and direction by the vector

$$\begin{pmatrix} 2 \\ 1 \\ 3 \end{pmatrix}.$$

If the force is applied at the point (3, 5, 0) relative to axes having the centre of the millstone as origin, calculate the turning moment on the millstone.

2. Suppose the force in Question 1 is applied at the point (–4, 2, 0), what is now the turning moment? At what point on the rim of the stone (distance 1 m from centre) should the same force be applied (a) for maximum turning moment, (b) for minimum effect?

3. Given that a force

$$\begin{pmatrix} F \\ F \\ 2F \end{pmatrix}$$

acting through (2, 1, 3) has a moment of 18 units about an axis through (1, 1, 2) with direction

$$\begin{pmatrix} -1 \\ 1 \\ 1 \end{pmatrix}.$$

Find the value of F.

4. Suppose **a**, **b** and **c** are three mutually perpendicular vectors. Simplify $\mathbf{a}.(\mathbf{b}\wedge\mathbf{c})$. What is the geometrical significance of your answer? Suppose **a**, **b** and **c** are linearly independent but not mutually perpendicular, what does $\mathbf{a}.(\mathbf{b}\wedge\mathbf{c})$ represent now? What happens when **a**, **b** and **c** are linearly dependent?

5. Show that in any scalar triple product $\mathbf{a}.(\mathbf{b}\wedge\mathbf{c})$, the value is the same if the 'dot' and 'vec' are interchanged (i.e. $\mathbf{a}.(\mathbf{b}\wedge\mathbf{c}) = (\mathbf{a}\wedge\mathbf{b}).\mathbf{c}$). Show also that any cyclic interchange of **a**, **b**, and **c** gives the same scalar triple product. Verify that

$$\mathbf{a}.(\mathbf{b}\wedge\mathbf{c}) = \begin{vmatrix} a_1 & a_2 & a_3 \\ b_1 & b_2 & b_3 \\ c_1 & c_2 & c_3 \end{vmatrix}$$

6. Use the results of the above two questions to calculate the volume of the parallelepiped with one vertex at the origin such that the three edges meeting there are represented by the vectors $7\hat{\mathbf{i}}$, $-8\hat{\mathbf{k}}$ and $5\hat{\mathbf{j}}$.

7. Repeat Question 6 using the three vectors: $5\hat{\mathbf{i}} + 6\hat{\mathbf{j}} - 2\hat{\mathbf{k}}$, $3\hat{\mathbf{i}} + 9\hat{\mathbf{k}}$ and $2\hat{\mathbf{i}} + 2\hat{\mathbf{j}}$.

8. A tetrahedral shaped building is to be erected. Taking the vertex as origin the three edges of the building are represented by the vectors $5\hat{\mathbf{i}} + 2\hat{\mathbf{k}}$, $3\hat{\mathbf{i}} + 7\hat{\mathbf{j}} + 5\hat{\mathbf{k}}$ and $13\hat{\mathbf{i}} - 7\hat{\mathbf{j}} + 9\hat{\mathbf{k}}$. Find the volume of the building.

5. GEOMETRICAL APPLICATIONS

We have restricted our use of the vector product to representing velocities and moments, but the general definition (3.1) enables us to apply it to geometrical problems. The vector product is useful because it produces a vector $(\mathbf{a}\wedge\mathbf{b})$ which is perpendicular to the two given vectors **a** and **b**. Examples of its use are given below.

5.1 Equation of a plane

We are familiar with the equation of a plane as $\mathbf{r}.\mathbf{n} = d$ (or as $ax + by + cz = d$). In many situations this is not the most convenient form. Suppose we are given the position vectors of three points and wish to find the equation of the plane passing through the points. We could substitute the three points in turn into the equation $ax + by + cz = d$ and solve it as three equations in three unknowns. (it contains three effective unknowns if we divide throughout by a non-zero coefficient, say d.) This process is very tedious, whereas the vector product can simplify the working.

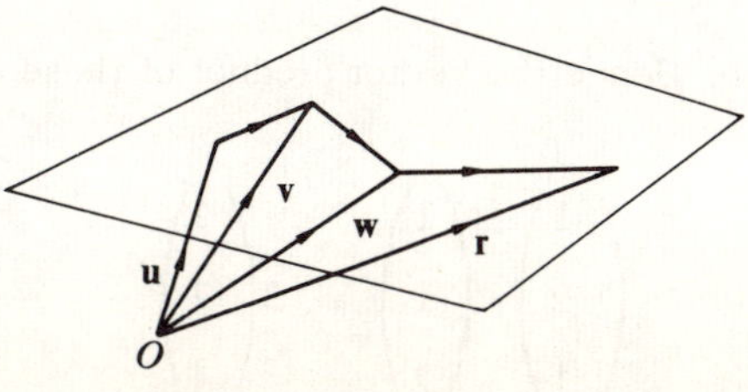

Fig. 20

Let $\mathbf{u}$, $\mathbf{v}$ and $\mathbf{w}$ be the three position vectors, then $(\mathbf{v}-\mathbf{u})$ and $(\mathbf{w}-\mathbf{v})$ lie in the plane — any two can be linked.

So $(\mathbf{v}-\mathbf{u})\wedge(\mathbf{w}-\mathbf{v})$ is a vector perpendicular to the plane.

Also if $\mathbf{r}$ is the position vector of any point on the plane then $(\mathbf{r}-\mathbf{w})$ lies in the plane and is always perpendicular to $(\mathbf{v}-\mathbf{u})\wedge(\mathbf{w}-\mathbf{v})$.

Therefore $(\mathbf{r}-\mathbf{w}).[(\mathbf{v}-\mathbf{u})\wedge(\mathbf{w}-\mathbf{v})] = 0$ (2)

Note that the scalar triple product is zero $\Rightarrow$ no volume. But $\mathbf{r}$ is a variable vector so the equation (2) is the equation of the plane.

If we write $(\mathbf{v}-\mathbf{u})\wedge(\mathbf{w}-\mathbf{v}) = \mathbf{n}$ (say), then the equation is of the form:

$$(\mathbf{r}-\mathbf{w}).\mathbf{n} = 0$$

or

$$\mathbf{r}.\mathbf{n} = \mathbf{w}.\mathbf{n} = d \text{ (say)},$$

which is the standard form for the equation of a plane.

Example 10. Find the equation of the plane passing through the points (1, 1, 1), (2, 0, 2) and (2, –1, 1).

Let $\mathbf{u} = \hat{\mathbf{i}} + \hat{\mathbf{j}} + \hat{\mathbf{k}}$, $\mathbf{v} = 2\hat{\mathbf{i}} + 2\hat{\mathbf{k}}$ and $\mathbf{w} = 2\hat{\mathbf{i}} - \hat{\mathbf{j}} + \hat{\mathbf{k}}$

then $(\mathbf{v}-\mathbf{u}) = \hat{\mathbf{i}} - \hat{\mathbf{j}} + \hat{\mathbf{k}}$ and $(\mathbf{w}-\mathbf{v}) = -\hat{\mathbf{j}} - \hat{\mathbf{k}}$.

Now applying the above formula,

$$(\mathbf{v}-\mathbf{u})\wedge(\mathbf{w}-\mathbf{v}) = 2\hat{\mathbf{i}} + \hat{\mathbf{j}} - \hat{\mathbf{k}},$$

and hence the equation of the plane is: $(\mathbf{r}-\mathbf{w})\cdot(2\hat{\mathbf{i}} + \hat{\mathbf{j}} - \hat{\mathbf{k}}) = 0$

Putting $\mathbf{r} = \begin{pmatrix} x \\ y \\ z \end{pmatrix}$ we obtain the scalar form $\begin{pmatrix} x \\ y \\ z \end{pmatrix} . \begin{pmatrix} 2 \\ 1 \\ -1 \end{pmatrix} = \begin{pmatrix} 2 \\ -1 \\ 1 \end{pmatrix} . \begin{pmatrix} 2 \\ 1 \\ -1 \end{pmatrix}$,

i.e.

$$2x + y - z = 2$$

Example 11. Find the equation of the plane containing the lines $\mathbf{r} = (\hat{\mathbf{i}} + \hat{\mathbf{j}}) + p(-\hat{\mathbf{i}} + 2\hat{\mathbf{j}} + \hat{\mathbf{k}})$ and $\mathbf{r} = (\hat{\mathbf{i}} + \hat{\mathbf{j}}) + q(\hat{\mathbf{i}} + \hat{\mathbf{j}} + 2\hat{\mathbf{k}})$.

Here the problem can be solved by using the perpendicular property of the vector product. The vector directions of the lines must be parallel to the plane containing the lines.

So the vector $\begin{pmatrix} -1 \\ 2 \\ 1 \end{pmatrix}$ and the vector $\begin{pmatrix} 1 \\ 1 \\ 2 \end{pmatrix}$

are parallel to the plane. Hence the vector product of these two must be perpendicular to the plane:

$$\begin{pmatrix} -1 \\ 2 \\ 1 \end{pmatrix} \wedge \begin{pmatrix} 1 \\ 1 \\ 2 \end{pmatrix} = 3\begin{pmatrix} 1 \\ 1 \\ -1 \end{pmatrix}.$$

So the vector

$$\begin{pmatrix} 1 \\ 1 \\ -1 \end{pmatrix}$$

is perpendicular to the required plane and hence the equation of the plane must be $x + y - z = d$. To find d we must substitute in this equation a point we know lies on the plane – in this case the point of intersection of the two lines, (1, 1, 0). (The reader should check that this is the point of intersection, put $p = q = 0$.)

Substituting: $1 + 1 - 0 = d$, so the required equation is $x + y - z = 2$.

5.2 Intersection of planes

The vector product can be used for many practical problems involving the intersections of planes. Suppose we have a large modern building one end of which is formed by three intersecting planes. Relative to a convenient coordinate system the sides of the building lie in the planes $3x - 3y + z = 6$, $-x + y + 2z = 12$ and $6x + 6y - z = 0$ respectively. What are the angles at the corner where the three planes meet?

Note that the first two planes have a horizontal line of intersection passing through the points (–1, –1, 6) and (1, 1, 6). This line intersects the third plane at the point $(\frac{1}{2}, \frac{1}{2}, 6)$. This is a check that the three planes do in fact have a point of intersection.

In order to solve this problem we need the vector directions of the three edges, knowing these we can find the angles between them by using the scalar product method in the usual way.

The plane $3x - 3y + z = 6$ is perpendicular to

$$\begin{pmatrix} 3 \\ -3 \\ 1 \end{pmatrix}$$

and the plane $-x + y + 2z = 12$ is perpendicular to

$$\begin{pmatrix} -1 \\ 1 \\ 2 \end{pmatrix}.$$

The line of intersection of the planes must therefore be perpendicular to both these vectors and its direction is given by the vector product of the two:

$$\begin{pmatrix} 3 \\ -3 \\ 1 \end{pmatrix} \wedge \begin{pmatrix} -1 \\ 1 \\ 2 \end{pmatrix} = -7 \begin{pmatrix} 1 \\ 1 \\ 0 \end{pmatrix}$$

Similarly the second and third planes have a line of intersection with direction

$$\begin{pmatrix}-1\\1\\2\end{pmatrix}\wedge\begin{pmatrix}6\\6\\-1\end{pmatrix}=\begin{pmatrix}-13\\11\\-12\end{pmatrix}.$$

The angle between these two directions can now be calculated (this is left as an exercise for the reader). This gives us one angle at the corner, the other two angles can be obtained by the same method.

EXERCISE E

1. Find the equation of the plane containing the points (0, 1, 4), (0, –4, 2) and (1, 2, 1).

2. Find the equation of the plane through the point (2, 1, 0) parallel to the lines $\mathbf{r} = \hat{\mathbf{i}} + p(2\hat{\mathbf{i}} + 3\hat{\mathbf{j}} + \hat{\mathbf{k}})$ and $\mathbf{r} = \hat{\mathbf{k}} + q(7\hat{\mathbf{i}} + 4\hat{\mathbf{k}})$.

3. Find the general equation of the line through the point (2, –1, –5) and perpendicular to the vector

$$\begin{pmatrix}3\\2\\-1\end{pmatrix}.$$

4. Do the points (–1, 2, 3), (4, 3, –2), (–1, –3, –4) and (1, 1, 0) lie on one plane?

5. Find the direction of the line of intersection of the plane $\mathbf{r}.(\hat{\mathbf{i}} - 3\hat{\mathbf{j}}) = 4$ and the plane parallel to the vectors

$$\begin{pmatrix}3\\1\\2\end{pmatrix} \text{ and } \begin{pmatrix}4\\2\\3\end{pmatrix}$$

passing through (1, 1, 0).

6. Show that the direction of the line of intersection of a plane parallel to the vectors $\mathbf{a}$ and $\mathbf{b}$ and another plane parallel to the vectors $\mathbf{c}$ and $\mathbf{d}$ is $(\mathbf{a}\wedge\mathbf{b})\wedge(\mathbf{c}\wedge\mathbf{d})$.

7. Find the equation of the line through (1, –2, 4) perpendicular to and intersecting the line $\mathbf{r} = 4\hat{\mathbf{j}} - \hat{\mathbf{k}} + t(3\hat{\mathbf{i}} + 2\hat{\mathbf{j}} + \hat{\mathbf{k}})$.

8. Derive the equation of a plane passing through 3 points whose position vectors are $\mathbf{a}$, $\mathbf{b}$ and $\mathbf{c}$. Show by expanding the triple product that this equation can be written in the form $\mathbf{r}\cdot\mathbf{n} = \mathbf{a}\cdot(\mathbf{b}\wedge\mathbf{c})$ and find $\mathbf{n}$ in terms of $\mathbf{a}$, $\mathbf{b}$ and $\mathbf{c}$.

9. Given that $\mathbf{u}$ is a unit vector show that $\mathbf{u}\wedge(\mathbf{F}\wedge\mathbf{u})$ is the vector component of $\mathbf{F}$ in a direction perpendicular to $\mathbf{u}$.

10. A pyramid has three faces which (taking the vertex as origin) have equations

$$3x + 2y + 4z = 0, \qquad 2x - 3y + 2z = 0 \quad\text{and}\quad -3x - y + 3z = 0.$$

Find the three angles made by adjacent edges at the vertex.

11. $\mathbf{a}\wedge(\mathbf{b}\wedge\mathbf{c})$ is called the *vector triple product* of the vectors, $\mathbf{a}$, $\mathbf{b}$ and $\mathbf{c}$. Show that it is a vector in the plane of $\mathbf{b}$ and $\mathbf{c}$. By writing it in the form $\mathbf{a}\wedge(\mathbf{b}\wedge\mathbf{c}) = \lambda\mathbf{b} + \mu\mathbf{c}$ and taking the scalar product of both sides with $\mathbf{a}$, show that $\lambda : \mu = (\mathbf{a}\cdot\mathbf{c}) : -(\mathbf{a}\cdot\mathbf{b})$. Hence prove the result that

$$\mathbf{a}\wedge(\mathbf{b}\wedge\mathbf{c}) = (\mathbf{a}\cdot\mathbf{c})\mathbf{b} - (\mathbf{a}\cdot\mathbf{b})\mathbf{c}.$$

This result shows that the vector product is *not* associative.

6. DYNAMICS OF A PARTICLE

In this section we return to the problem posed at the beginning of the chapter – how to link up the applied forces with their rotational effect. We can now answer this question in simple cases.

6.1 Satellite problem

Suppose a satellite is orbiting the earth under the force of gravity and no other forces – what can we discover about its motion? Firstly if $\mathbf{r}$ is the position vector of the satellite relative to the centre of the earth and $\mathbf{F}$ is the force on the satellite due to gravity, then $\mathbf{r}$ and $\mathbf{F}$ are in the same line. Thus $\mathbf{r}\wedge\mathbf{F} = \mathbf{0}$ is always true for the motion of the satellite. Unfortunately, however, this equation does not tell us anything directly about the velocity of the satellite. If we substitute for $\mathbf{F}$, using Newton's Second Law

$$\mathbf{F} = \frac{\mathrm{d}}{\mathrm{d}t}(m\mathbf{v}),$$

then the equation becomes

$$\mathbf{r}\wedge\frac{\mathrm{d}}{\mathrm{d}t}(m\mathbf{v}) = \mathbf{0}. \qquad (3)$$

This equation clearly is important and gives us some information about the velocity. In the above form, however, all it tells us is that the *rate of change* of the velocity is in the direction of $\mathbf{r}$; how can we find out about $\mathbf{v}$ itself?

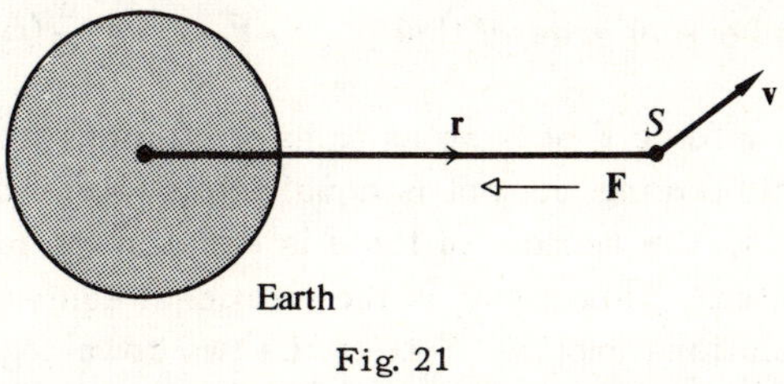

Fig. 21

This is a mathematical problem, and we must look around for a mathematical solution. We want to re-express the above equation in a more convenient form involving the velocity. The solution to the problem was discovered by considering the expression $(\mathrm{d}/\mathrm{d}t)\,(\mathbf{r}\wedge m\mathbf{v})$, which can easily be shown to be identical with $\mathbf{r}\wedge(\mathrm{d}/\mathrm{d}t)(m\mathbf{v})$:
using the Product Law (see Exercise F, Question 10)

$$\frac{d}{dt}(\mathbf{r}\wedge m\mathbf{v}) = \mathbf{r}\wedge\frac{d}{dt}(m\mathbf{v}) + \left(\frac{d}{dt}\mathbf{r}\right)\wedge m\mathbf{v},$$

$$= \mathbf{r}\wedge\frac{d}{dt}(m\mathbf{v}) + \mathbf{v}\wedge m\mathbf{v},$$

$$= \mathbf{r}\wedge\frac{d}{dt}(m\mathbf{v}), \quad (\text{as } \mathbf{v}\wedge\mathbf{v} = 0).$$

And so, substituting in equation (3), in the case of the satellite we can say that

$$\frac{d}{dt}(\mathbf{r}\wedge m\mathbf{v}) = \mathbf{0}.$$

This equation can be solved by integrating both sides with respect to time:

$$\mathbf{r}\wedge m\mathbf{v} = \text{a constant vector (say } \mathbf{H}).$$

This result therefore tells us that the velocity of the satellite is always in a direction perpendicular to some fixed vector $\mathbf{H}$, and so is $\mathbf{r}$. That is, $\mathbf{r}$ and $\mathbf{v}$ always lie in the same plane, perpendicular to $\mathbf{H}$. Thus the motion of the satellite under the *central force* due to gravitation is in a fixed plane. The above result also tells us that for any point on the orbit of the satellite the vector product $\mathbf{r}\wedge m\mathbf{v}$ is constant in magnitude. We call this quantity the *moment of momentum*† $\mathbf{H}$, and it is an extremely useful concept in solving problems of rotational motion.

Note:

$$\mathbf{H} = \mathbf{r}\wedge m\mathbf{v}$$

$$= m\mathbf{r}\wedge(\dot{r}\hat{\mathbf{r}} + r\dot{\theta}\hat{\mathbf{u}})$$

$$= mr^2\dot{\theta}\hat{\mathbf{e}}$$

$$\Longrightarrow H = mh,$$

where $h(=r^2\dot{\theta})$ was constant for the orbits of Chapter 2.

Definition. In general the *moment of momentum* $\mathbf{H}$, is defined to be the vector $\mathbf{r}\wedge m\mathbf{v}$. In the special case of the satellite's orbit, we found $\mathbf{H}$ to be constant.

This result suggests a solution to the general problem of relating a force to its resultant rotational motion. The rotational effect, or moment, of a force is $\mathbf{r}\wedge\mathbf{F}$, but we proved above *in general* that $\mathbf{r}\wedge\mathbf{F} = \mathbf{r}\wedge\frac{d}{dt}(m\mathbf{v}) = \frac{d}{dt}(\mathbf{r}\wedge m\mathbf{v})$.

So we can say that if a force $\mathbf{F}$ acts so as to have a turning moment $\mathbf{r}\wedge\mathbf{F}$ about some point O, then this turning moment is equal to the rate of change of the vector $\mathbf{r}\wedge m\mathbf{v}$. In words, 'the moment of force is equal to the rate of change of the moment of momentum'. This result is the rotational equivalent to Newton's Second Law for translational motion. Setting the two down together, for a force $\mathbf{F}$ acting on a particle and producing a velocity $\mathbf{v}$, then:

(a) $$\mathbf{F} = \frac{d}{dt}(m\mathbf{v}) \tag{4}$$

(b) $$\mathbf{r}\wedge\mathbf{F} = \frac{d}{dt}(\mathbf{r}\wedge m\mathbf{v}) = \dot{\mathbf{H}}. \tag{5}$$

† Often called the *angular momentum*.

These formulae summarise the theory of dynamics and in the next chapter they will be extended to apply to any number of forces acting on any system of particles.

6.2 Systems of forces

A space station consists of a light, rigid framework, at the centre of which is a small control unit of mass m. Propulsive rockets of negligible mass are situated at points on the extremity of the space station. What is the total effect of one or more rockets being fired?

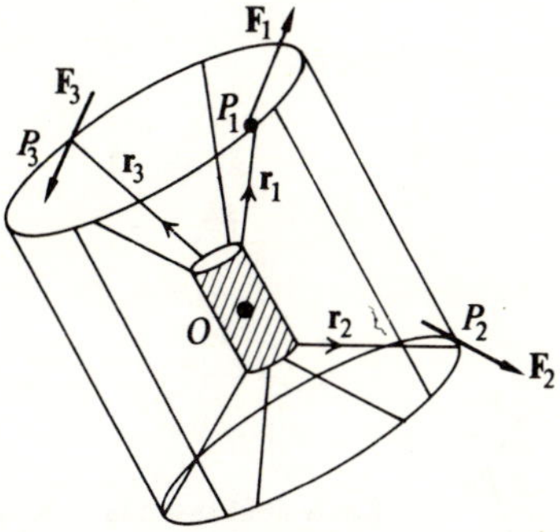

Fig. 22

The space station approximates to a model of a particle mass at O acted on by forces situated at P_1, P_2, etc. transmitted by weightless struts.

Consider first the case of the rocket at P_1 (its position vector is $\mathbf{r}_1$) which exerts a propulsive force $\mathbf{F}_1$. Except when the line of action of $\mathbf{F}_1$ happens to pass through the origin O it causes some rotation about O of moment $\mathbf{r}_1 \wedge \mathbf{F}_1$. Considering the space station as a whole we would also expect $\mathbf{F}_1$ to cause some translational motion given by Newton's Second Law.

In order to clarify the effects of this one force $\mathbf{F}_1$ we introduce two equal and apposite forces ($+\mathbf{Q}$ and $-\mathbf{Q}$) acting at O such that $\mathbf{Q}$ is equal in magnitude and direction to $\mathbf{F}_1$ (see Figure 23).

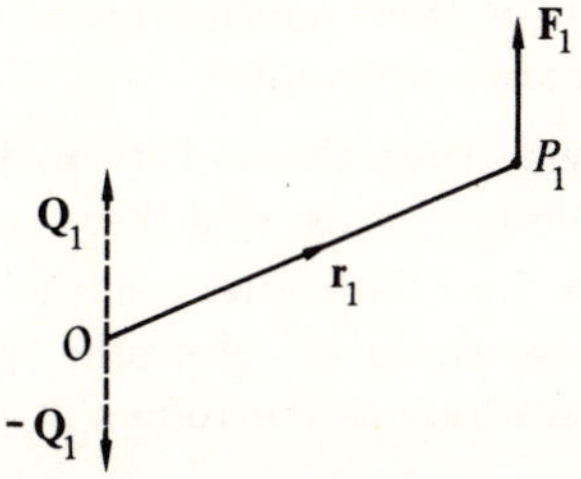

Fig. 23

The introduction of these forces (which have no effect on the space station) enables us to see the effect of $\mathbf{F}_1$ on the origin O. $\mathbf{F}_1$ and $-\mathbf{Q}$ together form a *couple* with no translational effect but they exert a turning moment about O (the reader should check that this turning moment is given by the vector $\mathbf{r}_1 \wedge \mathbf{F}_1$). The remaining force $\mathbf{Q}$ acts *at O* and hence its effect on O is purely translational.

Thus the force $\mathbf{F}_1$ (equivalent to forces $\mathbf{F}_1$, $\mathbf{Q}$ and $-\mathbf{Q}$, as in Figure 24) has a turning effect of $\mathbf{r}_1 \wedge \mathbf{F}_1$ about O and a translational effect of $\mathbf{Q}(=\mathbf{F}_1)$ *at O*.

This analysis can be repeated for any number of other forces $\mathbf{F}_2$, $\mathbf{F}_3$, ... acting at P_2, P_3, ... with position vectors $\mathbf{r}_2$, $\mathbf{r}_3$, ... respectively. Assuming we can add the vector moments, we deduce that a system of forces acting on the space station is equivalent in effect to (a) a translational force

$$\sum_1^n \mathbf{F}_i$$

acting at O and (*b*) a rotational moment

$$\sum_1^n \mathbf{r}_i \wedge \mathbf{F}_i \text{ about } O.$$

(See Figure 24.)

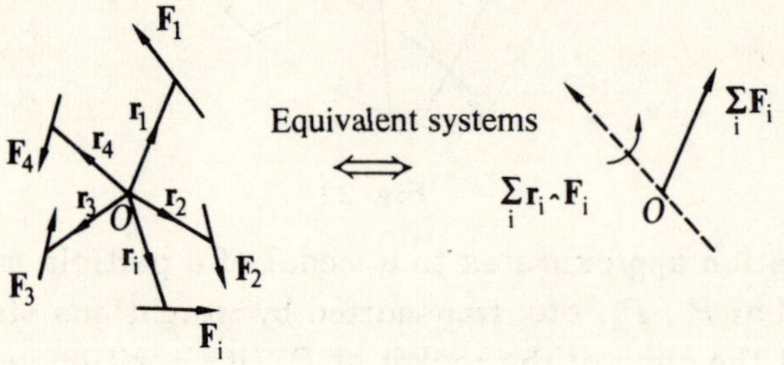

Fig. 24

This is a very important result with wide applications.

6.3 Applications

At this stage we consider general force systems applied to a single particle and in the next chapter the application will be extended to systems of particles and rigid bodies. It is worth bearing in mind that we will always be using the same theory, embodied in equations (4) and (5). Those formulae summarise the whole of Newtonian dynamics. It is in their application to more complicated physical situations that the work becomes difficult.

Example 12. A space station fires three of its rockets, located at the points (1, 1, 0), (0, −1, 1) and (1, 1, 1). If the forces exerted there are respectively $3\hat{i} + 2\hat{k}$, $4\hat{i} + 2\hat{j} + \hat{k}$ and $2\hat{i} + \hat{j} + \hat{k}$ find their effect on the origin O. Can this effect be achieved by a single rocket firing at some other point on the station?

Firstly we determine the effect of the forces at O. The translational effect on O is

$$\sum_i \mathbf{F}_i = 9\hat{\imath} + 3\hat{\jmath} + 4\hat{k}$$

The moment of the forces is :

$$\begin{pmatrix}1\\1\\0\end{pmatrix} \wedge \begin{pmatrix}3\\0\\2\end{pmatrix} + \begin{pmatrix}0\\-1\\1\end{pmatrix} \wedge \begin{pmatrix}4\\2\\1\end{pmatrix} + \begin{pmatrix}1\\1\\1\end{pmatrix} \wedge \begin{pmatrix}2\\1\\1\end{pmatrix} = \begin{pmatrix}2\\-2\\-3\end{pmatrix} + \begin{pmatrix}-3\\4\\4\end{pmatrix} + \begin{pmatrix}0\\1\\-1\end{pmatrix} = \begin{pmatrix}-1\\3\\0\end{pmatrix}.$$

Therefore $$\sum_i \mathbf{r}_i \wedge \mathbf{F}_i = -\hat{\mathbf{i}} + 3\hat{\mathbf{j}}$$

Secondly we wish to know if we can produce both these effects by just one force situated at some other point of the space craft.

It should be clear that this force must be represented in magnitude and direction by the force $\mathbf{F} = 9\hat{\mathbf{i}} + 3\hat{\mathbf{j}} + 4\hat{\mathbf{k}}$ in order to have the correct translational effect on O. The only freedom we have is in choosing the line of action of this force. Can we situate this force to produce a vector moment equal to $-\hat{\mathbf{i}} + 3\hat{\mathbf{j}}$? Suppose we put the line of action of $\mathbf{F}$ so that the position vector from O is $\mathbf{r}$. Then we must have $\mathbf{r} \wedge \mathbf{F} = -\hat{\mathbf{i}} + 3\hat{\mathbf{j}}$. Notice that even with complete freedom to choose $\mathbf{r}$ this equation will not in general have a solution – it can only be solved if $\mathbf{F}$ is perpendicular to $(-\hat{\mathbf{i}} + 3\hat{\mathbf{j}})$. That is, the resultant force must lie in a plane perpendicular to the axis of rotation. In this case we note that

$$\begin{pmatrix}9\\3\\4\end{pmatrix} \cdot \begin{pmatrix}-1\\3\\0\end{pmatrix} = 0,$$

so that condition is satisfied. It is left as an exercise for the reader to show

(by putting $\mathbf{r} = \begin{pmatrix}x\\y\\z\end{pmatrix}$ and solving $\begin{pmatrix}x\\y\\z\end{pmatrix} \wedge \begin{pmatrix}9\\3\\4\end{pmatrix} = \begin{pmatrix}-1\\3\\0\end{pmatrix}$)

that the line of action of the force has direction

$$\begin{pmatrix}9\\3\\4\end{pmatrix}$$

and passes through, for example, the point $(0, 0, \frac{1}{3})$.

Example 13. What are the effects of the forces in Example 12 on the point (1, 1, 0) in the space station? What general rule holds for the point with position vector $\mathbf{p}$?

Intuitively we should expect that the rotational effect would vary from point to point – think of the merry-go-round. Note that the translational force is the same for all points on the space station – this is what we mean by translational motion. To calculate $\sum_i (\mathbf{r}_i \wedge \mathbf{F}_i)$ for the point (1, 1, 0) we need the 'relative' positions of the rockets which are (0, 0, 0), (–1, –2, 1) and (0, 0, 1) respectively. In this case therefore the moment of the forces is:

$$\begin{pmatrix}0\\0\\0\end{pmatrix}\wedge\begin{pmatrix}3\\0\\2\end{pmatrix}+\begin{pmatrix}-1\\-2\\1\end{pmatrix}\wedge\begin{pmatrix}4\\2\\1\end{pmatrix}+\begin{pmatrix}0\\0\\1\end{pmatrix}\wedge\begin{pmatrix}2\\1\\1\end{pmatrix}=\begin{pmatrix}-4\\5\\6\end{pmatrix}+\begin{pmatrix}-1\\2\\0\end{pmatrix}=\begin{pmatrix}-5\\7\\6\end{pmatrix}.$$

For a general point P with position vector $\mathbf{p}$, suppose the vector moment of the forces about the origin is $\mathbf{G}$, then the vector moment of the forces about P is

$$\begin{aligned}\sum_i(\mathbf{r}_i-\mathbf{p})\wedge\mathbf{F}_i &= \sum_i \mathbf{r}_i\wedge\mathbf{F}_i-\mathbf{p}\wedge\sum_i\mathbf{F}_i\\ &= \sum_i(\mathbf{r}_i\wedge\mathbf{F}_i)-\mathbf{p}\wedge\sum_i\mathbf{F}_i\\ &= \mathbf{G}-\mathbf{p}\wedge\sum_i\mathbf{F}_i.\end{aligned}$$

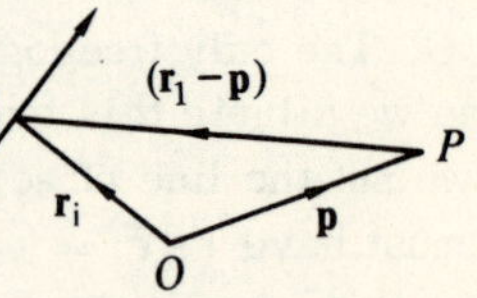

Fig. 25

The result in words is: if the effect of a system of forces is $\sum_i \mathbf{F}_i$ acting on a point and a moment $\mathbf{G}$ about that point, then the rotation moment about any other point (with position vector $\mathbf{p}$) is given by $\mathbf{G}$ minus the moment of $\mathbf{F}$ about P. In the above example

$$\mathbf{G}=\begin{pmatrix}-1\\3\\0\end{pmatrix},\qquad \mathbf{p}=\begin{pmatrix}1\\1\\0\end{pmatrix}\quad\text{and}\quad \mathbf{F}=\begin{pmatrix}9\\3\\4\end{pmatrix}.$$

Thus
$$\mathbf{p}\ \sum_i\mathbf{F}_i=\begin{pmatrix}4\\-4\\-6\end{pmatrix}\quad\text{and}\quad \mathbf{G}-\mathbf{p}\wedge\sum_i\mathbf{F}_i=\begin{pmatrix}-5\\7\\6\end{pmatrix}$$

as calculated above.

6.4 A wrench

You may recall from films of space flights that objects ejected from space craft often move with a rolling motion, spinning about their line of flight as they move away. In fact we can show that *every* force system is equivalent to a translational force $\mathbf{F}$ and a rotational couple $\mathbf{G}$ in the direction of $\mathbf{F}(\mathbf{G}=\lambda\mathbf{F})$.

Example 14. Find the effect of the following force system on the origin. Show that the system is equivalent to a force, and couple in the same direction, acting at some other point:

Force $\hat{\mathbf{j}}+\hat{\mathbf{k}}$	acting at (1, 1, 0).
Force $2\hat{\mathbf{i}}-\hat{\mathbf{j}}-3\hat{\mathbf{k}}$	acting at (2, 1, 0).
Force $-\hat{\mathbf{i}}+2\hat{\mathbf{k}}$	acting at (0, 0, 2).

The above forces are equivalent to a force $\hat{\mathbf{i}}$ acting at the origin and a couple of moment $-2\hat{\mathbf{i}} + 3\hat{\mathbf{j}} - 3\hat{\mathbf{k}}$ (check this). Note that these vectors are not perpendicular and hence we cannot reduce the system to a single force. We wish to situate the force $\mathbf{F} = \hat{\mathbf{i}}$ at some other point so that its moment about the origin, combined with a couple $\lambda\mathbf{i}$ will equal the vector $-2\hat{\mathbf{i}} + 3\hat{\mathbf{j}} - 3\hat{\mathbf{k}}$. That is, we want a $\mathbf{p}$ and λ such that $-2\hat{\mathbf{i}} + 3\hat{\mathbf{j}} - 3\hat{\mathbf{k}} = \mathbf{p} \wedge \hat{\mathbf{i}} + \lambda\hat{\mathbf{i}}$

$$\Longrightarrow \mathbf{p} \wedge \mathbf{i} = (-2\hat{\mathbf{i}} + 3\hat{\mathbf{j}} - 3\hat{\mathbf{k}} - \lambda\hat{\mathbf{i}}).$$

First we must find λ such that $-2\hat{\mathbf{i}} + 3\hat{\mathbf{j}} - 3\hat{\mathbf{k}} - \lambda\hat{\mathbf{i}}$ is perpendicular to $\hat{\mathbf{i}}$. Clearly $\lambda = -2$ satisfied this condition leaving

$$3\hat{\mathbf{j}} - 3\hat{\mathbf{k}} = \mathbf{p} \wedge \hat{\mathbf{i}} \text{ to be solved for } \mathbf{p}.$$

Putting $\mathbf{p} = \begin{pmatrix} x \\ y \\ z \end{pmatrix}$ and solving $\begin{pmatrix} 0 \\ 3 \\ -3 \end{pmatrix} = \begin{pmatrix} x \\ y \\ z \end{pmatrix} \wedge \begin{pmatrix} 1 \\ 0 \\ 0 \end{pmatrix}$ gives $\mathbf{p} = \begin{pmatrix} x \\ 3 \\ 3 \end{pmatrix}$.

As the line of the force $\mathbf{F}$ is $\hat{\mathbf{i}}$ then we should expect the solution for $\mathbf{p}$ to have an arbitrary first coordinate (check various values for x).

We have therefore shown that the original force system *has the same effect* as a force $\hat{\mathbf{i}}$ acting at the point (0, 3, 3) combined with a couple represented by the vector $-2\hat{\mathbf{i}}$.

This motion is therefore along a 'corkscrew path' or helix; the combination of force and couple with the same direction is called a *wrench*.

EXERCISE F

1. Find the rate of change of angular momentum, $\dot{\mathbf{H}}$, about the origin, due to a force $3\hat{\mathbf{i}} - 7\hat{\mathbf{j}} + \hat{\mathbf{k}}$ acting on a body at the point (1, 0, −2).

2. The acceleration produced by a force acting on a satellite is represented in magnitude and direction by the vector

$$\begin{pmatrix} 3 \\ 1 \\ 1 \end{pmatrix}.$$

If the position vector of the satellite relative to the earth is (7, −5, 4) calculate the rate of change of angular momentum relative to the earth given that the mass of the satellite is 12 units.

3. Given that the rate of change of angular momentum in Question 2 is represented by a vector

$$\begin{pmatrix} 4 \\ 2 \\ 1 \end{pmatrix}$$

for a satellite positioned at the point (–2, 0, 8), find the acceleration.

4. Find the resultant effect of the three forces

$$\begin{pmatrix}0\\2\\3\end{pmatrix}, \quad \begin{pmatrix}7\\-6\\0\end{pmatrix} \quad \text{and} \quad \begin{pmatrix}0\\0\\5\end{pmatrix}$$

acting respectively at the points (2, 4, 0), (0, 1, 3) and (0, 3, 0), (a) at the origin (b) at the point (5, 5, 6). For (b) check your answer by the two methods as set out in Example 13.

5. A space station is acted on by the following forces acting at the following points:

$$\begin{aligned} &\hat{\mathbf{i}} + \hat{\mathbf{k}} && \text{acting at } (1, 1, 0),\\ &\hat{\mathbf{i}} + \hat{\mathbf{j}} && \text{acting at } (1, 1, 1),\\ -&3\hat{\mathbf{j}} + \hat{\mathbf{k}} && \text{acting at } (1, 0, 1). \end{aligned}$$

Determine the effect of these on the origin and find if this effect can be neutralised by a single force acting at some other point.

6. What is the effect on the origin of the following force system?

$$\begin{aligned} &\text{A force } 2\hat{\mathbf{i}} + 3\hat{\mathbf{j}} + 4\hat{\mathbf{k}}, \text{ acting at } (1, 0, 0),\\ &\text{A force } 4\hat{\mathbf{i}} + 2\hat{\mathbf{j}} + \hat{\mathbf{k}}, \text{ acting at } (0, 1, 0).\\ &\text{A force } 6\hat{\mathbf{i}} + \hat{\mathbf{j}} + 3\hat{\mathbf{k}}, \text{ acting at } (0, 0, 1). \end{aligned}$$

Find a force and couple in the same direction equivalent to the above three forces.

7. A system of forces acting on a body is said to be in equilibrium if it has no resultant translational and rotational effect. State these criteria in terms of vector equations and show that any system is in equilibrium if the resultant moments about three non-collinear points are all zero.

8. Are the following four forces in equilibrium?

Force	$3\hat{\mathbf{i}} - 2\hat{\mathbf{j}} - 4\hat{\mathbf{k}}$	$-\hat{\mathbf{i}} + \hat{\mathbf{j}}$	$-\hat{\mathbf{i}} + \hat{\mathbf{j}}$	$-\hat{\mathbf{i}} + 4\hat{\mathbf{k}}$
Acting at	(1, 0, 1)	(0, 0, 1)	(0, 1, 1)	(1, 1, 1)

9. Suppose a system of forces acting on a space craft is equivalent to a force

$$\begin{pmatrix}1\\0\\-1\end{pmatrix} \text{ acting at the origin and a couple } \begin{pmatrix}2\\1\\0\end{pmatrix}.$$

Find the wrench equivalent to this system.

***10.** From first principles justify the product law for differentiating a vector product:

$$\frac{d}{dt}(\mathbf{a} \wedge \mathbf{b}) = \frac{d(\mathbf{a})}{dt} \wedge \mathbf{b} + \mathbf{a} \wedge \frac{d(\mathbf{b})}{dt}.$$

*11. A system of forces reduces to a couple **G** and a force **F** at the origin and we wish to find the equivalent wrench: i.e. to find **p** and λ such that $\mathbf{G} = \mathbf{p} \wedge \mathbf{F} + \lambda\mathbf{F}$ Show by taking dot products that $\lambda = \mathbf{F}\cdot\mathbf{G}/\mathbf{F}\cdot\mathbf{F}$. Check the answers in questions above using this formula.

7. SUMMING VECTOR PRODUCTS

Throughout this chapter we have been using vector products to represent moments and adding and subtracting them like vectors to find *resultant* moments. Why are we justified in doing this? In this final section we shall try to show that even in the case of two skew forces acting at different points, their turning moments about some other point may be represented by vector products and their resultant moment is given by the vector sum of the vector products. That is, we will show from first principles that $(\mathbf{r}_1 \wedge \mathbf{F}_1 + \mathbf{r}_2 \wedge \mathbf{F}_2)$ represents the resultant turning effect of $\mathbf{F}_1$ and $\mathbf{F}_2$.

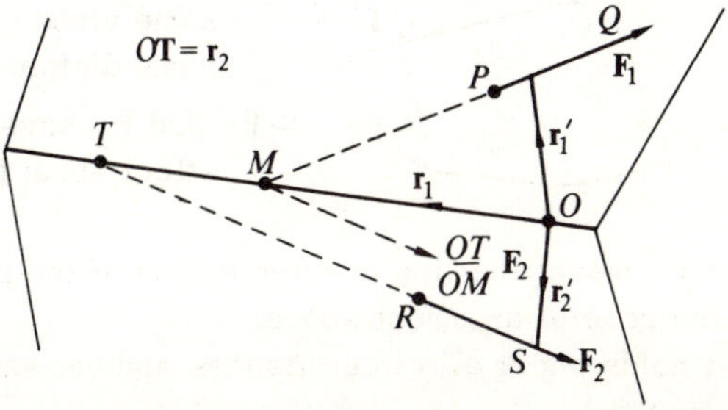

Fig. 26

From Figure 26, let $\mathbf{F}_1$ and $\mathbf{F}_2$ be two forces whose lines of action are skew. If O is the point about which we are taking moments then PQO is the plane of rotation of $\mathbf{F}_1$ and RSO the plane for $\mathbf{F}_2$. These planes have a line of intersection which passes through O. Extend the lines of action of $\mathbf{F}_1$ and $\mathbf{F}_2$ so that they intersect this line of intersection at M and T (the case when they are parallel to it will be considered later), as in Figure 26.

The problem is to calculate the total turning effect of $\mathbf{F}_1$ and $\mathbf{F}_2$. If $\mathbf{F}_1$ and $\mathbf{F}_2$ acted at the same point this would be easy, but from elementary work we know that the turning effect of $\mathbf{F}_2$ acting at T is equivalent to a larger force parallel to $\mathbf{F}_2$ acting at M. Taking moments about O gives us this larger force as $(OT/OM)\mathbf{F}_2$. Thus the original system is rotationally equivalent to the two forces $\mathbf{F}_1$ and $(OT/OM)\,\mathbf{F}_2$ acting at M. From earlier work we know that the resultant effect is

$$\mathbf{r}_1 \wedge \left(\mathbf{F}_1 + \frac{OT}{OM}\mathbf{F}_2\right).$$

This is the resultant turning effect calculated from first principles. Do we get the same answer by adding the vector products $\mathbf{r}'_1 \wedge \mathbf{F}_1 + \mathbf{r}'_2 \wedge \mathbf{F}_2$?

Clearly we do because

$$\mathbf{r}'_1 \wedge \mathbf{F}_1 = \mathbf{r}_1 \wedge \mathbf{F}_1 \quad \text{and} \quad \mathbf{r}'_2 \wedge \mathbf{F}_2 = \mathbf{r}_2 \wedge \mathbf{F}_2 .$$

But $\mathbf{r}_1$ and $\mathbf{r}_2$ are in the same line such that $\mathbf{r}_2 = (OT/OM)\mathbf{r}_1$.

So $$\mathbf{r}_1 \wedge \mathbf{F}_1 + \mathbf{r}_2 \wedge \mathbf{F}_2 = \mathbf{r}_1 \wedge \mathbf{F}_1 + \left(\frac{OT}{OM}\mathbf{r}_1\right) \wedge \mathbf{F}_2 = \mathbf{r}_1 \wedge \left(\mathbf{F}_1 + \frac{OT}{OM}\mathbf{F}_2\right)$$

using the Distributive Law.

The reader should check that the same result holds when the forces cut the line of intersection of planes on opposite sides of O, and also that the above working applies to the case when one or both forces are parallel to the line of intersection. One quick check is that a force parallel to the line of intersection is equivalent in *rotational* effect to a force acting at right angles to the line of intersection (see Figure 27).

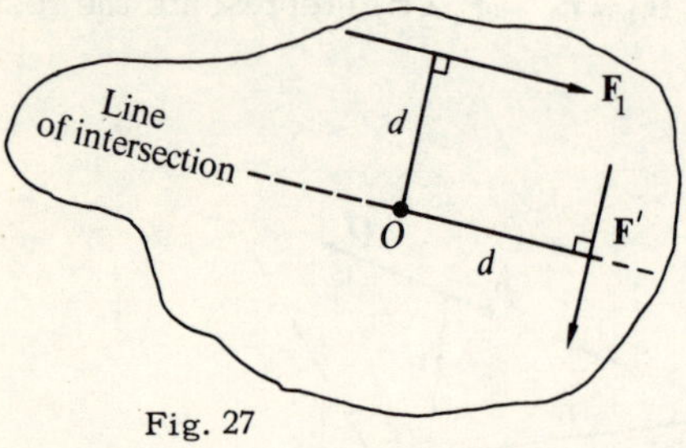

Fig. 27

$\mathbf{F}'$ has the same magnitude as $\mathbf{F}_1$.

The lines of $\mathbf{F}'$ and $\mathbf{F}_1$ are in the same plane containing 0 and the same distance from 0.

$\Rightarrow \mathbf{F}'$ and $\mathbf{F}_1$ have the same rotational effect about 0.

The line of action of $\mathbf{F}'$ meets the line of intersection of the planes of rotation, so we can now use the general argument above.

Hence the result holds under all circumstances and our assumptions throughout this chapter are justified.

SUMMARY

The vector product $\mathbf{r} \wedge \mathbf{F}$ is defined as the vector $rF \sin\theta\, \hat{\mathbf{e}}$, where $\hat{\mathbf{e}}$ is a unit vector perpendicular to $\mathbf{r}$ and $\mathbf{F}$ (in a right-hand corkscrew sense) and θ is the angle between them. When $\mathbf{r}$ is any position vector from O to the line of $\mathbf{F}$, it represents the turning moment of a force $\mathbf{F}$ about O.

Properties of vector product

1. Distributive over addition $\mathbf{a} \wedge (\mathbf{b} + \mathbf{c}) = \mathbf{a} \wedge \mathbf{b} + \mathbf{a} \wedge \mathbf{c}$.
2. Scalars can be multiplied through $\mathbf{a} \wedge p\mathbf{b} = p\mathbf{a} \wedge \mathbf{b} = p(\mathbf{a} \wedge \mathbf{b})$, etc.
3. The vector product is neither commutative nor associative.

Components

$\begin{pmatrix} a \\ b \\ c \end{pmatrix} \wedge \begin{pmatrix} P \\ Q \\ R \end{pmatrix}$ can be expanded in the determinant form $\begin{vmatrix} \hat{\mathbf{i}} & \hat{\mathbf{j}} & \hat{\mathbf{k}} \\ a & b & c \\ P & Q & R \end{vmatrix}$.

A couple is two equal and opposite forces situated at a perpendicular distance $d(\neq 0)$ apart. Any force system producing rotation and no translation is equivalent to a couple.

The angular velocity vector $\boldsymbol{\omega}$ for a body rotating about a fixed axis is given by $\mathbf{v} = \boldsymbol{\omega} \wedge \mathbf{r}$ where $\mathbf{v}$ and $\mathbf{r}$ are the velocity and position vector respectively of a point on the body.

Plane passing through three points with position vectors $\mathbf{u}$, $\mathbf{v}$ and $\mathbf{w}$ has equation:

$$(\mathbf{r} - \mathbf{w})\cdot((\mathbf{v} - \mathbf{u}) \wedge (\mathbf{w} - \mathbf{v})) = 0.$$

Rotational equation of motion. For a force $\mathbf{F}$ acting on a particle of mass m, with velocity $\mathbf{v}$ and position vector $\mathbf{r}$ then:

$$\mathbf{r} \wedge \mathbf{F} = \frac{d}{dt}(\mathbf{r} \wedge m\mathbf{v}) = \dot{\mathbf{H}} \quad (\mathbf{H} \text{ is called the moment of momentum}).$$

All force systems can be reduced to a translational force acting at a point and a couple acting about the point. In special cases force systems can be reduced to one force only acting at a certain distance from the point. They may also be represented by a wrench, the combination of a force and a couple with the same direction.

4. Rigid Bodies

1. TRANSLATION

A space craft of total mass M is acted on by a force **F** as in Figure 1(a). What is the resultant rotational motion of the craft about the point O?

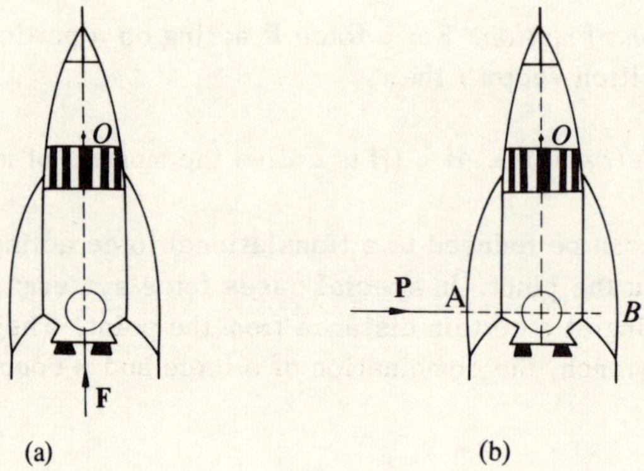

Fig. 1

We know, from rocket launchings, that if **F** is due to the main propulsive rocket then the craft will usually move with translational motion only. Suppose, however, that the space craft had used up all the fuel in the tanks on the right-hand side of the ship and that the left-hand side fuel tanks were full (putting virtually all the *mass* on one side). Would you now expect the force in Figure 1(a) to rotate the craft? What is usually true about the mass distribution in a space craft taking off from the earth?

It appears, therefore, that it is not enough to know the total mass of the craft—its rotational motion depends also on how the mass is distributed. Consider the force **P** acting on the craft as in Figure 1(b). Would you expect the craft to rotate about O under this force? Intuitively the answer is 'yes', but this assumes a 'usual' uniform mass distribution. Suppose the same mass M of the craft was concentrated along the line AB (the rest being a light rigid framework). Would we now expect the rocket to rotate about O? It should now be clear that the situations discussed in Chapter 3 to illustrate rotational motion were rather special. They only dealt with *one* particle and did not analyse the situation arising from a system of forces applied to a large body of mass M. If we are to explain the rotational motion of cars, aeroplanes, and space-ships, we must develop the theory to account for 'systems of particles'. Our object in this chapter is to explain the rotational motion of a system of n particles, when each particle is acted on by a separate force. From this we build up a mathematical model of the motion of rigid bodies, for a rigid body may be considered as an infinite number of particles 'stuck together'; calculus techniques can be used to overcome this difficulty and the general theory of rotational motion of a rigid body can be set out. Thus our task is to explain the rotational motion of rigid bodies acted on by systems of forces. Before we can do this we first have to derive the equations for linear motion.

1.1 Linear motion (internal forces)

Consider any two particles. They may be two small magnets attracting or repelling one another; they may be small blobs joined by an elastic string; they may be rigidly connected as are the ends of a dumb-bell; or they may not be connected at all. Any forces which they experience on account of their mutual interaction are called *internal forces,* denoted by $\mathbf{F}_1'$ and $\mathbf{F}_2'$ in Figure 2. They may also be subjected to other *external forces,* denoted by $\mathbf{F}_1$ and $\mathbf{F}_2$.

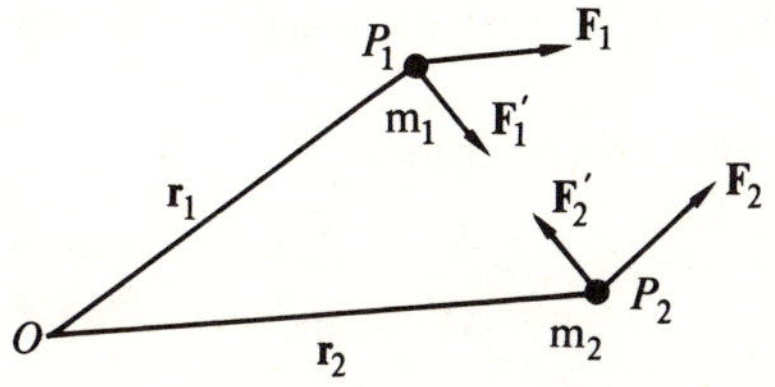

Fig. 2

Then Newton's Second Law applied to each particle gives

$$\begin{aligned} \mathbf{F}_1 + \mathbf{F}_1' &= m_1\ddot{\mathbf{r}}_1, \\ \mathbf{F}_2 + \mathbf{F}_2' &= m_2\ddot{\mathbf{r}}_2, \end{aligned} \tag{1}$$

whence adding: $\mathbf{F}_1 + \mathbf{F}_2 = m_1\ddot{\mathbf{r}}_1 + m_2\ddot{\mathbf{r}}_2,$

since the total interaction force $\mathbf{F}_1' + \mathbf{F}_2'$ is zero by Newton's Third Law. The sum of the external forces is thus equal to the sum of the mass accelerations.

Symbolically: $$\sum \mathbf{F} = \sum m\ddot{\mathbf{r}}. \tag{2}$$

What is the situation when there are three particles? The mutual interaction may give rise to as many as six internal forces. However, by Newton's Third Law, the sum of the internal forces will still be zero. It is easy to see that this will be true for any number of particles. So for any number of particles

$$\sum \mathbf{F} = \sum m\ddot{\mathbf{r}}.$$

This is an interesting result, since it seems to imply that the acceleration of any system of particles is not influenced by any internal forces there may be. But it really tells us nothing about the fate of any individual particle; for this we must go back to our first equations, which do involve the internal forces. However, it does give us some valuable information about the overall motion of the system. [Can you decide what?]

1.2 Mass centre

We can easily add the two vectors $m_1\mathbf{r}_1$ and $m_2\mathbf{r}_2$ in equation (2) to get a resultant vector, but it is more convenient to write

$$m_1\mathbf{r}_1 + m_2\mathbf{r}_2 = (m_1 + m_2)\bar{\mathbf{r}},$$

Where will the point C with position vector $\bar{\mathbf{r}}$ be in relation to P_1 and P_2? How would this be affected by a change of origin?

Differentiating: $$m_1\ddot{\mathbf{r}}_1 + m_2\ddot{\mathbf{r}}_2 = (m_1 + m_2)\ddot{\bar{\mathbf{r}}}.$$

Symbolically: $\Sigma(m\ddot{\mathbf{r}}) = M\ddot{\bar{\mathbf{r}}}$, where M is the sum of the masses,

but
$$\sum \mathbf{F} = m_1\ddot{\mathbf{r}}_1 + m_2\ddot{\mathbf{r}}_2,$$
$$\sum \mathbf{F} = (m_1 + m_2)\ddot{\bar{\mathbf{r}}},$$

so there is a point C, the *mass centre* (or centroid), whose acceleration $\ddot{\bar{\mathbf{r}}}$ is the same as it would have had if the particles and the forces acting on them had all been located at C.

Similarly for any number of particles.

Symbolically: $\sum \mathbf{F} = \sum (m\ddot{\mathbf{r}})$, $\mathbf{P} = M\ddot{\bar{\mathbf{r}}}$, where M is the sum of all the masses.

The total external force is equal to the total mass acceleration of all the particles concentrated at the mass centre.

So there is a mass centre C associated with a set of particles with position vector $\bar{\mathbf{r}}$ *given by*

$$M\bar{\mathbf{r}} = \sum (m\mathbf{r}) \tag{3}$$

(a) whose position is independent of the origin chosen,

(b) whose motion is independent of any internal forces,

(c) it is typical of the system as a whole since, if every particle were to have the same motion, it would be the motion of C,

(d) C lies within the convex polyhedron bounded by the particles,

(e) its motion is as if all the particles were concentrated at C with all the forces acting together at C on them.

It is well worth making sure you can prove all these remarkable properties for such a point. [See *SMP Advanced Mathematics*, Chapter 9]

Example 1. Two charged particles of mass 2 and 3, initially at the points (5, 0, 0) and (0, 5, 0) are subjected to external field forces of

$$\begin{pmatrix} 0 \\ -4 \\ 5 \end{pmatrix} \text{ and } \begin{pmatrix} 0 \\ -6 \\ -5 \end{pmatrix}.$$

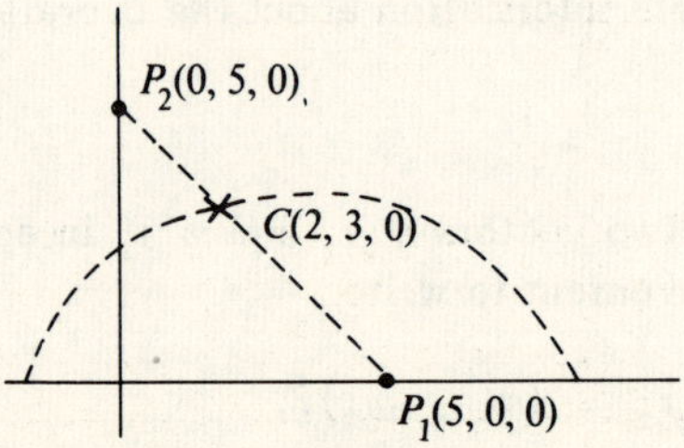

Fig. 3

The mass centre C has position vector $\bar{\mathbf{r}}$ given by

$$M\bar{\mathbf{r}} = m_1\mathbf{r}_1 + m_2\mathbf{r}_2$$

$$5\bar{\mathbf{r}} = 2\begin{pmatrix}5\\0\\0\end{pmatrix} + 3\begin{pmatrix}0\\5\\0\end{pmatrix} \Rightarrow C \text{ is the point } (2, 3, 0).$$

Also we know from the ratio theorem that C will divide P_1P_2 in the ratio 3 to 2.

For the motion of C: $M\ddot{\bar{\mathbf{r}}} = \Sigma\,\mathbf{F}$

$$5\ddot{\bar{\mathbf{r}}} = \begin{pmatrix}0\\-10\\0\end{pmatrix} \Rightarrow \ddot{\bar{\mathbf{r}}} = \begin{pmatrix}0\\-2\\0\end{pmatrix}.$$

So C will have a constant acceleration parallel to the y-axis. Its path will be a parabola or straight line, depending whether or not it had any initial velocity other than in the y-direction. We get quite a clear idea of the motion of C but the motion of the particles themselves can be pretty arbitrary so long as C is always 3/5 of the way from P_1 to P_2.

In fact, for a system of particles, C is no more than a very theoretical mean. It has little significance for a collection of flies, for example, and it is poor consolation to have thrown the mass centre successfully into the rubbish bin if all the rubbish actually lands on the floor!

1.3 Rigid body

Take a few awkwardly shaped objects – a pen, shoe, wastepaper basket – hold them at one end, toss them across the room and watch the end you were holding. The prospect of describing its motion is rather daunting. Now toss them again, but watch the mass centre. Can you really see it? Can you explain its motion?

For some objects the mass centre C is a definite point of the body. If we know the forces acting on such a body, even though we may not know where they act, there is this one point C whose motion we can readily calculate. We make a mathematical model of such objects by considering them to be composed of a collection of particles, the distance between any two of which is constant. We call such an object a *rigid body*. For instance, when the only significant external force is the gravitational attraction of the earth on each particle, we get $-\Sigma\,(mg)\hat{\mathbf{k}} = M\ddot{\bar{\mathbf{r}}}$, where $\hat{\mathbf{k}}$ is a unit vector in a vertically upward direction.

i.e. $$\ddot{\bar{\mathbf{r}}} = -g\hat{\mathbf{k}}.$$

C describes a parabolic path, whose exact shape depends on the initial velocity of C. [What if we had tossed these objects in outer space with negligible gravitational attraction?] So far our model has proved very satisfactory for depicting the motion of one particular point of a rigid body, its mass centre.

Try tossing your objects once again, but this time attempt to observe the end as well as the mass centre. Are you now able to describe the motion of one end?

1.4 Motion relative to mass centre

If we mentally place ourselves at the mass centre the motion of a body certainly looks simpler. So let us see what we can find out about the motion of a set of particles relative to their mass centre C.

Notation: We use stars to denote any quantity relative to C, and bars to denote mass centre quantities, e.g. $\mathbf{r}_1^*$ is the position of P_1 relative to C, so that $\mathbf{r}_1 = \bar{\mathbf{r}} + \mathbf{r}_1^*$ and $m_1\mathbf{r}_1 = m_1\bar{\mathbf{r}} + m_1\mathbf{r}_1^*$.

For three particles:

$$m_1\mathbf{r}_1 + m_2\mathbf{r}_2 + m_3\mathbf{r}_3 = (m_1 + m_2 + m_3)\bar{\mathbf{r}} + m_1\mathbf{r}_1^* + m_2\mathbf{r}_2^* + m_3\mathbf{r}_3^* .$$

Symbolically:

$$\sum(m\mathbf{r}) = \sum(m\bar{\mathbf{r}}) + \sum(m\mathbf{r}^*)$$

$$\Longrightarrow \sum(m\mathbf{r}) = M\bar{\mathbf{r}} + \sum(m\mathbf{r}^*). \qquad (4)$$

But $\sum(m\mathbf{r}) = M\bar{\mathbf{r}}$, by the definition of mass centre,

$$\Longrightarrow \sum m\mathbf{r}^* = 0,$$

which is true, similarly, for any number of particles. This tells us about the position of the system relative to C, but merely confirms that C is the mean of the distribution. In fact $\Sigma(m\mathbf{r}^*) = 0$ corresponds precisely to the statistical mean being zero if the assumed mean is taken as the actual mean.

Differentiating: $\sum m\mathbf{r}^* = 0$ gives $\sum m\dot{\mathbf{r}}^* = 0$ and $\sum m\ddot{\mathbf{r}}^* = 0$ (5)

so the total linear momentum relative to C is zero.

Symbolically: $\mathbf{L}^* = 0$ also $\dot{\mathbf{L}}^* = 0$.

Is there any other point for which this is true? This gives some insight into the symmetry of the motion relative to C.

We can summarise all the results for linear motion.

The mass centre C is given by: $\sum(m\mathbf{r}) = M\bar{\mathbf{r}}$.

Differentiating: $\sum(m\dot{\mathbf{r}}) = M\dot{\bar{\mathbf{r}}}$.

The total linear momentum is equal to the linear momentum of a system concentrated at C.

Symbolically: $\mathbf{L} = \bar{\mathbf{L}}$. (6)

So the total linear momentum is the same as if all the particles had been at C.

Also, differentiating again: $\sum\mathbf{F} = \sum(m\ddot{\mathbf{r}})$ $(= M\ddot{\bar{\mathbf{r}}})$, using equation (2)

So the total external force gives the total rate of change of linear momentum [which is the same as the rate of change of linear momentum of a system concentrated at C]

Symbolically: $\mathbf{P} = \dot{\mathbf{L}}$ $(= \dot{\bar{\mathbf{L}}})$. (7)

Note that all the results so far hold for any system of particles, although they may only be useful when the particles are suitably constrained so as to provide a rigid body model.

The summary on page 130 gives the notation used in this chapter, and also all important results.

EXERCISE A

1. Discuss the motion of the mass centre of a skater who loses his balance while standing on smooth ice.

2. Prove that the mass centre of three particles lies in their plane and locate its position if the masses are in the ratio 2 : 3 : 4.

3. Three similar ink-pots fly through the air. Their mass centre lands in the wastepaper basket and one of them is observed to land a few feet away. Is it possible from this to say where the others landed? Would it make any difference (a) if the masses were not equal, (b) if they were rigidly joined together?

4. A space-ship blasts off, powered only by an adjustable rocket which is kept pointing vertically downwards. How do the rates of lift of the mass centre compare when the rocket is located (a) centrally, or (b) off-centre? How do the rates of lift of the tip of the nose compare?

5. Show that the rate of change of linear momentum of a body is zero relative to any point with the same velocity as the mass centre.

6. A police traffic cone is gripped with both hands and is thrown with a straight arm swing. 'All things being equal', where should it be gripped to propel it the farthest?

7. Discuss the motion of mass centre of (a) a long jumper, (b) a high jumper, once they have left the ground. Show how, at least in theory, it is possible for the mass centre of the high jumper to pass beneath the bar although he goes over it.

2. ROTATIONAL MOTION

Much wisdom and satisfaction can be acquired by kicking a large cardboard box downstairs. So long as the magnitude and direction of kick are constant the time of flight is much the same no matter where the foot be applied. This you can explain in terms of its mass centre. However, a kick off-centre causes some rotation which, if the box slides before take-off, will be about a vertical axis and may indeed provide greater stability.

If you flick your pen along your desk how far will it travel? Does it matter what point of the pen you flick? Was the disagreement an imperfection in your theory or in your desk? Are you sure? We had better consider the turning effect when forces are applied to a system of particles and try to obtain a model for the rotational motion of rigid bodies. Let us start with the familiar forces of gravitational attraction.

2.1 Gravitational attraction

We have already seen that the linear motion of mass centre is independent of the location of the forces and that, if $\mathbf{g}$ is towards the centre of the earth the gravitational attraction acting on a system of particles is:

for three particles	*symbolically (for any number of particles)*
$m_1\mathbf{g} + m_2\mathbf{g} + m_3\mathbf{g}$	$\Sigma(m\mathbf{g})$
$= (m_1 + m_2 + m_3)\mathbf{g}$	$= (\Sigma m)\mathbf{g}$ (A) since $\mathbf{g}$ is constant
$= M\mathbf{g}$	$= M\mathbf{g}$

So the translational effect of the gravitational attraction is the same as if the whole gravitational attraction were acting on the total mass concentrated at the mass centre C.

The rotational effect of the gravitational attraction about the origin O is:

for three particles	*symbolically (for any number of particles)*
$\mathbf{r}_1\wedge m_1\mathbf{g} + \mathbf{r}_2\wedge m_2\mathbf{g} + \mathbf{r}_3\wedge m_3\mathbf{g}$	$\Sigma(\mathbf{r}\wedge m\mathbf{g})$
$= m_1\mathbf{r}_1\wedge\mathbf{g} + m_2\mathbf{r}_2\wedge\mathbf{g} + m_3\mathbf{r}_3\wedge\mathbf{g}$	$= \Sigma(m\mathbf{r}\wedge\mathbf{g})$ (B) since m is scalar
$= (m_1\mathbf{r}_1 + m_2\mathbf{r}_2 + m_3\mathbf{r}_3)\wedge\mathbf{g}$	$= (\Sigma m\mathbf{r})\wedge\mathbf{g}$ (C) distributive since $\mathbf{g}$ is constant
$= M\bar{\mathbf{r}}\wedge\mathbf{g}$	$= M\bar{\mathbf{r}}\wedge\mathbf{g}$ definition of $\bar{\mathbf{r}}$
$= \bar{\mathbf{r}}\wedge M\mathbf{g}$	$= \bar{\mathbf{r}}\wedge M\mathbf{g}$ (B)

So the rotational effect of the gravitational attraction is the same as if the whole gravitational attraction were acting on the total mass concentrated at the mass centre C. This is why the mass centre is often called the centre of gravity. The result only holds when $\mathbf{g}$ is the same for each particle, which is approximately true for small bodies.

Note the symbolic manipulation with the Σ sign, particularly the three steps labelled (A), (B), (C), which frequently occur. The justification is obtained by writing the steps out in full, as shown on the left.

2.2 System of particles

We know how to combine moments of forces, but what effect do they have on a system of particles? Consider first two particles (cf. Section 1.1)

$$\mathbf{F}_1 + \mathbf{F}_1' = m_1\ddot{\mathbf{r}}_1,$$
$$\mathbf{F}_2 + \mathbf{F}_2' = m_2\ddot{\mathbf{r}}_2.$$

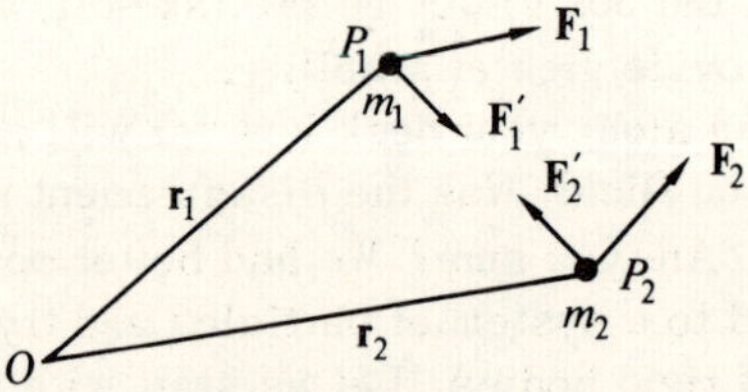

(Fig. 2 again)

To get the moment about O we form a vector product giving:

$$\mathbf{r}_1\wedge\mathbf{F}_1 + \mathbf{r}_1\wedge\mathbf{F}_1' = \mathbf{r}_1\wedge m_1\ddot{\mathbf{r}}_1,$$
$$\mathbf{r}_2\wedge\mathbf{F}_2 + \mathbf{r}_2\wedge\mathbf{F}_2' = \mathbf{r}_2\wedge m_2\ddot{\mathbf{r}}_2.$$

Now the sum of the second terms, the moments of the internal forces,

$$= \mathbf{r}_1 \wedge \mathbf{F}_1' + \mathbf{r}_2 \wedge \mathbf{F}_2',$$

$$= (\mathbf{r}_1 - \mathbf{r}_2) \wedge \mathbf{F}_1', \text{ using Newton's Interaction Law,}$$

$$= 0$$

since the interaction $\mathbf{F}_1'$ is along the line $(\mathbf{r}_1 - \mathbf{r}_2)$ joining the particles,

whence $$\mathbf{r}_1 \wedge \mathbf{F}_1 + \mathbf{r}_2 \wedge \mathbf{F}_2 = \mathbf{r}_1 \wedge m_1\ddot{\mathbf{r}}_1 + \mathbf{r}_2 \wedge m_2\ddot{\mathbf{r}}_2.$$

The moment of the external forces is the sum of the moments of the mass-accelerations.

Symbolically: $$\sum \mathbf{r} \wedge \mathbf{F} = \sum \mathbf{r} \wedge m\ddot{\mathbf{r}}, \qquad (8)$$

and this result holds for any number of particles, since all the moments of the internal forces will cancel in pairs, as above. This is the fundamental equation for rotational motion.

Again this is a most interesting result for it tells us something about the motion of the system which is quite independent of any internal forces there may be, and which is caused entirely by the turning effect of the external forces on the system.

However, it is hard to see how a knowledge of the value of $\Sigma(\mathbf{r} \wedge m\ddot{\mathbf{r}})$ is of any practical use whatever. But this was the same problem as faced us in Section 6 of the previous chapter. There, with one particle, we found we could rewrite $\mathbf{r} \wedge m\ddot{\mathbf{r}}$ in a far more convenient form.
So making use of the fact that

$$\sum \mathbf{r} \wedge m\ddot{\mathbf{r}} = \sum \frac{d}{dt}(\mathbf{r} \wedge m\dot{\mathbf{r}}) \quad \text{(Verify this by diffentiation)}$$

$$= \frac{d}{dt} \sum (\mathbf{r} \wedge m\dot{\mathbf{r}}), \quad \text{since differentiation may be carried out}$$

before or after addition. We finally get a very important alternative way of expressing the fundamental rotational equation.

$$\sum \mathbf{r} \wedge \mathbf{F} = \frac{d}{dt} \sum (\mathbf{r} \wedge m\dot{\mathbf{r}})$$
$$= \frac{d}{dt} \sum (\mathbf{r} \wedge m\boldsymbol{v}). \qquad (9)$$

The moment of the external forces is the rate of change of the total moment of momentum.

Symbolically: $$\mathbf{G} = \dot{\mathbf{H}}.$$

The moment of the forces $\mathbf{G}$ is often called the *couple* or *torque*. Note, in particular that $\mathbf{G} = 0 \Rightarrow \mathbf{H}$ is a constant, so that if there is a point about which the external forces have no torque then the moment of momentum about that point is constant.

So if we know what forces are acting we can calculate something about the moment of momentum. This seems convenient since we are already familiar with the linear momentum from the previous section. Nevertheless, it is still hard to see how to interpret this result in a practical situation.

The reason is, of course, that we never can determine the motion of disconnected particles without full knowledge of their interactions, indeed it is hardly meaningful to talk of their rotation. But once they are connected their velocities will be related and our model will be of use, particularly if there is a suitable fixed point to choose as our origin.

Example 2. A space station consists essentially of four masses of 1000 kg at the corners of a square of diagonal length 20 m. It is to rotate at 1 rad/s about the axis of symmetry perpendicular to the square. What forces (using rockets) would you design to accelerate the space station to this angular velocity? State where you would place the rockets, in what direction they should point and for how long they should fire.

Solution. Two (or four) rockets should be used firing in opposite directions so as not to change the overall linear momentum of the system.

Their torque will be greatest if they are placed at the ends of a diagonal and so as to fire at right angles to the diagonal.

In order to set up an angular speed ω of 1 rad/s they must cause an angular acceleration $\dot{\omega}$ of 1 rad/s^2 for 1 s or of 0·5 rad/s^2 for 2 s, etc.

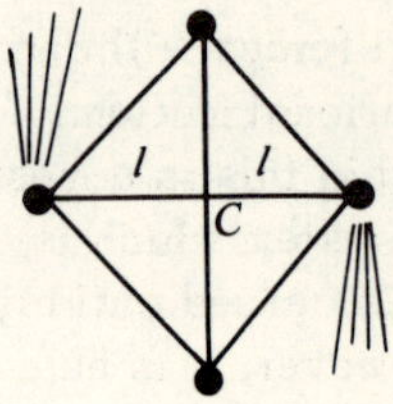

Fig. 4

Let us assume that two rockets are to be fired for 10 s with force of magnitude F causing an angular acceleration of 0·1 rad/s^2.

$$\overset{\curvearrowleft}{C}: \qquad \sum \mathbf{r} \wedge \mathbf{F} = \sum \mathbf{r} \wedge m\ddot{\mathbf{r}}, \text{ using equation (8),}$$

$$2lF = 4l\,ml\dot{\omega}, \text{ where } l \text{ is half the diagonal,}$$

$$F = 2ml\dot{\omega}$$

$$= 2 \times 1000 \times 10 \times \dot{\omega}$$

$$= 20\,000\,\dot{\omega}$$

So a thrust $F = 2000$ newtons from two such rockets for 10 s would provide the necessary angular speed.

EXERCISE B

1. Idealise a big wheel at a fair as being 10 particles of mass M equally spaced on the circumference of a circle of radius r. What torque is needed to accelerate the wheel at 0·1 rad/s^2?

2. A small model plane of mass M flies at speed v in a circle of radius a at a height h above the operator. Determine the force between (i) the string and the plane, (ii) the string and the operator.

3. In a square dance, 4 dancers hold hands so that they rotate in a ring at 1 rad/s. If their masses are 60 kg each and they are symmetrically 1·8 m apart, determine the tension in their arms. Ignore the reaction between their feet and the ground. State the assumptions you have made. Still rotating freely with arms straight,

two dancers move to the centre while the other two move further apart, what is now their angular speed and the tension in their arms?

4. A conker on the end of a string of length $2l$ is travelling in a horizontal circle when the middle of the string hits a circular lamp post of circumference c. By what factor has the speed of the conker increased when the string has wrapped itself once round the lamp post?

2.3 Solid body model

Take a long ruler, and use your compass point to bore a hole through it close to one end. Set it swinging and note the time needed for ten complete swings. Does it seem to make any difference whether the swings are large or small? Now tie some cotton round the middle of the ruler, suspend it and set it swinging so that it remains horizontal, parallel to the axis, with its mass centre C the same distance from the pivot O as before. Note the time needed for ten complete swings.

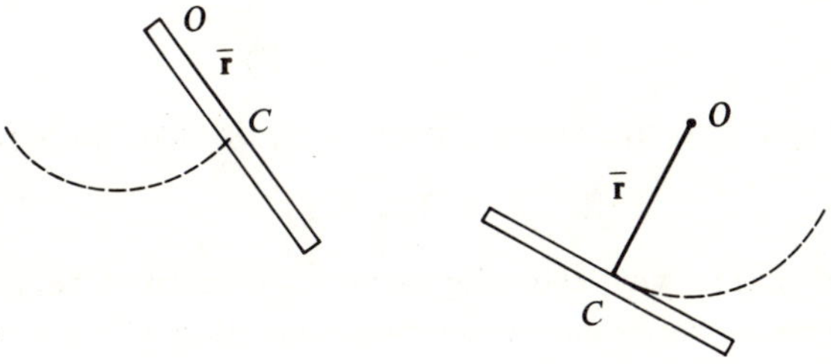

Fig. 5

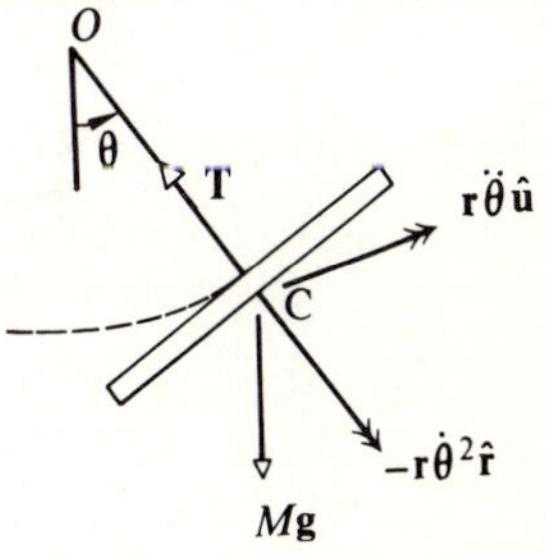

Fig. 6

You may find that the *period* (time required for one complete oscillation), although it appears to be independent of the size of the oscillation, is *not* the same in these two cases. Can our model account for these observations? Can you? With the notation of Figure 5, let OC be inclined at an angle θ to the downward vertical at time t. Then the acceleration of mass centre C will be, radially and transversely, $-r\dot{\theta}^2\hat{\mathbf{r}} + r\ddot{\theta}\hat{\mathbf{u}}$ (see Chapter 1, Section 4.4) since $\bar{\mathbf{r}}$ is constant. If the rod remains horizontal every point moves in the same way (about the axis of rotation) and thus has the same acceleration as the mass centre (assuming the ruler is thin and narrow). (See Figure 6.)

These accelerations are caused by the external forces, namely the tension $\mathbf{T}$ in the cotton, and the earth's attraction on each particle, which we have seen (Section 2.2) is equivalent to a force $M\mathbf{g}$ acting at C.

Applying the fundamental equation for rotational motion for the second case (Figure 6):

$$\sum \mathbf{r} \wedge \mathbf{F} = \sum \mathbf{r} \wedge m\ddot{\mathbf{r}}$$

$\Rightarrow \quad \bar{\mathbf{r}} \wedge (\mathbf{T} + M\mathbf{g}) = \bar{\mathbf{r}} \wedge M(-\bar{r}\dot{\theta}^2\hat{\mathbf{r}} + \bar{r}\ddot{\theta}\,\hat{\mathbf{u}}),$ since $\mathbf{r}$ is the same for all the particles,

$\Rightarrow \quad \bar{\mathbf{r}} \wedge M\mathbf{g} = (\bar{\mathbf{r}} \wedge (M\bar{r}\,\ddot{\theta})\hat{\mathbf{u}}),$ the other two moments being zero,

$\Rightarrow \quad -Mg\bar{r}\sin\theta\,\hat{\mathbf{k}} = (M\bar{r}^2\,\ddot{\theta})\,\hat{\mathbf{k}},$ where $\hat{\mathbf{k}}$ is directed normal to and out of the plane of motion of C,

$\Rightarrow \quad -Mg\bar{r}\sin\theta = M\bar{r}^2\,\ddot{\theta},$

$\Rightarrow \quad \ddot{\theta} + \dfrac{g}{\bar{r}}\sin\theta = 0,$

which can, in theory, be integrated to give the inclination θ at any time t.

In fact the integration requires a knowledge of elliptic integrals and an approximation is usually made. Writing $\sin\theta \approx \theta$, (reasonable for θ less than about 1/2 radian) $\ddot{\theta} + (g/\bar{r})\theta = 0$, which is an example of *simple harmonic motion* and integrates to give

$$\theta = A\sin(pt + B),$$

where $p = \sqrt{(g/\bar{r})}$ and A, B are arbitary constants, so that the *period* is

$$2\pi/p = 2\pi\sqrt{(\bar{r}/g)}.$$

So, suspended in this way, the ruler swings with a fixed period; which is the same as if all the mass were concentrated into one blob at the mass centre, called a *simple pendulum*.

Note that the equation for rotational motion has enabled us to calculate the angle θ of rotation at any time and hence, also, the angular speed $\dot{\theta}$ and angular acceleration $\ddot{\theta}$ for this rigid body.

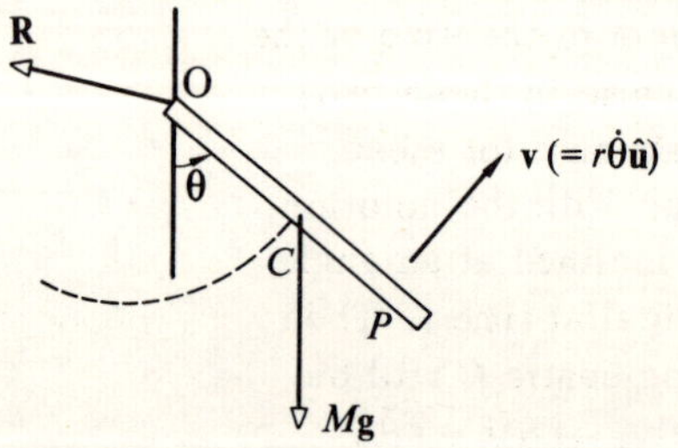

Fig. 7

When the ruler is pivoted about one end there are again two significant external forces, the (variable) force $\mathbf{R}$ of the pivot on the ruler and the gravitational force equivalent to $M\mathbf{g}$ at C [we are assuming that any air resistance and any resisting torque through friction at the pivot are insignificant.] This time, however, the points are at differing distances from the axis of rotation. But, because the ruler is rigid, we know that the velocity $\mathbf{v}$ of a typical point P with position vector $\mathbf{r}$ is given by [see Chapter 3, Section 3.4.]

$$\mathbf{v} = \boldsymbol{\omega} \wedge \mathbf{r}, \text{ where } \boldsymbol{\omega} \text{ is the angular velocity,}$$
$$= (\dot{\theta}\, r)\, \hat{\mathbf{u}}, \quad \text{where } \hat{\mathbf{u}} \text{ is in the transverse direction.}$$

It is because of this angular speed $\dot{\theta}$ common to all points that we are able to give a meaningful interpretation to the angular momentum of rigid bodies.

$$\mathbf{G} = \dot{\mathbf{H}}$$

$$\sum \mathbf{r} \wedge \mathbf{F} = \frac{\mathrm{d}}{\mathrm{d}t} \sum (\mathbf{r} \wedge m\mathbf{v}),$$

$\overset{\curvearrowleft}{O}$:
$$\mathbf{0} \wedge \mathbf{R} + \bar{\mathbf{r}} \wedge M\mathbf{g} = \frac{\mathrm{d}}{\mathrm{d}t} \sum (\mathbf{r} \wedge (mr\,\dot{\theta})\,\hat{\mathbf{u}}).$$

In this problem, as in many others, the ruler is swinging in a fixed plane and thus the direction $\hat{\mathbf{k}}$ of the vector product $\mathbf{r} \wedge \hat{\mathbf{u}}$ is the same for every particle and is perpendicular to the plane

$$\Rightarrow \quad -Mg\bar{r}\,\sin\theta\, \hat{\mathbf{k}} = \frac{\mathrm{d}}{\mathrm{d}t} \sum (mr^2\dot{\theta})\, \hat{\mathbf{k}}$$

$$\Rightarrow \quad -Mg\bar{r}\,\sin\theta = \frac{\mathrm{d}}{\mathrm{d}t} (\Sigma\, mr^2)\, \dot{\theta}$$
$$= (\Sigma\, mr^2)\ddot{\theta},$$

since neither the mass m nor the distance r from O of any particle changes.

There is still the expression $\Sigma\, mr^2$ to consider. We assume that there is an infinite number of 'particles' making up a *solid body* such as a ruler and thus we must use integration to 'sum' them. Treating the length of the ruler as our range of integration we want to add up the product mr^2 for every particle.
If the ruler has mass M and length l, then a portion of length δr will have mass $(M/l)\delta r$ and its contribution to the summation is thus approximately $(M/l)r^2\, \delta r$. Hence summing by integration we get:

$$\int_0^l \frac{M}{l} r^2\, \mathrm{d}r = \frac{M}{l}\left[\frac{r^3}{3}\right]_0^l$$
$$= \tfrac{1}{3} Ml^2$$
$$= \tfrac{4}{3} M\bar{r}^2.$$

So finally:
$$-Mg\bar{r}\,\sin\theta = \tfrac{4}{3} M\bar{r}^2\,\ddot{\theta},$$
$$\ddot{\theta} + \tfrac{3}{4}(g/\bar{r})\,\sin\theta = 0,$$

which again gives approximate simple harmonic motion but with period $2\pi\sqrt{(4\bar{r}/3g)}$.

So there is a significant difference in the two periods caused by the different distribution of the mass in relation to the axis of rotation. Note furthermore that, merely from our knowledge of the external force, we have been able to apply our mathematical model to get a complete insight into the motion. But was this just a special case or does this method have wider application?

At any instant for a rigid body the velocity $\mathbf{v}$ of any point with position vector $\mathbf{r}$ can be expressed as

$$\mathbf{v} = \boldsymbol{\omega} \wedge \mathbf{r},$$

where $\boldsymbol{\omega}$ is the angular velocity vector at that instant and is the same for all points of the body.

We have already seen how the idea of angular velocity gives a unity to the particles of a ruler.

In general
$$\mathbf{G} = \dot{\mathbf{H}}$$
$$= \frac{d}{dt} \sum (\mathbf{r} \wedge m\,\mathbf{v})$$
$$= \frac{d}{dt} \sum m (\mathbf{r} \wedge \mathbf{v}),$$
which, for a rigid body,
$$= \frac{d}{dt} \sum m \{ \mathbf{r} \wedge (\boldsymbol{\omega} \wedge \mathbf{r}) \}.$$

So, in theory, if we know the couple $\mathbf{G}$ applied to a rigid body we can calculate the resulting angular velocity $\boldsymbol{\omega}$ of the body. This together with our knowledge of the motion of the mass centre, completely describes the behaviour of the body at any instant and our investigations are at an end.

This is taken up again in the final section where the real problem of calculating $\boldsymbol{\omega}$ is indicated. Suffice to say that for general motion in three dimensions it is certainly not easy. Meanwhile, we shall confine our attention to situations in which $\boldsymbol{\omega}$ is perpendicular to all $\mathbf{r}$ and hence to so called *laminas* (bodies so thin that their points all lie in one plane) and whose angular velocity $\boldsymbol{\omega}$ may be written $\omega\hat{\mathbf{k}}$, where $\hat{\mathbf{k}}$ is in a fixed direction normal to the plane.

That is to say we shall only consider 'thin' bodies moving in a plane.

For such motion
$$\mathbf{G} = \frac{d}{dt} \{ \Sigma (mr^2) \} \,\omega \hat{\mathbf{k}}$$
$$= I\,\dot{\omega}\,\hat{\mathbf{k}}, \tag{10}$$

where $I = \Sigma\, mr^2$ is called the *moment of inertia* of the lamina about an axis through the origin perpendicular to the plane of the lamina, that is to say, parallel to $\hat{\mathbf{k}}$.

EXERCISE C.

1. Verify that $\theta = A \sin (pt + B)$ does satisfy the equation
$$\ddot{\theta} + p^2\theta = 0.$$

2. The ratio of the periods for a ruler swinging vertically and horizontally was found to be $2 : \sqrt{3}$. What will the ratio be for a ruler half as long?

3. How long must a ruler be to have a period of 1 second?

3. MOMENT OF INERTIA

The whole of Section 3 is devoted to the techniques of calculating this vital statistic for common objects.

3.1 Calculation of moment of inertia

The scalar quantity $\Sigma(mr^2)$ derived in the last section is called the moment of inertia. The quantity can be calculated and, in the special cases of rotation where **r** is always perpendicular to $\boldsymbol{\omega}$, used to find the motion of the body.

$$\mathbf{G} = \frac{\mathrm{d}}{\mathrm{d}t}\{(\Sigma\, mr^2)\,\omega\}\,\hat{\mathbf{k}}$$

$$= \frac{\mathrm{d}}{\mathrm{d}t}(I\omega)\,\hat{\mathbf{k}}. \tag{10}$$

This equation is the rotational analogue to Newton's Second Law, where the inertia, $\Sigma\, mr^2$, is a measure of the reluctance of the body to rotate under an applied couple **G**. A knowledge of their moment of inertia enables us to solve problems involving the rotation of thin rigid 'laminas' which rotate about an axis perpendicular to their plane (i.e. ω is perpendicular to **r**).

Example 3. A circular flywheel of mass 10 kg and radius 20 cm is fixed to rotate in a horizontal plane and a couple of moment 12 kgm is applied to rotate it. What is its angular acceleration?

We can apply equation (10) above, if we imagine the flywheel as a uniform circular disc mass M, radius a, rotating about a vertical axis through its centre (Figure 8). For now $\boldsymbol{\omega}$ is always perpendicular to **r** for all 'particles' of the disc.

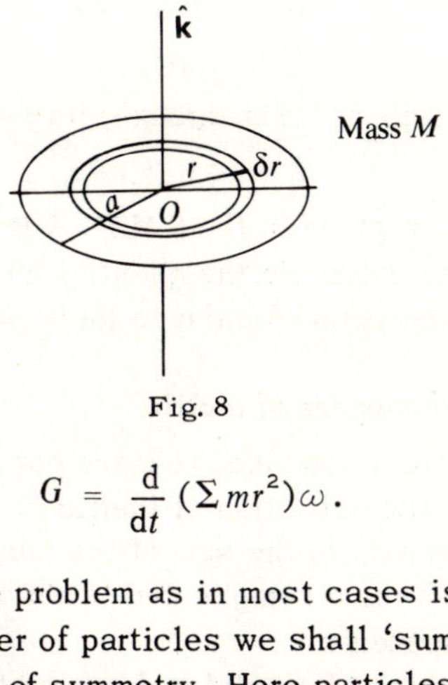

Fig. 8

$$G = \frac{\mathrm{d}}{\mathrm{d}t}(\Sigma\, mr^2)\omega.$$

G is given as 12 kgm but the problem as in most cases is to find the quantity $\Sigma\, mr^2$. As there is an infinite number of particles we shall 'sum' by integration. Whenever possible use considerations of symmetry. Here particles the same distance from the axis can be grouped together by considering a narrow ring of width δr and radius from r to $r + \delta r$, centre O, the centre of the disc.

The density per unit area is $M/\pi a^2$. The moment of inertia of the ring about the axis is thus approximately $(M/\pi a^2)(2\pi r\,\delta r)r^2$

$$I = \lim_{\delta r \to 0} \sum \frac{2Mr^3\,\delta r}{a^2}$$

$$= \frac{2M}{a^2} \int_0^a r^3\,dr$$

$$= \frac{2M}{a^2} \left[\frac{r^4}{4}\right]_0^a$$

$$= \frac{Ma^2}{2}.$$

In this case $M = 10\,\text{kg}$ and $a = 0{\cdot}2\,\text{m}$. So, if $\hat{\mathbf{k}}$ is a unit vector in the direction of the axis of the flywheel,

$$\mathbf{G} = \frac{Ma^2}{2}\dot{\omega}\,\hat{\mathbf{k}}$$

$$\Rightarrow \quad 12\hat{\mathbf{k}} = \frac{10\cdot(0{\cdot}2)^2}{2}\dot{\omega}\,\hat{\mathbf{k}}$$

$$\Rightarrow \quad \dot{\omega} = 60.$$

So the angular acceleration of the flywheel is 60 rad/s^2.

The moment of inertia of a lamina about an axis is a property of the particular lamina in question. We have already carried out the calculation for two common objects:

Uniform rod, length l, about (axis through) one end

$$I = \tfrac{1}{3}Ml^2.$$

Uniform disc, radius a, about (axis through) its centre

$$I = \tfrac{1}{2}Ma^2.$$

These and other results are given in the S.M.P. A-level tables. Using a similar calculus technique we can calculate the quantity Σmr^2 for laminas of various shapes about different axes perpendicular to their plane.

3.2 Additive property of moment of inertia

If two simple laminas are combined to make one, more complex, lamina, it follows immediately from the definition of inertia ($= \Sigma\, mr^2$) that the inertia of the combined lamina about an axis is the sum of the inertia of the two individual laminas about that axis. Thus a complicated lamina may be considered split up into a set of simpler components.

Furthermore we can think of a solid body as a stack of laminas whose inertia about an axis is again the sum of the inertia of the individual laminas. For example a cylinder, radius a, rotating about its axis can be taken to be a pile of discs each with $I = \tfrac{1}{2}Ma^2$ where M is the mass of the disc.

Hence inertia of cylinder $= \tfrac{1}{2}M_1a^2 + \tfrac{1}{2}M_2a^2 + \ldots = \tfrac{1}{2}Ma^2$ where M is now the mass of the cylinder. Similarly the inertia of any prism about any axis perpendicular to the cross-section is the same expression as for its cross-section lamina; it is merely the mass that differs in the two cases.

Note: Although this enables us to calculate the inertia of a solid body about an axis we are *not*, however, justified in assuming $\mathbf{G} = (\Sigma mr^2)\dot{\boldsymbol{\omega}}$ since this was based on the assumption that $\boldsymbol{\omega}$ was perpendicular to all $\mathbf{r}$. If you attempt to spin a mug on a smooth table it will wobble and probably fall over however careful you are. In fact in general it is just not true that a torque $\mathbf{G}$ about a vertical axis will merely cause an angular acceleration $\dot{\omega}$ about the vertical axis. However, it is true for a lamina, and can also be shown to be true for prisms and solid bodies with symmetry about the axis of rotation. Test this by trying to spin some suitable objects. Further details are given in the last section. (Page 120 onwards.)

We can now extend the definition of inertia to a solid body thus: the inertia of a solid body about an axis fixed in relation to it, is Σmr^2 where r is the distance of the particle from the *axis* and *not* from the origin.

Example 4. Determine the inertia of a sphere of mass M and radius a about a diameter. Let the density be ρ and consider the inertia about the y-axis (Figure 9). Imagine the sphere split up into a large number of circular discs all perpendicular to the y-axis. The inertia of each can be written down and then summed:

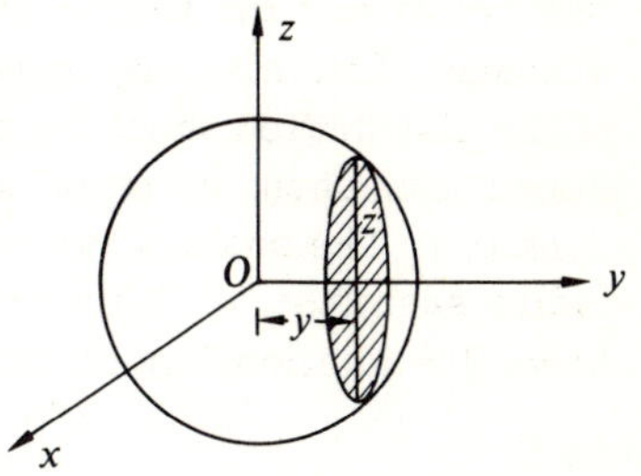

Fig. 9

Inertia about Oy of typical disc $\approx \frac{1}{2} m z^2$

$$= \tfrac{1}{2}(\rho\pi z^2 \delta y) z^2.$$

Summing for the whole sphere, $I = \lim_{\delta y \to 0} \Sigma \frac{1}{2} \rho\pi z^4 \delta y$.

In the limit, $I = 2\int_0^a \frac{1}{2}\rho\pi z^4 \,dy$, using the symmetry of the sphere.

But $$y^2 + z^2 = a^2.$$

Hence
$$\begin{aligned}
I &= \rho\pi \int_0^a (a^2 - y^2)^2 \,dy \\
&= \rho\pi \left[a^4 y - 2\frac{a^2 y^3}{3} + \frac{y^5}{5}\right]_0^a \\
&= \rho\pi \left[a^5 - \frac{2a^5}{3} + \frac{a^5}{5}\right] \\
&= \tfrac{8}{15}\rho\pi a^5 \\
&= \tfrac{2}{5} Ma^2,
\end{aligned}$$

since $$M = \tfrac{4}{3}\rho\pi a^3.$$

3.3 Parallel axis rule

Simplification of working often follows by referring motion to the mass centre. This is true too of the moment of inertia of any body. Thus using $\mathbf{r} = \bar{\mathbf{r}} + \mathbf{r}^*$, that is, the position of mass centre + position relative to mass centre.

$$\begin{aligned}\sum mr^2 &= \sum m(\bar{\mathbf{r}} + \mathbf{r}^*)\cdot(\bar{\mathbf{r}} + \mathbf{r}^*)\\ &= \sum (m\bar{\mathbf{r}}\cdot\bar{\mathbf{r}}) + 2\sum(m\bar{\mathbf{r}}\cdot\mathbf{r}^*) + \sum(m\mathbf{r}^*\cdot\mathbf{r}^*)\\ &= (\Sigma m)\bar{r}^2 + 2\bar{\mathbf{r}}\cdot\sum(m\mathbf{r}^*) + \sum(mr^{*2})\\ &= M\bar{r}^2 + 0 + \sum mr^{*2}\\ \Rightarrow I_0 &= Md^2 + I_C.\end{aligned}$$

The inertia about an axis through O = the inertia about a parallel axis through the mass centre $+Md^2$, where d is the distance OG between the two axes. Incidentally this shows that the inertia about an axis through the mass centre is always a minimum. This also emphasises the statistical analogy with variance. The inertia of the distribution about the mass centre being equivalent to the variance of a distribution about its mean, with the mass density m replacing the frequency density f. The analogy is even closer with the *radius of gyration* k, which is the radius such that, if all the mass were at this distance, the moment of inertia and hence the rotational motion would be unchanged,

i.e. $$Mk^2 = \sum(mr^2).$$

Compare this with the standard deviation s for which

$$s^2 = \sum(fx^2)/\sum f.$$

EXERCISE D.

1. Write down the inertia of a circular ring of mass M and radius a about the axis of symmetry perpendicular to its plane.

2. Write down the inertia of a circular pipe of mass M, radius a and length l about its central axis of symmetry.

3. Determine the inertia of a rod of mass M and length l about an axis through one end and perpendicular to the rod. Hence write down the inertia of a rod of mass M and length l about an axis through an end making an angle α with the rod.

4. By considering elementary cylinders of radius r and thickness δr determine the inertia of a uniform solid sphere of mass M and radius a about an axis of symmetry.

5. Determine the inertia of a uniform rectangular lamina of mass M, length l and breadth b about the axis of symmetry parallel to the edge l. Write down the inertia of the lamina about the axis of symmetry parallel to the edge b.

6. Hence, or otherwise, obtain the inertia of the lamina in Question 5 about the axis of symmetry perpendicular to the lamina.

7. The result of Question 6 suggests the *perpendicular axis rule*. This is that if the inertia of a lamina about two perpendicular axes in its plane are I_x and I_y respectively, then the inertia I_z about the axis perpendicular to the lamina through the intersection of the axes is $I_x + I_y$. By considering a particle m at (x, y) in the plane of a lamina, prove this result.

8. Write down the inertia of (i) a disc about an axis through the edge of the disc perpendicular to the disc, (ii) a solid sphere about a tangent. In each case take the mass to be M and the radius to be a.

9. Write down the inertia of the lamina in Question 5 (i) about a long edge as axis, (ii) about an axis perpendicular to the lamina, through one corner.

10. A pendulum consists of a circular disc of radius a and mass M attached to a rod of length l and mass m, which is rigidly attached to the disc along the radius of the disc so that one end of the rod A is $l + a)$ from the centre of the disc. The pendulum swings in the plane of the disc about an axis through A perpendicular to the plane of the disc. Determine the inertia of the system about the axis.

11. A space satellite may be assumed to consist of a hollow cylinder, without ends, of length l and radius r. Determine the initial acceleration caused by a force F applied at the end of the satellite and on its periphery (i) longitudinally, (ii) tangentially. Take the origin at the centre of the cylinder, the x-axis as the longitudinal axis of symmetry, and the y-axis as the direction of the tangential force. Take the mass of the satellite to be M, and its inertia about the y-axis as I.

12. Determine the inertia of a star of mass M and radius R, about an axis through the centre, given that the density of its material varies inversely as the distance from the centre of the star.

4. MASS-ACCELERATION PROBLEMS IN 2-DIMENSIONS

Now that we can calculate moments of inertia we are in a position to investigate problems involving rate of change of moment of momentum $\mathbf{H}$.

4.1 Example

Example 5. A pulley, of inertia I about its axle and radius r, has a light string hung over it. Attached to the ends of the string are masses m and $2m$ respectively. Determine the acceleration of the masses.

In Figure 10 are shown all the *external* forces acting on the system (why is the tension not involved?). Let the acceleration of the masses be of magnitude f. Then the angular acceleration of the pulley will be f/r.

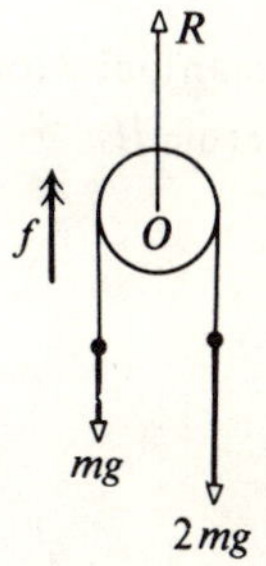

Fig. 10

Applying $\mathbf{G} = \dot{\mathbf{H}}$,

$$\circlearrowleft: \quad (2mgr - mgr)\hat{\mathbf{k}} = (2mfr + mfr + If/r)\hat{\mathbf{k}},$$

$$f = \frac{mgr^2}{3mr^2 + I}.$$

EXERCISE E

1. Determine the angular acceleration of a uniform sphere mass M and radius r about an axis of symmetry when a couple L is applied about this axis and a frictional couple G opposes motion.

2. Find the ratio of the angular acceleration of a rod subject to the same couple when it is pivoted (a) about its centre, (b) about an end.

3. Find the ratio of the angular acceleration of a rectangular lamina of length l and breadth b pivoted (i) about the axis of symmetry parallel to the edge b, (ii) about the axis of symmetry perpendicular to its plane when it is subject to a couple of the same magnitude about its axis of rotation.

4. A wheel (which may be considered to be a uniform disc) of radius r has a belt round half its circumference. If its mass is M and the tensions in the belt are T_1 and T_2 where $T_1 > T_2$, determine the angular acceleration of the wheel.

5. A pulley wheel of radius r and mass m mounted on a horizontal axis has a light string hung over it, to one end of which is attached a mass $2m$ and to the other a mass $3m$. Determine the angular acceleration of the wheel if there is no slipping.

6. The rear wheel of a bicycle is held off the ground and is assumed to weigh 1·5 kg concentrated at the rim of radius 0·4 m. A force of 45 newtons is applied at right angles to the crank (of length 12 cm). If the gear wheels are 9 cm and 4 cm in radius respectively, determine the acceleration of the wheel. What approximations have you made?

4.2 Rotation relative to mass centre

So far we have always had a convenient fixed point as a pivot. When a wheel rolls down a ramp or a chair is thrown through the window this is not so, and so we are led to consider the motion relative to the mass centre. Again using stars to denote any quantity relative to the mass centre:

$$\mathbf{r}_1 = \bar{\mathbf{r}} + \mathbf{r}_1^*.$$

[The manipulation steps below are justified as in Section 2.2.] The moment of momentum H

$$= \sum(\mathbf{r} \wedge m\dot{\mathbf{r}})$$

$$= \sum(\bar{\mathbf{r}} + \mathbf{r}^*) \wedge m(\dot{\bar{\mathbf{r}}} + \dot{\mathbf{r}}^*)$$

$$= \sum(\bar{\mathbf{r}} \wedge m\dot{\bar{\mathbf{r}}}) + \sum(\mathbf{r}^* \wedge m\dot{\bar{\mathbf{r}}}) + \sum(\bar{\mathbf{r}} \wedge m\dot{\mathbf{r}}^*) + \sum(\mathbf{r}^* \wedge m\dot{\mathbf{r}}^*),$$

using distributive law

$$= \bar{\mathbf{r}} \wedge \sum m\dot{\bar{\mathbf{r}}} + \sum(m\mathbf{r}^*) \wedge \dot{\bar{\mathbf{r}}} + \bar{\mathbf{r}} \wedge \sum(m\dot{\mathbf{r}}^*) + \sum(\mathbf{r}^* \wedge m\dot{\mathbf{r}}^*)$$

$$= \bar{\mathbf{r}} \wedge M\dot{\bar{\mathbf{r}}} + \mathbf{0} \wedge \dot{\bar{\mathbf{r}}} + \bar{\mathbf{r}} \wedge \mathbf{0} + \sum(\mathbf{r}^* \wedge m\dot{\mathbf{r}}^*).$$

$$= \bar{\mathbf{r}} \wedge M\dot{\bar{\mathbf{r}}} + \sum(\mathbf{r}^* \wedge m\dot{\mathbf{r}}^*)$$

Symbolically: $$\mathbf{H} = \bar{\mathbf{H}} + \mathbf{H}^*.$$

The moment of momentum is the moment of momentum of the system concentrated at C and moving with the velocity of C together with the moment of momentum of the system relative to C.

Whence $$\mathbf{G} = \dot{\mathbf{H}}$$

$\Rightarrow$ $$\mathbf{G} = \dot{\bar{\mathbf{H}}} + \dot{\mathbf{H}}^*.$$

The moment of the external forces is equal to the rate of change of the moment of momentum of the system concentrated at C moving with the velocity of C together with the rate of change of the moment of momentum of the system relative to C.

$$\sum \mathbf{r} \wedge \mathbf{F} = \frac{d}{dt}(\bar{\mathbf{r}} \wedge M\dot{\bar{\mathbf{r}}}) + \frac{d}{dt}\sum(\mathbf{r}^* \wedge m\dot{\mathbf{r}}^*). \tag{11}$$

The whole point of deriving this equation is that it can simplify our work. About a fixed origin O it is true that $\mathbf{G} = \dot{\mathbf{H}}$, but it is often useful to know that the right-hand side of this equation, the sum of the rates of change of moment of momentum about O, can be calculated as $\dot{\bar{\mathbf{H}}} + \dot{\mathbf{H}}^*$. In the special case of rigid laminas we know $\dot{\mathbf{H}}^*$, or it is not difficult to find, in the form $I\ddot{\theta}$ and $\dot{\bar{\mathbf{H}}}$ is easy to calculate. It also leads to a convenient means of representing the motion on a diagram, as in the next example.

4.3 Choice of origin

We have tacitly assumed the existence of a fixed origin O. What are the implications of a change to origin O', where $\mathbf{OO}' = \mathbf{a}$, so that $\mathbf{r} = \mathbf{a} + \mathbf{r}'$?

$$\sum \mathbf{F} = \sum m\ddot{\mathbf{r}}^*$$

$$\Rightarrow \sum \mathbf{F} = \sum m\ddot{\mathbf{r}}' + \sum m\ddot{\mathbf{a}}$$

$$= \sum m\ddot{\mathbf{r}}' + M\ddot{\mathbf{a}}.$$

So the linear results would still be true so long as $\ddot{\mathbf{a}} = \mathbf{0}$, that is so long as the new origin were not accelerating relative to the old origin.

Also:
$$\sum \mathbf{r} \wedge \mathbf{F} = \sum \mathbf{r} \wedge m\ddot{\mathbf{r}}$$

$$\Rightarrow \sum(\mathbf{r}' + \mathbf{a}) \wedge \mathbf{F} = \sum(\mathbf{r}' + \mathbf{a}) \wedge m\ddot{\mathbf{r}}$$

$$\Rightarrow \sum(\mathbf{r}' \wedge \mathbf{F}) = \sum(\mathbf{r}' \wedge m\ddot{\mathbf{r}})$$

$$= \sum(\mathbf{r}' \wedge m\ddot{\mathbf{r}}') + \sum(\mathbf{r}' \wedge m\ddot{\mathbf{a}})$$

$$= \sum(\mathbf{r}' \wedge m\ddot{\mathbf{r}}') + \left(\sum m\mathbf{r}'\right) \wedge \ddot{\mathbf{a}}.$$

So the rotational results would still be true so long as $(\sum m\mathbf{r}') \wedge \ddot{\mathbf{a}} = \mathbf{0}$, that is so long as the new origin were not accelerating or if the new origin were the mass centre. So not only can we apply the equations

$$\mathbf{F} = \dot{\mathbf{L}}_o$$

$$\mathbf{G}_o = \dot{\mathbf{H}}_o,$$

using any origin O *either* fixed *or* having constant velocity, but we can also apply the latter equation to the mass centre C.

$$\mathbf{G}_C = \dot{\mathbf{H}}^*,$$

$$\sum \mathbf{r}^* \wedge \mathbf{F} = \frac{d}{dt}\sum(\mathbf{r}^* \wedge m\dot{\mathbf{r}}^*). \tag{12}$$

So the moment of the forces about C equals the rate of change of momentum about C whatever the motion of C may be. This also shows clearly that the rotational motion about C is completely independent of the motion of C.

Thus the motion of a body is completely specified by the linear motion of C and the rotational motion about C and can be represented for laminas on a diagram by the linear components of the mass-acceleration of C together with $I\ddot{\theta}$ about C. If the external force vector system is drawn on a second diagram, the two can be equated. The systems are completely equivalent, the forces in the one giving rise to the mass-accelerations of the other. This is particularly convenient if it is necessary to investigate the motion of a system of bodies, though we shall confine our attention to solitary objects.

Example 6. A rigid body is transfixed to a wall. Investigate the motion and reaction if it is allowed to swing freely. If the inertia about the pivot O is I, the mass M and $OC = \bar{\mathbf{r}}$, then the situation is as shown in Figure 11, where $\mathbf{R}$ denotes the reaction at the pivot, θ is the inclination of OC to the downward vertical and the components of acceleration of mass centre C are shown radially and transversely.

The motion is completely specified by the linear and rotational equations.

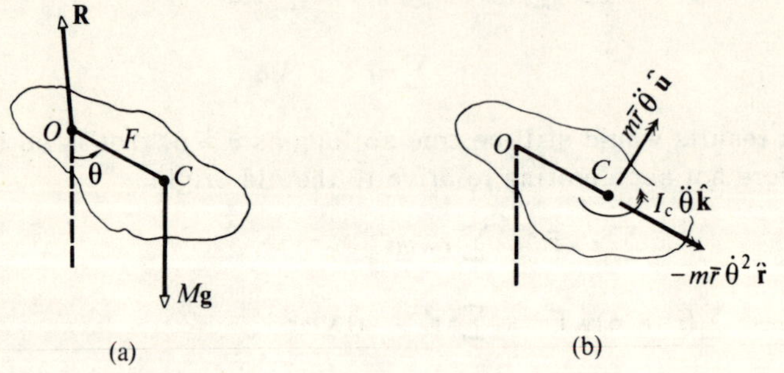

Fig. 11

Linear $$\mathbf{R} + M\mathbf{g} = M\ddot{\bar{\mathbf{r}}}.$$

Rotational $$\bar{\mathbf{r}} \wedge M\mathbf{g} = I\ddot{\theta}\,\hat{\mathbf{k}}.$$

The second, in fact, gives us the angular acceleration directly

$\circlearrowleft O$: $$-Mg\bar{r}\sin\theta = I\ddot{\theta}$$

$$\Rightarrow \quad Mg\bar{r}\cos\theta = \tfrac{1}{2}I\dot{\theta}^2 + c, \text{ by integration.}$$

The constant of integration depends on the initial conditions. In particular, if $\theta = \alpha$ when $\dot{\theta} = 0$ then $c = Mg\,\bar{r}\cos\alpha$.

The first equation now gives us the unknown reaction $\mathbf{R}$

$$\mathbf{R} + M\mathbf{g} = M[\bar{r}\dot{\theta}^2\hat{\mathbf{r}} + \bar{r}\ddot{\theta}\,\hat{\mathbf{u}}],$$

$$\Rightarrow \quad \mathbf{R} = \frac{M^2 g\bar{r}^2}{I}\,[\,2(\cos\theta - \cos\alpha)\hat{\mathbf{r}} - \sin\theta\,\hat{\mathbf{u}}\,] - M\mathbf{g}.$$

If, for example, we need to know the vertical force at the pivot we take the component in the vertical direction.

$$\uparrow: \qquad R_v = \frac{M^2 g\bar{r}^2}{I}[-2(\cos\theta - \cos\alpha)\cos\theta - \sin\theta\sin\theta] + Mg.$$

Thus for a rod, for which $I = \frac{1}{3}Ml^2$ and $\bar{r} = \frac{1}{2}l$,

$$R_v = \tfrac{3}{4}Mg[2\cos\theta\cos\alpha - \cos^2\theta - 1] + Mg.$$

Similarly for the component of the reaction in any other direction.

Example 7. A uniform circular disc, radius a and mass M, rolls down a ramp of gradient $\tan\alpha$. (i) If it does not slip, determine the acceleration. (ii) If the coefficient of friction is μ (less than the critical value), determine the linear and angular accelerations.

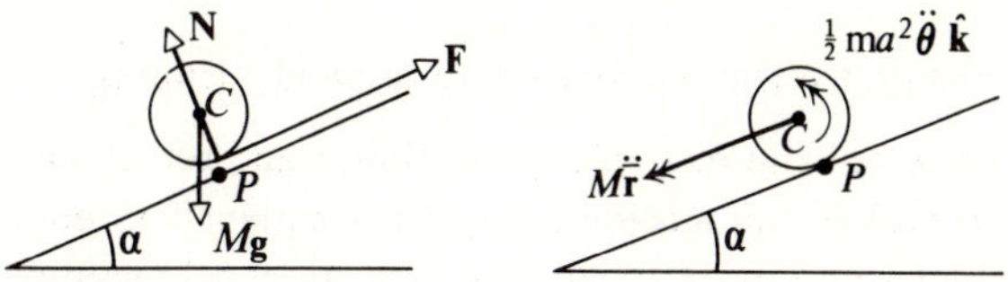

Fig. 12

Figure 12(a) shows the external forces and (b) the resulting mass-accelerations where $\ddot{\theta}\,\hat{\mathbf{k}}$ is the angular, and $\ddot{\mathbf{r}}$ the linear acceleration. $\mathbf{R}$ is the unknown reaction at the point of contact P and $CP = \mathbf{a}$. In this situation we have no convenient fixed point to take as origin. However, the equations of linear and rotational motion about C give

Linear $\qquad \mathbf{R} + M\mathbf{g} = M\ddot{\mathbf{r}}.$

Rotational $\qquad \mathbf{a}\wedge\mathbf{R} = \frac{1}{2}Ma^2\,\ddot{\theta}\,\hat{\mathbf{k}}.$

Without further information we cannot solve for the unknowns $\mathbf{R}$, $\ddot{\mathbf{r}}$ and $\ddot{\theta}$ since $\ddot{\mathbf{r}}$ and $\ddot{\theta}$ are quite independent for a body which is not pivoted.

(i) *If there is no slipping*: then the point of contact P must be, momentarily, stationary

$$\Rightarrow \quad \ddot{r} - a\ddot{\theta} = 0,$$
$$\Rightarrow \quad \ddot{r} = a\ddot{\theta}.$$

Substituting for $\mathbf{R}$ and for $a\ddot{\theta}$ in the rotational equation gives

$$\mathbf{a}\wedge(M\ddot{\mathbf{r}} - M\mathbf{g}) = \tfrac{1}{2}Ma\ddot{r}\,\hat{\mathbf{k}}$$
$$\Rightarrow \quad -Ma\ddot{r} + Mga\sin\alpha = \tfrac{1}{2}Ma\ddot{r}$$
$$\Rightarrow \quad \ddot{r} = 2/3\, g\sin\alpha.$$

(ii) *If it does slip* we shall need to know something about the nature of the surfaces in contact.

If the coefficient of friction is μ and there is slipping: then $F = \mu N$, where N and F are the normal and tangential components of the reaction **R**.

But $$\mathbf{R} = M\ddot{\mathbf{r}} - M\mathbf{g}.$$

Hence $$(-M\ddot{r} + Mg\sin\alpha) = \mu(Mg\cos\alpha),$$

$$\Rightarrow \qquad \ddot{r} = g(\sin\alpha - \mu\cos\alpha).$$

The rotational equation gives

$$aF = \tfrac{1}{2}Ma^2\ddot{\theta},$$

$$\Rightarrow \ddot{\theta} = 2(-M\ddot{r} + Mg\sin\alpha)/Ma,$$

$$= 2\mu\, g\cos\alpha/a.$$

Of course it will stop slipping if $a\ddot{\theta} = \ddot{r}$

$$\Rightarrow \mu = 1/3\tan\alpha.$$

This gives the minimum friction necessary to prevent slipping.

Note that, as with most of the examples, the linear and rotational equations which give the complete model of the motion are quite simple. It is essential not to lose sight of this fact when extra conditions and algebraic manipulation tend to cloud the principles.

EXERCISE F.

1. Draw two diagrams in each of the following cases, one to show the mass-accelerations, the other to show the external forces.

(a) A uniform hoop of radius r and mass M hangs over a horizontal knife-edge and is allowed to make small oscillations in a plane perpendicular to the knife-edge.

(b) A uniform square plate of side l and mass M, pivoted about one corner at right angles to the plane of the plate, is released when an edge through the pivot is vertical. Take the position at time t when the angle turned through is θ and the angular acceleration is $\ddot{\theta}$.

(c) A uniform cylinder of mass m and radius a has a light string wrapped around and attached to its circumference. The cylinder is pivoted about its axis horizontally, and a mass m is attached to the other end of the string and is released from rest when the string is just taut.

(d) A compound pendulum consists of a uniform disc of mass $4m$ and radius a and a uniform rod of mass m and length $4a$ attached to the circumference of the disc so that the one end of the rod is $5a$ from the centre of the disc. The pendulum is pivoted about this end of the rod and swings in the plane of the disc. Take the angle turned through to be θ at time t from the equilibrium position.

2. Use the results of Question 1 as follows.

In (a) determine the period of small oscillations;

in (b) determine the vertical component of the force on the pivot at the lowest part of the swing;

in (c) determine the acceleration of the mass and the reaction at the pivot;

in (d) determine the period of small oscillations, and the horizontal component of the reaction at the pivot when the pendulum is vertical.

3. A cotton-reel is placed on a smooth table and the end of the cotton is pulled with a constant horizontal force. How does the speed of the end of the cotton compare with that of the centre of the reel?

5. MOMENTUM

It is frequently the case that velocities are more accessible or of more interest than accelerations and the basic equations are best modified to meet these needs.

5.1 Impulse

For the linear motion of a system we know that

$$\sum \mathbf{F} = \sum \frac{d}{dt}(m\dot{\mathbf{r}}) \quad (= \dot{\mathbf{L}}),$$

whence, integrating:

$$\int \sum \mathbf{F}\, dt = \left[\sum (m\dot{\mathbf{r}})\right] \quad (= [\mathbf{L}]),$$

where the square brackets indicate that the difference of the initial and final conditions must be taken. Hence, writing $\sum \int \mathbf{F}\, dt$ for $\int \sum \mathbf{F}\, dt$ as they have the same values, we get the (Linear) Momentum Equation.

$$\sum \int \mathbf{F}\, dt = \left[\sum (m\dot{\mathbf{r}})\right] \quad (= [\mathbf{L}]). \tag{13}$$

The sum of the external Impulses equals the change of momentum. In particular, $\sum \mathbf{F} = \mathbf{0} \Leftrightarrow \mathbf{L}$ remains constant. The *impulse* $\int \mathbf{F}\, dt$ is the net effect of a force acting for a time. It is frequently the case that the precise variation of $\mathbf{F}$ is not known as a function of time, as when a nail is struck with a hammer. But an observation of the change in momentum will give the average force acting in the time.

5.2 Moment of impulse

We can develop a relation between moment of momentum and impulse in just the same way.

Starting with

$$\mathbf{G} = \dot{\mathbf{H}},$$

i.e.

$$\sum \mathbf{r} \wedge \mathbf{F} = \frac{d}{dt} \sum (\mathbf{r} \wedge m\dot{\mathbf{r}}).$$

Integrating we get the (Angular) Momentum Equation

$$\sum \int \mathbf{r} \wedge \mathbf{F}\, dt = \left[\sum (\mathbf{r} \wedge m\dot{\mathbf{r}})\right]. \tag{14}$$

Symbolically:

$$\int \mathbf{G}\, dt = [\mathbf{H}].$$

The effect of the external couples acting for a time is to change the angular momentum.

In particular $\mathbf{G} = \mathbf{0} \Leftrightarrow \mathbf{H}$ remains constant. Furthermore, as long as all $\mathbf{r}$ are constant for the time under consideration,

$$\sum \int \mathbf{r} \wedge \mathbf{F}\, dt = [\mathbf{H}], \text{ may be written}$$

$$\sum \left(\mathbf{r} \wedge \int \mathbf{F}\, dt \right) = [\mathbf{H}].$$

This will be true for forces applied at fixed locations, such as a rope round a pulley. It is also approximately true for a particular type of impulse which we call a *jerk* $\mathbf{J}$ in which a large force acts for such a short time that the change in position of the point of application during this time is negligible.

Thus for jerks: $$\sum \mathbf{r} \wedge \mathbf{J} = [\mathbf{H}]. \tag{15}$$

'The sum of the moments of the jerks equals the change in moment of momentum.'

In practice it often helps to work in terms of the mass centre (see Section 4.2) and apply this equation in the form:

$$\sum \mathbf{r} \wedge \mathbf{J} = [\bar{\mathbf{H}}] + [\mathbf{H}^*].$$

'The sum of the moments of the jerks equals the change in moment of momentum of the whole mass concentrated at the mass centre together with the change in moment of momentum relative to the mass centre.'

Example 8. Two cog wheels A and B, of inertia M and N about their axes, have radii m and n respectively and are mounted on parallel axes of negligible inertia. If A is rotating with angular velocity ω and is then brought into mesh with B, which is stationary, determine the resultant angular velocities of the wheels.

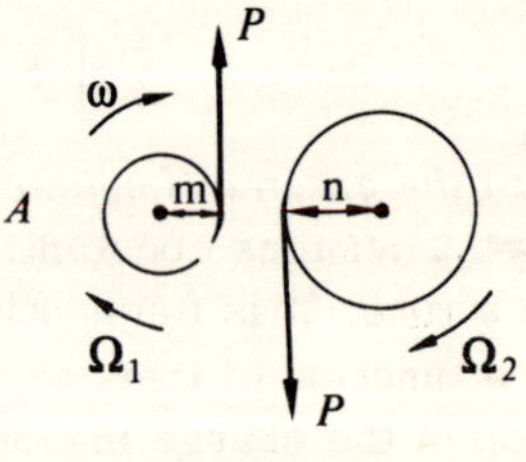

Fig. 13

Let these be Ω_1 and Ω_2 respectively, as shown. During the meshing there will be a force between the two wheels. This will be equal and opposite on each and acting for the same time. Thus the impulse on each will be equal and opposite. Let the tangential component be P. (What effect does any radial component have?)

Angular momentum: $$\sum \mathbf{r} \wedge \mathbf{J} = [\mathbf{H}].$$

For A: $$-mP = M(\Omega_1 - \omega).$$

For B: $$nP = -N\Omega_2.$$

$\Rightarrow$ on eliminating P, $$nM\omega = nM\Omega_1 - mN\Omega_2.$$

But since the wheels are meshed after the impact, the speeds at the point of contact on each must be the same.

Hence $$m\Omega_1 = -n\Omega_2.$$

Solving for Ω_1 and Ω_2: $\Omega_1 = \dfrac{n^2 M\omega}{n^2 M + m^2 N}$ and $\Omega_2 = -\dfrac{mnMw}{n^2 M + m^2 N}$.

Note that the total angular momentum before the meshing was $M\omega$ and after the meshing it is $nM\omega(nM - mN)/(n^2M + m^2N)$. Why are these momenta different? Also, why are we justified in applying the equation for jerks in this case?

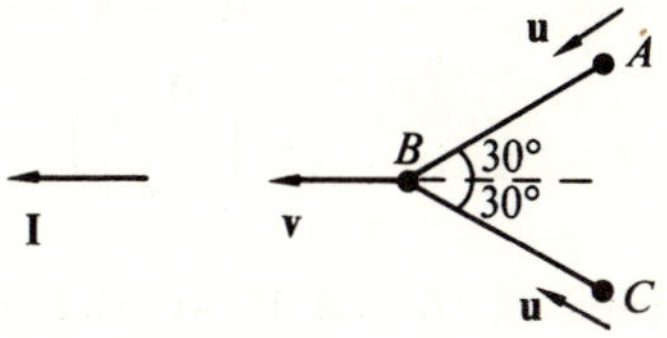

Fig. 14

Example 9. Three particles A, B and C, each of mass m are connected by equal taut strings AB and BC of length l. A, B and C lie at the corners of an equilateral triangle on a smooth horizontal table. B is given an impulse I along the bisector of ABC in the direction away from A and C.

(i) What is the initial impulse in the strings?

(ii) Describe the subsequent motion of the system.

We assume that the impulse I acts for such a short time that it changes the momentum of the system without changing the position of the particles, i.e. that it is a jerk. Then initially: A and C can only start to move along the line of their strings with initial velocity $\mathbf{u}$. Also, by symmetry (or by component of momentum equation perpendicular to the direction of I) the initial velocity $\mathbf{v}$ of B is in the direction of I.

Linear Momentum: $$\mathbf{I} = 2m\,\mathbf{u} + m\mathbf{v},$$

$$\Rightarrow I/m = 2u\cos 30 + v.$$

It also implies that the mass centre has velocity $I/3m$. This is insufficient to enable us to solve for u and v and a rotational equation is of little help as the system is not rigid.

However, we must make use of the fact that A, B, C are connected by taut strings,

i.e. speed of A in direction AB = speed of B in direction AB

$$\Rightarrow u = v\cos 30.$$

From these two equations we find that the system starts to move with

$$v = \frac{2I}{5m} \quad \text{and} \quad u = \frac{\sqrt{3}I}{5m};$$

and hence the initial impulse mu in the strings was of magnitude $[\sqrt{(3)}/5]I$. In the subsequent motion no external force acts on the system.

$\Rightarrow$ Mass centre has a constant velocity $(= I/3m)$.

Also moment of momentum about the mass centre is constant (= 0). Again this is little help, but the fact that AB and AC are taut means that A and C must move in circles relative to B and with constant angular speed ω since no force (there are tensions in the strings) has any moment about B.

$$\text{Velocity of } A \text{ relative to } B = \mathbf{u} - \mathbf{v}$$

$$= \begin{cases} (u - v\cos 30) & \text{along } AB \\ (\;\; - v\sin 30) & \text{perp. to } AB \end{cases}$$

$$= \begin{pmatrix} 0 \\ -\tfrac{1}{2}v \end{pmatrix} \quad \begin{matrix} \text{along } AB \\ \text{perp. to } AB \end{matrix}$$

The constant angular speeds of AB and AC are thus $v/2l$ ($=I/5ml$) towards each other. When A and C collide all particles will be moving forward with the same speed. If the collision is perfectly elastic then the angular velocities will be reversed in direction and the particles A and C will swing around colliding next in front of B and the process of collision will continue fore and aft of B, each collision occurring after $\pi/(I/5ml)$ sec. If the coefficient of restitution is e, then the angular velocity will be reduced by a factor e and the time between each collision will increase by a factor $1/e$ but the centre ot mass will continue at its constant rate. How would the motion differ if the same impulse had been applied but in the course of a far greater length of time?

EXERCISE G.

1. A torque of 0·1 Nm is applied for 2 min to a flywheel of inertia 0·005 kg m^2 about its axis; what is the change in angular speed of the gyro?

2. If an astronaut were to apply a torque T to tighten a nut on his spaceship, what would happen to him if his inertia about the axis of the torque is I? Design a device to tighten a nut without an equal and opposite torque acting on the applier.

3. Two flywheels of inertia I_1 and I_2 about their axis are rotating on the same axis with angular speeds ω_1 and ω_2 when they are brought into contact so that they continue with the same speed. Determine the speed. If the connection between flywheels is by means of a friction clutch which slips as long as the couple applied to it is greater than L, determine the time for which slipping persists.

4. A rigid light rod of length l has masses m attached to each end. It is rotating about its centre with angular velocity $\boldsymbol{\omega}$ when one end is suddenly fixed. With what angular speed does the rod continue to move?

5. The torque on a shaft of moment of inertia I, increases uniformly with time for T sec, from 0 to L. Determine the angular velocity reached in this time.

6. A boy holds a 3-kg brick in each outstretched hand. He rotates at 1 rev in 2 s and then lowers the bricks to his sides. Determine his subsequent angular speed; assume that his inertia is 0·5 kg m^2 about his axis of rotation and that the bricks are 1·5 m apart when his arms are outstretched and 0·5 m apart when by his sides.

7. A meteor of mass m with speed v, strikes the earth. What is the greatest

resulting fractional change in the earth's speed of rotation? Assume the earth is of radius R and uniform density ρ.

8. A cricket bat of mass 1 kg has inertia of 0·05 kg m^2 about an axis parallel to the axis of rotation, but through its centre of mass, 50 cm below the top of its handle. It is swung about a point 60 cm above the handle and drives a cricket ball of mass 0·16 kg with the same speed, 25 m/s, with which it hits the bat 60 cm below the top of the handle. What is the impulse on the ball, and the change of angular velocity of the bat? Ignore the angular momentum of the arms – is this a reasonable assumption?

9. A uniform rod of mass M and length l hangs from a pivot at one end. It is struck at right angles to the rod and the pivot by a particle of mass m travelling with speed v at a distance h from the pivot. Assuming perfect elasticity, determine the initial angular velocity of the rod and the impulse at the pivot. What is the value of h for this impulse to be a minimum. This value determines the centre of percussion. Whereabouts is this for a cricket bat?

10. A penny of mass m travelling with speed v, slides along a smooth table and hits a square sheet of cardboard, mass M and side a, at one corner in the direction of one edge. Describe the subsequent motion of the lamina on the assumption $e = 1/2$ (that is, assume the relative velocity of separation of the points of impact perpendicular to the surfaces which impact equals half the relative velocity of approach).

11. A cricket ball of mass m and radius a hits the ground with speed v and no spin at an angle α. If the ground is so rough so that there is no slipping of the ball and the coefficient of restitution is e, determine the angle at which the ball leaves the ground.

12. Three particles A, B, C lie in order on a straight line on a smooth table. $AB = BC = l$ and they are connected by (i) strings of length l, (ii) strings of length $5l/4$. B is now given a velocity $\mathbf{v}$ perpendicular to ABC. Determine the initial velocities of the particles when they start to move and describe the subsequent motion of each system on the assumption that the impacts are perfectly elastic.

13. Two particles A and B are connected by a light string of length l, and rest on a smooth table. If the string is just taut when A is struck with an impulse I at right angles to AB, describe the subsequent motion (a) if the particles are of equal mass, (b) if A has mass m and B mass $2m$.

6. KINETIC ENERGY

We have seen that it is sometimes convenient to consider the integrated effect of forces acting for a known *time* on a system by means of the momentum equation. Similarly it is helpful to develop a direct means of investigating the effect of forces acting for a known *displacement* of a system.

6.1 The energy equation

A man helps to push a car which is skidding on boggy ground. The direction of the motion of the car and the direction and magnitude of the force he exerts may vary considerably, yet all will influence the overall effect he has on the motion of the car. However, we can take the motion approximately to consist of small displacements $\delta\mathbf{r}$ over each of which the force $\mathbf{F}$ is constant and consider $\mathbf{F}\cdot\delta\mathbf{r}$, the product of the displacement and the component of the force in the direction of the displacement. We can sum this for all such displacements to get the *work done* $\Sigma\,\mathbf{F}\cdot\delta\mathbf{r}$, or $\int \mathbf{F}\cdot d\mathbf{r}$ in the limit. This seems as though it should be a useful quantity to investigate, but what contribution does it make to the motion?

For a single particle acted on by a net force F,

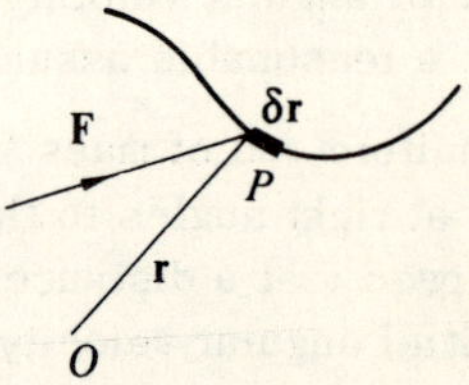

Fig. 15

$$\mathbf{F} = m\ddot{\mathbf{r}}$$

$$\Rightarrow \int \mathbf{F}\cdot d\mathbf{r} = \int m\ddot{\mathbf{r}}\cdot d\mathbf{r}$$

$$= m\int \ddot{\mathbf{r}}\cdot\dot{\mathbf{r}}\,dt$$

$$= [\tfrac{1}{2}m\,\dot{\mathbf{r}}\cdot\dot{\mathbf{r}}]$$

$$= [\tfrac{1}{2}m\,\dot{r}^2].$$

In words 'the work done equals the change in *kinetic energy*.'

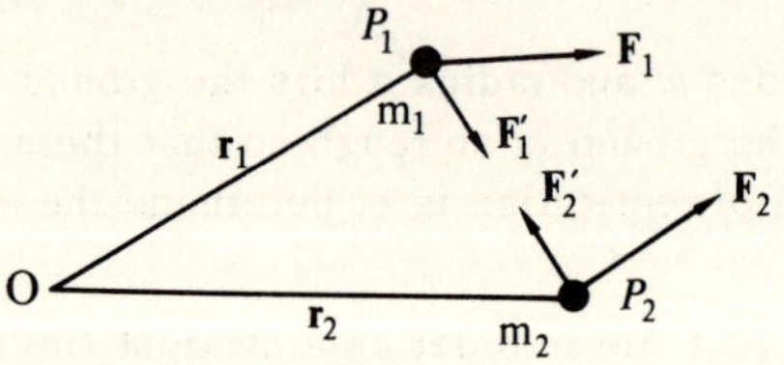

Fig. 16

For two particles:

$$\int \mathbf{F}_1\cdot d\mathbf{r}_1 + \int \mathbf{F}_1'\cdot d\mathbf{r}_1 = [\tfrac{1}{2}m\dot{r}_1^2],$$

$$\int \mathbf{F}_2\cdot d\mathbf{r}_2 + \int \mathbf{F}_2'\cdot d\mathbf{r}_2 = [\tfrac{1}{2}m\dot{r}_2^2],$$

where $\mathbf{F}_1'$ and $\mathbf{F}_2'$ are their mutual interactive forces. Whence adding we get: The work done by the external forces plus the work done by the internal forces is equal to the total charge of kinetic energy.

Now the contribution from the internal forces is

$$\int \mathbf{F}_1'\cdot d\mathbf{r}_1 + \int \mathbf{F}_2'\cdot d\mathbf{r}_2\,,$$

$$= \int \mathbf{F}_1'\cdot\dot{\mathbf{r}}_1\,dt + \int -\mathbf{F}_1'\cdot\dot{\mathbf{r}}_2\,dt, \text{ since } \mathbf{F}_1' + \mathbf{F}_2' = 0,$$

$$= \int \mathbf{F}_1'\cdot(\dot{\mathbf{r}}_1 - \dot{\mathbf{r}}_2)\,dt,$$

which is *not* necessarily zero.

For example if P_2 is fixed and P_1 moves directly towards P_2. However, if the particles are rigidly connected, so that the distance $P_1 P_2$ is constant, the work done by their internal force will be zero since no relative motion is possible. Similarly for any number of particles, for which the internal forces must be considered in pairs.

Thus for a *rigid body*:

The work done by the external force = the total change of kinetic energy

$$\sum \int \mathbf{F} \cdot d\mathbf{r} = \sum [\tfrac{1}{2} m r^2], \tag{16}$$

which is known as the *energy equation*.

Note that this equation does not always hold. In particular, in a collision, the distance between the particles of the bodies will not remain constant and the work done by the internal forces will not be zero.

6.2 K.E. referred to the mass centre

The kinetic energy T may be written:

$$\sum \tfrac{1}{2} m (\dot{\bar{\mathbf{r}}} + \dot{\mathbf{r}}^*)^2$$

$$= \tfrac{1}{2}\left(\sum m\right) \dot{\bar{\mathbf{r}}} \cdot \dot{\bar{\mathbf{r}}} + \left(\sum m \dot{\mathbf{r}}^*\right) \cdot \dot{\bar{\mathbf{r}}} + \tfrac{1}{2} \sum (m \dot{\mathbf{r}}^* \cdot \dot{\bar{\mathbf{r}}}^*)$$

$$= \tfrac{1}{2} M \dot{\bar{r}}^2 + \tfrac{1}{2} \sum m \dot{r}^{*2} \tag{17}$$

The total K.E. = The K.E. of mass concentrated at C + K.E. relative to C.

Symbolically:

$$T = \bar{T} + T^*.$$

If further the system consists of a rigid body, then

$$\dot{\mathbf{r}}^* = \boldsymbol{\omega} \wedge \mathbf{r}^*$$

and for two-dimensional motion the K.E. becomes

$$\tfrac{1}{2} M \dot{\bar{r}}^2 + \left(\tfrac{1}{2} \sum m r^{*2}\right) \omega^2 = \tfrac{1}{2} M \dot{\bar{r}}^2 + \tfrac{1}{2} I \dot{\theta}^2. \tag{18}$$

That is, the K.E. of the whole mass concentrated at the mass centre and moving with the velocity of the mass centre together with the K.E. of the system relative to the mass centre.

Example 10. To start an outboard motor, an angular speed of 2 rev/s must be built up. If the motor is started by pulling on a rope wrapped around an axle of radius 3 cm, how large an effective inertia can the motor have if the force applied to the rope is 100 N for 0·7 m?

The work done = K.E. given to the motor

$$100 \times 0{\cdot}7 = \tfrac{1}{2} I (2.2\pi)^2$$

$$I = 140/(4\pi)^2$$

$$= 0{\cdot}89 \text{ kg m}^2.$$

Example 11. A cylindrical chimney-pot of mass m and radius a rolls from rest, without slipping, down a roof of gradient $\tan\alpha$ for distance h. What speed does it achieve? Describe its subsequent motion as it leaves the roof.

The normal and frictional forces do not work as there is no motion in the direction of these forces. The only work done by the external forces is that by gravity, which is $mgh \sin\alpha$.

Let the speed achieved be v, then the angular speed achieved is v/a

$$\text{Work done} = \text{change in K.E.}$$

$$\int \mathbf{F}\cdot d\mathbf{r} = \bar{T} + T^*$$

$$\Rightarrow \quad mgh \sin\alpha = \tfrac{1}{2} mv^2 + \tfrac{1}{2}(ma^2)(v/a)^2$$

$$\Rightarrow \quad mgh \sin\alpha = mv^2$$

$$\Rightarrow \quad v = \sqrt{(gh \sin\alpha)}.$$

After leaving the slope, the only force acting is gravity, this has no moment about the centre of mass, so the angular velocity of

$$\frac{v}{a} = \frac{\sqrt{(gh \sin\alpha)}}{a}$$

is preserved. The horizontal velocity is similarly constant. The vertical velocity increases linearly, i.e. the motion is parabolic.

6.3 Applications

It is pleasing to find such a simple set of results for handling dynamical problems and now, for two-dimensional movement at least, we have the equipment to handle a wide variety of situations (see summary on page 130).

Example 12. A flywheel of unknown moment of inertia, I, has an inextensible string attached to, and wrapped around, its axle, whose radius is a. A weight mg is attached to the other end of the string and takes time t to fall from rest through a distance h when the string frees itself from the axle. After a further time T, the flywheel comes to rest. Assuming a constant retarding torque L determine the inertia of the flywheel.

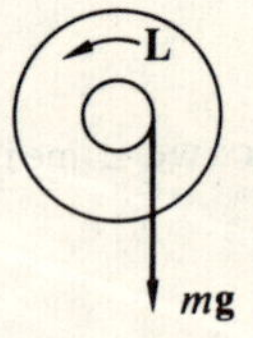

Fig. 17

We know the work done during acceleration so that we can write down an energy equation. During retardation, however, we know the impulse of the weight so we can use a momentum equation.

The angle turned through during acceleration = h/a radians.

Let the speed of m be v after time t.

Equating energies and work done during acceleration

$$mgh = \tfrac{1}{2} mv^2 + \tfrac{1}{2} I(v/a)^2 + L(h/a). \tag{A}$$

Since the forces are constant, the acceleration of m is constant and its final velocity = 2 × (average velocity) = $2\cdot(h/t) = v$.

Hence substituting in equation (A):

$$mgh = 2mh^2/t^2 + 2\,Ih^2/a^2t^2 + Lh/a. \qquad \text{(B)}$$

During retardation $LT = I \cdot 2h/at$.
Substituting for L in equation (B):

$$m\left(gh - \frac{2h^2}{t^2}\right) = I\left(\frac{2h^2}{a^2t^2} + \frac{2h^2}{a^2Tt}\right),$$

$$\Longrightarrow \qquad I = \frac{ma^2(gt^2 - 2h)T}{2h(T+t)}.$$

Example 13. A vertical rocket fails to fire as its supports are withdrawn and topples over. Simulate this situation by a uniform rigid rod of length l and mass m on a smooth surface. Determine the angular velocity when it has turned through an angle θ. In what direction will the centre of mass move? Will the bottom of the rocket leave the ground?

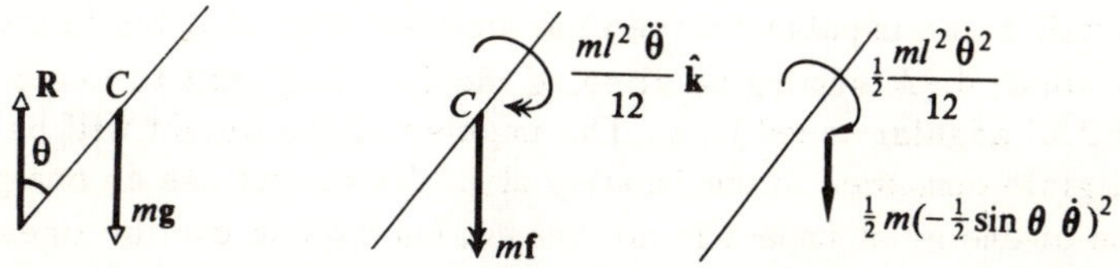

Fig. 18

Figure 18 shows the forces, mass-accelerations and energy at time t when the rocket has turned through an angle θ.

To determine $\dot{\theta}$ we need an equation not involving **R**. We could just write down the linear and rotational equations of motion, but this will introduce $\ddot{\theta}$ necessitating integration, so we try the energy equation. First though, we must express the motion of the centre of mass (why is this vertical?) in terms of θ.

Let z be the height of the centre of mass C at time t.

$$z = \tfrac{1}{2}l\cos\theta$$

so long as the base is in contact with the ground.

Differentiating:
$$\dot{z} = -\tfrac{1}{2}l\sin\theta\,\dot{\theta}.$$

Equating the work done by the force $m\mathbf{g}$ (does **R** do any work?) to the gain in kinetic energy:
$$\int m\mathbf{g}\cdot d\mathbf{r} = \bar{T} + T^*,$$

$$mg\,\tfrac{1}{2}l(1-\cos\theta) = \tfrac{1}{2}m(-\tfrac{1}{2}l\sin\theta\,\dot{\theta})^2 + \frac{1}{2}\frac{ml^2\dot{\theta}^2}{12}$$

$$= \frac{ml^2\dot{\theta}^2}{24}(3\sin^2\theta + 1)$$

$$\Rightarrow \quad \dot{\theta} = \sqrt{\left(\frac{12g(1-\cos\theta)}{l(1+3\sin^2\theta)}\right)}$$

The centre of mass moves vertically since there is no external horizontal force.

Now we need an equation for R and the simplest is rotational

$$\overset{\frown}{C}: \qquad \frac{Rl}{2}\sin\theta = \frac{ml^2}{12}\ddot{\theta}.$$

Differentiating the expression for $\dot{\theta}$ we get, after simplification,

$$\ddot{\theta} = \frac{6g\sin\theta\,\{3(\cos\theta - 1)^2 + 1\}}{l(1 + 3\sin^2\theta)^2}$$

which is > 0 for $0 < \theta < \frac{1}{2}\pi$.

Hence $\ddot{\theta} > 0$. $\Rightarrow R > 0$, that is, contact is never lost with the ground.

Example 14. A circular disc of radius a and mass m rolls, without slipping, with speed V towards a step of height $a/2$. Show that the minimum speed for the disc to surmount the step is $\sqrt{(3ag)}$. If $V = 2\sqrt{(ag)}$ determine the subsequent speed of the disc.

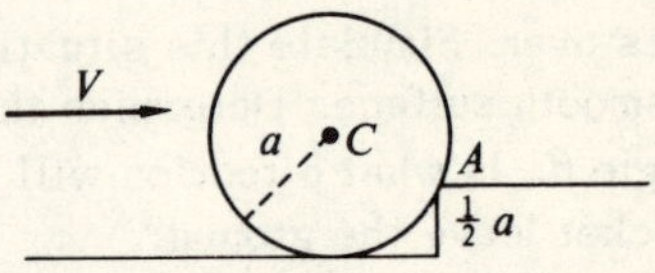

Fig. 19

There will be an impulse between the disc and step at A but this will have no moment about A. Assuming no slipping the disc will start to rotate about A. Let this initial angular speed be ω. The impulse of the weight will be ignored as being negligible compared to the impulse at A. We cannot use an energy equation for the loss of energy at impact is not known, but we can use the linear and angular momentum equations to find any change in velocities.

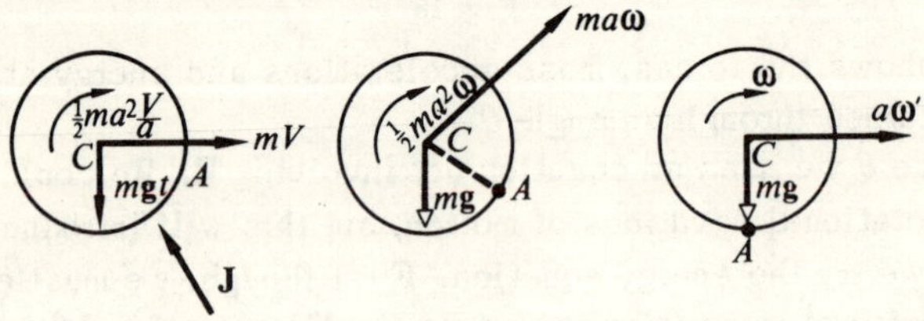

Fig. 20

Rotational: $\sum \mathbf{r} \wedge \mathbf{J} = [\bar{\mathbf{H}} + \mathbf{H}^*]$

About A: $$0 = \left(ma^2\omega + \frac{1}{2}ma^2\omega\right) - \left(\frac{a}{2}mV + \frac{1}{2}ma^2\frac{V}{a}\right),$$

$$\Rightarrow \quad \tfrac{3}{2}ma^2\omega = maV,$$

$$\Rightarrow \quad \omega = \frac{2}{3}\frac{V}{a}.$$

By taking moments about A, rather than C, the unknown impulse $\mathbf{J}$ has not been involved. It would be possible to solve for $\mathbf{J}$ if we wished, by using the linear momentum equation.

After the impact we wish to relate the velocity with the distance the disc rises, so the energy equation is the most appropriate to establish the condition for it to surmount the step. Let ω' be the angular speed as it just surmounts the step.

$$\sum \int \mathbf{F}\cdot d\mathbf{r} = [\bar{T} + T^*]$$

$$\Rightarrow -\tfrac{1}{2}mga = (\tfrac{1}{2}m(a\omega')^2 + \tfrac{1}{2}(\tfrac{1}{2}ma^2)\omega'^2) - (\tfrac{1}{2}m(a\omega)^2 + \tfrac{1}{2}(\tfrac{1}{2}ma^2)\omega^2)$$

$$= \tfrac{3}{4}ma^2\omega'^2 - \tfrac{3}{4}ma^2\omega^2.$$

$$\Rightarrow a^2\omega'^2 = a^2\omega^2 - \tfrac{2}{3}ag.$$

$$\text{Surmounts step} \Leftrightarrow \omega' > 0$$

$$\Leftrightarrow a^2\omega^2 > \tfrac{2}{3}ag$$

$$\Leftrightarrow \tfrac{4}{9}V^2 > \tfrac{2}{3}ag$$

$$\Leftrightarrow V > \sqrt{(\tfrac{3}{2}ag)}.$$

If this is satisfied and v is the subsequent speed after surmounting the step then

$$v^2 = a^2\omega^2 - \tfrac{2}{3}ag,$$

$$= \tfrac{4}{9}V^2 - \tfrac{2}{3}ag.$$

Whence

$$V = 2\sqrt{(ag)} \Rightarrow v = \sqrt{(\tfrac{10}{9}ag)}.$$

EXERCISE H

1. A bullet of mass m is fired with speed v into a cubical block of edge a and mass M. The block is suspended by strings so that its centre is a distance l from the axis of support. Determine the angle the block swings through if it swings without rotation.

2. The flywheel of a gyroscope consists of a disc 6 cm in diameter and 0·2 cm thick. It is made of metal of density 8000 kg/m^3. Determine its inertia about the axle ignoring the inertia of the axle. If the gyroscope is started by pulling on a chord wrapped around the axle with a force of 100 N for 0·5 m, determine the resulting speed of the gyroscope.

3. A metre rule of mass M is freely pivoted about a horizontal axis through its centre. It is initially horizontal and stationary. A lump of putty of mass m falls through a height h and sticks to the end of the rule. Determine (i) the subsequent angular velocity, (ii) the minimum value of h for the rule to make complete revolutions.

4. A shell of mass M kg is travelling at V m/s when there is an internal explosion and the shell splits into two parts; one of mass m moves off at v m/s at an angle θ to the original line of travel.

(i) Show that the direction of motion of the other part makes an angle ϕ with the original direction of travel, where

$$\tan\phi = \frac{mv\sin\theta}{MV - mv\cos\theta},$$

and determine the magnitude of its velocity.

(ii) Determine in terms of M, m, v, V and θ, the overall change in kinetic energy. Show that your expression has the same sign whatever the numerical values and hence state whether the change is a gain or loss.

5. A boy has mass 70 kg and his body has inertia of 1 kg m^2 about his axis of symmetry. His arms add an additional 0·2 kg m^2 when at his sides and 2 kg m^2 when extended horizontally. He grasps a dumbell of mass 3 kg in each hand. With his arms outstretched so the dumbells are 1·5 m apart, he pirouettes at ½ rev/s. He now lowers his arms to his sides. What is his new angular velocity and what energy will he expend in achieving the new velocity, if his arms are 0·5 m apart when by his sides?

6. A solid uniform cylinder of radius a and mass m rolls down a slope of inclination α. Determine the ratio of its translational to its rotational energy. Compare the same situation for a hollow cylinder, radius a mass m, of negligible thickness.

7. A hollow tube of length l and mass M is pivoted at one end so that it can revolve freely in a horizontal plane. A particle of mass M is halfway along the stationary tube when the tube is given a sudden impulse causing it to revolve at ω rad/s. With what velocity does the particle emerge from the tube?

8. An inelastic uniform sphere of radius r rolls down a rough inclined plane of inclination θ to the horizontal. The sphere strikes a step of height $7r/10$ normal to the plane. Assuming that the sphere does not slip on the edge of the step, show that, in order to mount the step, it must roll from rest a distance down the plane of at least:

$$4r \operatorname{cosec} \theta - \frac{6r \cot \theta}{5} - \frac{2r}{5}\sqrt{91}.$$

9. A uniform solid cylinder rolls down a slope of angle θ with the horizontal with no slipping. If r is the radius of the cylinder, and M its mass, show that the spin couple acting on the centre of mass is $(Mrg \sin\theta)/3$ while the resultant force on the centre of mass is $(2Mg \sin\theta)/3$. Prove that slipping will not occur as long as the coefficient of friction is not less that $(\tan\theta)/3$.

10. A uniform solid sphere slides along a smooth horizontal table with velocity v and no angular momentum. It slides onto a rough inclined plane of angle ϕ with the horizontal, the coefficient of friction being $(\tan\phi)/2$. Prove that after a time $(v/g) \sin\phi$ the sphere will begin to roll down the plane.

11. A uniform solid cylinder of mass M and radius r is rolling towards the edge of a step with velocity v perpendicular to the edge of the step. Assuming the cylinder does not slip at the edge, prove that it will leave horizontally if $v^2 > gr$, otherwise it will turn about the edge before dropping off.

*7. THREE-DIMENSIONAL MOTION

So far we have restricted our attention to applications in which the motion of the mass centre is in a plane and for which any rotation is about an axis normal to this plane. Furthermore, most of our work was with laminas, but extended to a few solids. In this section we extend our ideas to far more general motion to give some appreciation of the methods and problems involved.

7.1 Moment of momentum

We take a fixed origin O and (orthogonal) axes OX, OY, OZ, and consider a general set of forces **F** acting on a rigid body. The linear motion of the mass centre is straight forward, its acceleration $\ddot{\mathbf{r}}$ being given by

$$\sum \mathbf{F} = M\ddot{\mathbf{r}}. \tag{19}$$

The rotational motion, however, is much harder to determine. Let $\boldsymbol{\omega}$ be the angular velocity vector at some instant. Then we want to express $\boldsymbol{\omega}$ or $\dot{\boldsymbol{\omega}}$ in terms of the forces.

About O:

$$\mathbf{G} = \dot{\mathbf{H}}.$$

The moment of the forces equals the rate of change of moment of momentum. So we look more closely at the moment of momentum **H**.

$$\mathbf{H} = \sum \mathbf{r} \wedge m\dot{\mathbf{r}}, \text{ summed for all points } \mathbf{r} \text{ of the body,}$$

$$= \sum \mathbf{r} \wedge m(\boldsymbol{\omega} \wedge \mathbf{r}), \text{ for a rigid body,}$$

$$= \left(\sum mr^2\right)\boldsymbol{\omega} - \sum (m\mathbf{r}\cdot\boldsymbol{\omega})\mathbf{r}.$$ See Chapter 3, Exercise E, Question 11.

It is awkward to extricate $\boldsymbol{\omega}$ from this since $\mathbf{r}$ is not constant for the summation. So we look at the components of this expression.

$$\begin{pmatrix} H_x \\ H_y \\ H_z \end{pmatrix} = \sum mr^2 \begin{pmatrix} \omega_x \\ \omega_y \\ \omega_z \end{pmatrix} - \sum m(x\omega_x + y\omega_y + z\omega_z)\begin{pmatrix} x \\ y \\ z \end{pmatrix}$$

where ω_x is the component of angular velocity about the x-axis.

$$= \sum mr^2 \begin{pmatrix} \omega_x \\ \omega_y \\ \omega_z \end{pmatrix} - \sum \begin{pmatrix} mx^2\omega_x + mxy\omega_y + mxz\omega_z \\ mxy\omega_x + my^2\omega_y + myz\omega_z \\ mxz\omega_x + myz\omega_y + mz^2\omega_z \end{pmatrix}$$

$$= \sum m(x^2 + y^2 + z^2) \begin{pmatrix} \omega_x \\ \omega_y \\ \omega_z \end{pmatrix} - \sum \begin{pmatrix} mx^2 & mxy & mxz \\ mxy & my^2 & myz \\ mxz & myz & mz^2 \end{pmatrix} \begin{pmatrix} \omega_x \\ \omega_y \\ \omega_z \end{pmatrix}$$

$$\Rightarrow \qquad \mathbf{H} = \begin{pmatrix} A & -F & -E \\ -F & B & -D \\ -E & -D & C \end{pmatrix} \boldsymbol{\omega},$$

where $A = \sum m(y^2 + z^2) \qquad D = \sum myz$

$B = \sum m(z^2 + x^2) \qquad E = \sum mzx$

$C = \sum m(x^2 + y^2) \qquad F = \sum mxy$

called the *moments* (*A*, *B*, *C*) and *products* (*D*, *E*, *F*) of inertia.

Note: For solid bodies the summation is replaced by integration and the particle mass *m* by a density function.

Whence:

$$\mathbf{G} = \frac{d}{dt}(\mathbf{I})\boldsymbol{\omega}, \tag{20}$$

where (*I*) is the *inertia matrix* $\begin{pmatrix} A & -F & -E \\ -F & B & -D \\ -E & -D & C \end{pmatrix}$.

So we have finally succeeded in getting a direct relation between the couple applied and the resulting angular velocity. Thus equations (19) and (20) give a complete description of the resulting motion in terms of the applied forces. However, (*I*) is not constant but changes with time, and this makes for difficulties in even the simplest applications.

7.2 Constant angular velocity

If we skim a plate across the room, or throw a discus, there is usually a fixed direction for its axis of rotation. Consider the simplest case of an object whose angular velocity is constant, in magnitude as well as direction. At any instant take fixed axes with the z-axis as the axis of rotation. Then $\omega_x = 0$, $\omega_y = 0$, ω_z = constant. Equation (20) gives the necessary couples to be applied about the axes:

$$G_x = \frac{d}{dt}(-E\omega_z), \quad G_y = \frac{d}{dt}(-D\omega_z), \quad G_z = \frac{d}{dt}(C\omega_z)$$

$$= -\dot{E}\omega_z, \qquad = -\dot{D}\omega_z, \qquad = \dot{C}\omega_z.$$

The interpretation is surprising. One might expect that, once the body had been set spinning, no force would be necessary to maintain a constant angular velocity ω_z about the z-axis. And in fact the moment of inertia $C = \Sigma m(x^2 + y^2)$ about the z-axis is constant since the distance $\sqrt{(x^2 + y^2)}$ of a particle from the z-axis does not change. So $\dot{C} = 0$ and the couple G_z required about the z-axis is zero. However, the products of inertia *E* and *D*, in general will change with time. Hence in order to maintain a constant angular velocity about the z-axis it is necessary to provide couples G_x about the x-axis and G_y about the y-axis which are *not* zero!

Try skimming a heavy-handled saucepan along the floor or a tea-cup along a smooth table to confirm that they will not spin about a vertical axis.

However, for many objects there is frequently symmetry about some axis. And if the *XY* plane is a plane of symmetry both *E* and *D* are zero at all times, since for every point (x, y, z) there is also a point $(x, y, -z)$. [We assume that the density is uniform.]

All the two-dimensional motion of the earlier sections was for a lamina, for which $z = 0$, or a special solid in which the XY plane through the mass centre was always a plane of symmetry, so that D and E were always zero.

Such objects will spin happily with $G_x = 0$ and $G_y = 0$ if the axis of rotation is suitably chosen. So a plate or book, but not a cup, may be sent skimming through the air, continuing to spin about a suitable Z-axis of constant direction (normal to these objects, but not necessarily vertical), while their mass centre describes its parabolic path quite independently.

7.3 Principal axes

Try spinning pebbles about some of their protuberances. Is it possible to spin a die or a matchbox about one corner? Must the axis of rotation always be vertical? Is there a particular direction associated with each body which must be chosen as the axis of rotation?

We have seen that the necessary and sufficient condition for steady rotation about the Z-axis under the action of no external forces is that the products of inertia D and E do not change with time. Furthermore, D and E are always zero for homogeneous bodies which have $z = 0$ as a plane of symmetry. But is this ever possible with non-symmetrical bodies?

We shall establish the remarkable result that, not only are there axes for any body about which the products of inertia are zero, but there are even suitable axes through whatever point we care to choose as origin.

Take fixed axes $OXYZ$ through any point O. We consider the effect on the inertia matrix $(\mathbf{I})$ of taking a different set $OX'Y'Z'$ of axes through O.

Any such change of axes may be expressed by a matrix transformation $\mathbf{r} \to Q\mathbf{r}$ $(= \mathbf{r}')$ where Q is an orthogonal matrix. And we find, under the transformation $\mathbf{r} \to Q\mathbf{r}$, that $(\mathbf{I}) \to Q(\mathbf{I})\tilde{Q} = (\mathbf{I}')$, where $\tilde{Q}$ is the transpose of Q.

Note: Superficially this looks like a familiar result used in the reduction of a quadratic form [see chapter on Eigenvalues†]. However, $(\mathbf{I})$ is not the matrix of coefficients of a quadratic form, but is actually a matrix whose elements are themselves quadratic forms. The similarity is remarkable and most convenient, but is purely fortuitous. It certainly does not hold for every matrix whose elements are quadratic forms.

Proof: We first express $(\mathbf{I})$ in a more convenient form for applying a transformation.

$$(\mathbf{I}) = \begin{pmatrix} A & -F & -E \\ -F & B & -D \\ -E & -D & C \end{pmatrix}$$

$$= \sum m \begin{pmatrix} x^2+y^2+z^2 & 0 & 0 \\ 0 & x^2+y^2+z^2 & 0 \\ 0 & 0 & x^2+y^2+z^2 \end{pmatrix} - \sum m \begin{pmatrix} x^2 & xy & xz \\ yx & y^2 & yz \\ zx & zy & z^2 \end{pmatrix}$$

† SMP Further Mathematics, *Linear Algebra and Geometry*

$$= \sum m(x\,y\,z)\begin{pmatrix}x\\y\\z\end{pmatrix} I - \sum m \begin{pmatrix}x\\y\\z\end{pmatrix}(x\,y\,z)$$

$$\Longrightarrow \qquad (\mathbf{I}) = \sum m\{\tilde{\mathbf{r}}\mathbf{r}I - \mathbf{r}\tilde{\mathbf{r}}\}. \qquad (21)$$

where $\tilde{\mathbf{r}}$ is the transpose of $\mathbf{r}$ and I is the 3×3 identity matrix.

Note: This expresses $(\mathbf{I})$ as the difference of two rather special quadratic forms, to which we can apply standard transformations.

If we now change to axes $OX'Y'Z'$ the new inertia matrix is

$$(\mathbf{I}') = \sum m\{\tilde{\mathbf{r}}'\mathbf{r}'I - \mathbf{r}'\tilde{\mathbf{r}}'\}$$

Note that the mass m of a typical particle does not change though its distances from the axes do.

Such a change can be represented by the rotation $\mathbf{r}' = Q\mathbf{r}$ where Q is some orthogonal unit 3×3 matrix (see Section 3 of the chapter on eigenvalues). Also $\tilde{\mathbf{r}}' = \tilde{\mathbf{r}}\tilde{Q}$.

Hence
$$\begin{aligned}(\mathbf{I}') &= \sum m\{\tilde{\mathbf{r}}\tilde{Q}Q\mathbf{r}I - Q\mathbf{r}\tilde{\mathbf{r}}\tilde{Q}\}\\ &= \sum m\{\tilde{\mathbf{r}}\mathbf{r}I - Q\mathbf{r}\tilde{\mathbf{r}}\tilde{Q}\}\ \tilde{Q}Q = I, \text{ since } Q \text{ is orthogonal,}\\ &= \sum m\{Q\tilde{\mathbf{r}}\mathbf{r}I\tilde{Q} - Q\mathbf{r}\tilde{\mathbf{r}}\tilde{Q}\}, \text{ since } \tilde{\mathbf{r}}\mathbf{r} \text{ is scalar,}\\ &= \sum m\, Q\{\tilde{\mathbf{r}}\mathbf{r}I - \mathbf{r}\tilde{\mathbf{r}}\}\tilde{Q}\\ &= Q(\mathbf{I})\tilde{Q}\\ &= Q\begin{pmatrix}A & -F & -E\\ -F & B & -D\\ -E & -D & C\end{pmatrix}\tilde{Q},\end{aligned}$$

and the result is proved.

But the inertia matrix is symmetric and so, by a suitable choice of orthogonal matrix Q, can be reduced to diagonal form. (See 'Eigenvalues', Section 4.) Thus, by a suitable choice of axes, we get

$$(\mathbf{I}') = \begin{pmatrix}A' & 0 & 0\\ 0 & B' & 0\\ 0 & 0 & C'\end{pmatrix}, \text{ with } D',\ E',\ F' \text{ all zero and}$$

where the new axes are in fact the eigenvectors of $(\mathbf{I})$. So for any point of any body there are *principal directions*, about which the products of inertia are zero.

We might now expect that it would be possible to spin any object on the floor with a chosen point in contact with the floor, so long as a principal direction through that point is chosen as axis of rotation.

Unfortunately, unless the axis happens to pass through the mass centre, the gravitational force will provide a couple, and this will give rise to rotation about the other axes as well.

However, for a body with an axis of symmetry through its mass centre, such an axis is a principal direction. This is why we have been able to treat the rotation of many solid bodies as essentially a two-dimensional problem. If we take our axes through O to be in the principal directions at O, the equations of rotational motion reduce to the particularly simple form:

$$G_x = \frac{d}{dt}(A'\omega_x'), \qquad G_y = \frac{d}{dt}(B'\omega_y'), \qquad G_z = \frac{d}{dt}(C'\omega_z'),$$

so long as D', E', F' remain zero.

However, our satisfaction is short-lived for as soon as the body starts to rotate, the principle directions will no longer be in the direction of our axes. So some, and possibly all of the moments and products of inertia will have changed. Thus the equations given above are just not valid at all, since allowance must be made for terms in $\dot{D}'$, $\dot{E}'$, $\dot{F}'$, even though D', E', F', are zero.

7.4 Rotating axes

The obvious way out of our difficulty over the rate of change of inertia is to make sure that there is no change. So our axes, instead of remaining fixed in space, must be *principal axes*, fixed at a point in the body in the principal directions at that point.

Thus, however the object moves, we always take principal axes, usually through the mass centre C, as our coordinate axes. Hence D', E', F' will always be zero, while A', B', C' are now constants which can be calculated for the body once and for all.

But this gives the body's point of view of its own motion, and is about as helpful as in the case of the two flies riding on a gramophone record merry-go-round, who think they are stationary if they stand still. He, at P, as he stands gazing into her eyes, at X', sees she is sitting waiting for him and breaks into a run. With her determining his principal axes $OX'Y'Z'$ he scuttles across the record with velocity $\dot{\mathbf{r}}'$, where $\mathbf{r}'$ is his position relative to these axes.

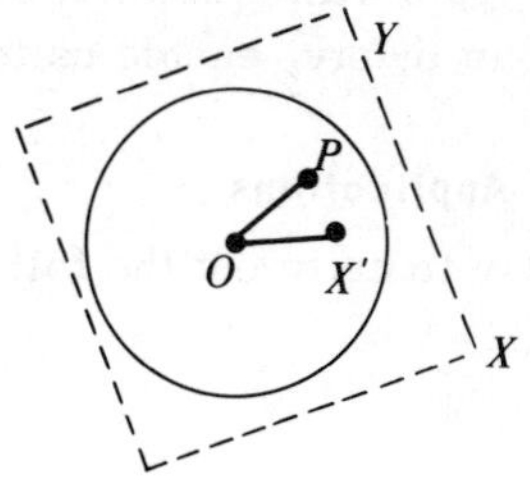

Fig. 21

But this is not the same as his velocity through the air (as he would soon find if he bumped into the pick-up). In fact he has an additional velocity $\boldsymbol{\omega}\wedge\mathbf{r}$, which is the velocity of his position on his groove relative to the cabinet; where $\mathbf{r}$ is his position relative to axes $OXYZ$ in the cabinet and $\boldsymbol{\omega}$ is the angular velocity of the record. So his actual velocity (at pick-up) is given by

$$\dot{\mathbf{r}} = \dot{\mathbf{r}}' + \boldsymbol{\omega}\wedge\mathbf{r}.$$

In the special case when the principal axes $OX'Y'Z'$, rotating with angular velocity $\boldsymbol{\omega}$, happen momentarily to coincide with the fixed axes $OXYZ$, then

$$\mathbf{r} = \mathbf{r}' \quad\text{and}\quad \dot{\mathbf{r}} = \dot{\mathbf{r}}' + \boldsymbol{\omega}\wedge\mathbf{r}',$$

(Note that just because $\mathbf{r} = \mathbf{r}'$ it does not mean that $\dot{\mathbf{r}} = \dot{\mathbf{r}}'$, since one set of axes is moving and the other is stationary.)

A similar analysis applies to the rate of change of any vector quantity relative to such axes. This is an important result because it gives an expression for the rate of change of the vector relative to fixed axes which momentarily coincide with the moving axes, but this rate of change is expressed in terms of the moving axes. In particular:

$$\dot{\mathbf{H}} = \dot{\mathbf{H}}' + \boldsymbol{\omega} \wedge \mathbf{H}'. \tag{22}$$

Now

$$\mathbf{H}' = \begin{pmatrix} A' & 0 & 0 \\ 0 & B' & 0 \\ 0 & 0 & C' \end{pmatrix} \boldsymbol{\omega},$$

$$\dot{\mathbf{H}}' = \begin{pmatrix} A'\dot{\omega}_x \\ B'\dot{\omega}_y \\ C'\dot{\omega}_z \end{pmatrix}.$$

Hence we finally get *Euler's Equations* for rotation:

$$\begin{aligned} G_x &= A'\dot{\omega}_x + (C' - B')\,\omega_y\,\omega_z, \\ G_y &= B'\dot{\omega}_y + (A' - C')\,\omega_z\,\omega_x, \\ G_z &= C'\dot{\omega}_z + (B' - A')\,\omega_x\,\omega_y, \end{aligned} \tag{23}$$

which completely relate the rotational motion to the applied torque about axes $OXYZ$ fixed in space and momentarily coinciding with the principal axes at the mass centre, or at a fixed point, of a rigid body.

Note that this only enables us to determine the behaviour of the object at one particular instant. At a different time it will have moved, and we shall have to start again with a new set of axes in the new principal directions. However, this does, in theory, enable us to build up a complete picture of the motion.

7.5 Applications

Try to carry out the following experiments.

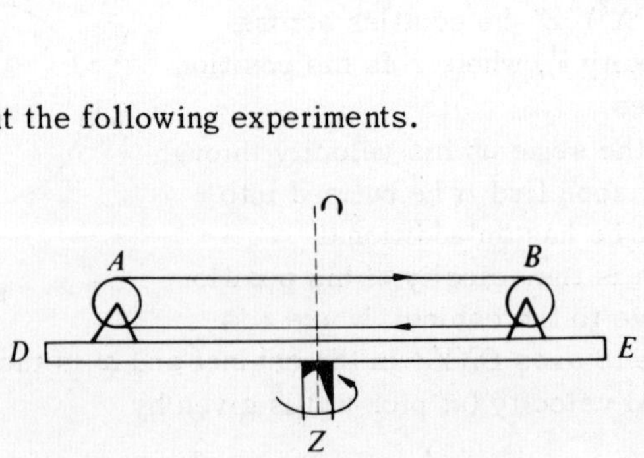

Fig. 22

(i) Mount two pulley wheels A and B on a bar or disc DE which can turn about a vertical axis OZ. Fasten a cord or band around the pulley wheels. If possible drive A or B by a small motor so that the pulley and cord revolve ; if not, choose heavy pulley wheels so that both will rotate for a few seconds. Now spin DE about its axis and observe the shape of the belt. Does it remain straight or does it bow? Does the same happen to both upper and lower sections?

(ii)

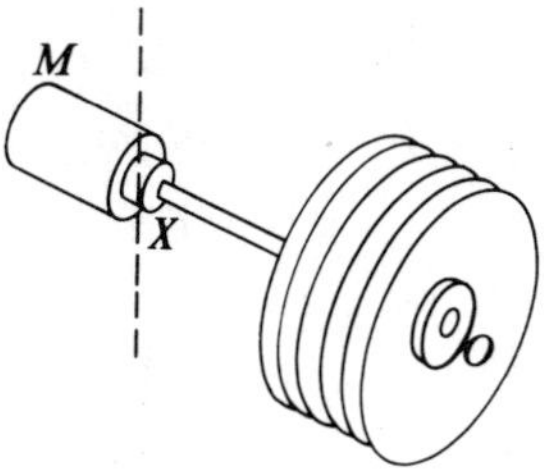

Fig. 23

Cut out about 6 discs from pad paper about 15 cm in diameter and clamp them together between small wheels on an axle OX perpendicular to the centre of the discs. Drive the axle by a motor M, or else make a frame to spin the discs by hand. Observe the shape of the paper discs as you rotate about a vertical axis, holding the motor in your hands.

Try to account for these results which, as indeed with most rotational effects, at first seem contrary to intuition.

Example 15. A thin book spins with constant angular velocity ω about a diagonal. What couple must act on the book in order to maintain this motion?

The principal axes through C will be $\hat{\mathbf{i}}$, $\hat{\mathbf{j}}$, parallel to the edges, and $\hat{\mathbf{k}}$, normal to the book.

Hence $A' = \frac{1}{3}Mb^2$, $\quad B' = \frac{1}{3}Ma^2$,

$$C' = \tfrac{1}{3}M(a^2 + b^2),$$

where M is the mass, $2a$ the length, $2b$ the breadth.

$\omega_x = \omega\cos\alpha$, $\omega_y = \omega\sin\alpha$, $\omega_z = 0$, where α is the angle between $\boldsymbol{\omega}$ and $\hat{\mathbf{i}}$.

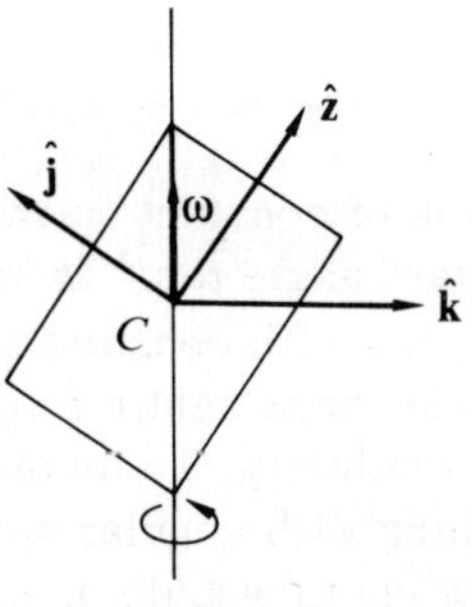

Fig. 24

Substituting these values into Euler's Equations (23) gives

$$G_x = 0, \qquad G_y = 0,$$

$$G_z = \tfrac{1}{3}M(a^2 - b^2)\omega^2 \sin\alpha\cos\alpha.$$

It is perhaps surprising to find that a couple is always needed normal to the book. This is why a matchbox will not spin about a diagonal but moves so as to align $\hat{\mathbf{j}}$ and $\boldsymbol{\omega}$.

Note that the result is independent of the inertia C' about $\hat{\mathbf{k}}$, and particularly that if $A' = B'$ then $G_z = 0$. Thus any body possessing symmetry such that $A' = B'$ will be able to spin freely with constant angular velocity $\boldsymbol{\omega}$, where $\boldsymbol{\omega}$ is perpendicular to $\hat{\mathbf{k}}$, without any couple at all being needed to maintain the motion.

The converse, however, is not true. A body with $A' = B'$, moving under the action of no external forces will not necessarily have constant (possibly zero) angular velocity!

Example 16. A space craft having an axis of symmetry is moving freely under the action of no external forces. What is its motion? At any instant take principal axes through the mass centre with OZ as the axis of symmetry.

Then $B' = A'$ and $\mathbf{G} = \mathbf{0}$.

Hence for the rotational motion, from Euler's Equations (23):

$$\left.\begin{aligned} A'\dot{\omega}_x + (C' - A')\omega_y\omega_z &= 0 \\ A'\dot{\omega}_y - (C' - A')\omega_z\omega_x &= 0 \\ C'\dot{\omega}_z &= 0 \end{aligned}\right\}$$

$$\left.\begin{aligned} \Rightarrow \quad \omega_z &= k, \text{ a constant,} \\ \dot{\omega}_x &= \frac{-(C' - A')}{A'} k\omega_y = -n\omega_y, \\ \dot{\omega}_y &= \frac{(C' - A')}{A'} k\omega_x = n\omega_x \end{aligned}\right\} \text{ where } n = k(C' - A')/A'.$$

Differentiating and eliminating $\dot{\omega}_y$ using the last two equations gives

$$\ddot{\omega}_x = -n\dot{\omega}_y = -n^2\omega_x, \text{ which is simple harmonic motion,}$$

$$\left.\begin{aligned} \Rightarrow \quad \omega_x &= a\cos(nt + b) \\ \omega_y &= a\sin(nt + b) \end{aligned}\right\} \text{ where } a, b \text{ are constants,}$$

$$\omega_z = k$$

$$\Rightarrow \quad \omega = \sqrt{(a^2 + k^2)}.$$

So $\boldsymbol{\omega}$ is of constant magnitude and makes a constant angle $\tan^{-1}(k/a)$ with OZ, about which it rotates with constant angular speed n.

The mass centre itself moves with constant linear velocity. To an observer the spacecraft is spinning with angular speed k about its axis while appearing to wobble about some other axis $\boldsymbol{\omega}$. Note that if $a = 0$ then the rotation is purely about OZ, and if $k = 0$ there is no rotation about OZ and the situation reduces to that of the previous example, with $\omega_x = a\cos b$, $\omega_y = a\sin b$.

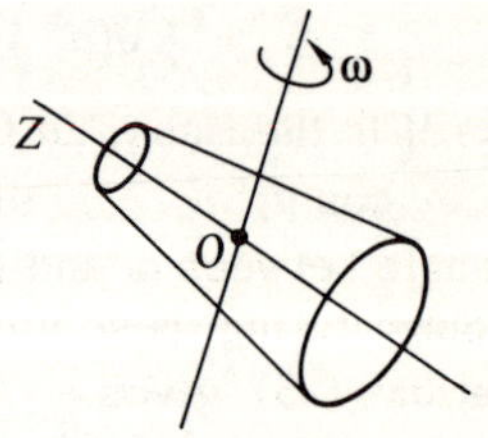

Fig. 25

Example 17. What happens if you are riding steadily along on a bicycle and turn the handlebars to the left about a vertical axis? Take a set of principal axes as shown in Figure 26. Where $\hat{\mathbf{i}}$, $\hat{\mathbf{j}}$ are fixed in the plane of the wheel and $\mathbf{k}$ is the axis of rotation.

At any instant let θ be the angle between the vertical and $\hat{\mathbf{i}}$, as shown.

The equations of motion of the front wheel are

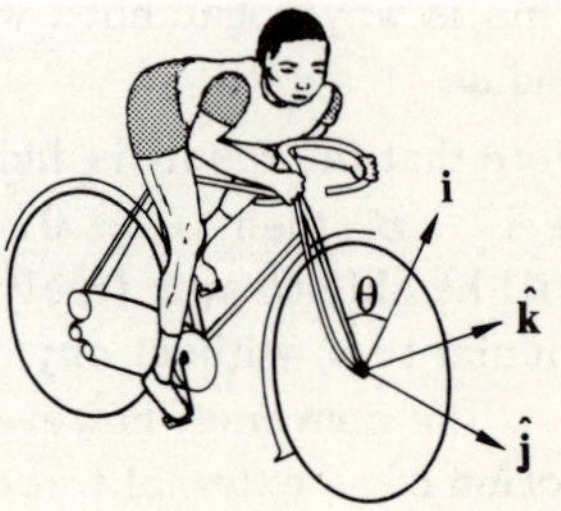

Fig. 26

the same as the previous example but with $G_x = \lambda\cos\theta,\ G_y = -\lambda\sin\theta$.

$$\text{Thus}\quad \omega_z = k$$

$$\dot{\omega}_x = -n\omega_y + \lambda\cos\theta/A', \text{ where } n = k(C' - A')/A',$$

$$\dot{\omega}_y = n\omega_x - \lambda\sin\theta/A'.$$

Differentiating and eliminating $\dot{\omega}_y$ as before, with $\dot{\theta} = k$

$$\ddot{\omega}_x = -n(n\omega_x - \lambda\sin\theta/A') - \lambda k\sin\theta/A',$$

$$\ddot{\omega}_x + n^2\omega_x = \lambda(n - k)\sin\theta/A',$$

which has the particular solution $\dfrac{\lambda}{\{A'(n+k)\}}\sin\theta$.

But $n = k(C' - A')/A'$, so the complete solution can be written

$$\omega_x = a\cos(nt + b) + \frac{\lambda}{kC'}\sin\theta.$$

Similarly
$$\omega_y = a\sin(nt + b) + \frac{\lambda}{kC'}\cos\theta.$$

If initially $\theta = 0$ so that z is vertical, and $\omega_x = \omega_y = 0$ [we could not merely take $\theta = 0$ so that $G_x = \lambda,\ G_y = 0$ from the beginning since we needed expressions for $\dot{G}_x$ and $\dot{G}_y$] then

$$G_x = \lambda,\quad G_y = 0,\quad G_z = 0$$

$$\omega_x = 0,\quad \omega_y = \lambda/kC',\quad \omega_z = k.$$

So when the wheel has angular speed k about OZ then a torque λ about OX causes a rotation about OY with angular speed λ/kC'.

Thus turning the handlebars to the *left* (applying a torque G_x) has the remarkable effect of merely tilting the whole wheel to the *right* (causes an angular speed ω_y).

There is another way of looking at this interesting result. If there is constant spin about the z-axis of magnitude ω_z then to cause a rotation of magnitude ω_y about the y-axis (this rotation is called precession) there must be a couple G_x of magnitude $C'\,\omega_y\,\omega_z$ about the x-axis, where C' is the moment of inertia about the z-axis. All these quantities are clockwise about the respective axis – i.e. spin, precession and couple.

This also accounts for the contrary nature of the gyroscope, of such use in navigation. It spins about one axis, you force it to rotate about a second perpendicular axis, and it responds, not by any action about these two axes, but by rotating about a third mutually perpendicular axis. But perhaps this is not so strange after all? In each case it will aim to align itself so that the axis of spin coincides with the axis of the applied couple.

So, happily, rather than attempting to turn the handlebars, we can cause the wheel to turn in the required direction by the simple expedient of leaning that way.

EXERCISE I

Investigate and account for the behaviour of the following:

1. A cricket ball in flight.
2. The earth's non-symmetric rotation.
3. A gyrocompass.
4. A billiard ball struck off-centre.
5. A spinning top.
6. An unusual bicycle, whose front wheel turns in the opposite direction to the handlebars.
7. The problem of getting out of bed on a rotating earth.

SUMMARY

Particle		*Notation*
Position $\mathbf{r}$	Mass m	Σ Summation for all particles.
Velocity $\dot{\mathbf{r}}$	Force $\mathbf{F}$	$\bar{\mathbf{r}}$ Bars denote mass centre quantities
Acceleration $\ddot{\mathbf{r}}$	Internal $\mathbf{F}'$	$\mathbf{r}^*$ Stars denote quantities relative to mass centre.

Linear motion

Total external force = Rate of change of linear momentum,

$$\Sigma\mathbf{F} = \Sigma m\ddot{\mathbf{r}}$$

$$= M\ddot{\bar{\mathbf{r}}}. \qquad M = \Sigma m \text{ Total mass.}$$

Symbolically: $\mathbf{P} = \dot{\mathbf{L}}$ $\qquad \mathbf{L} = \Sigma(m\dot{\mathbf{r}})$ Total linear momentum.

$$= \dot{\bar{\mathbf{L}}}. \qquad \mathbf{P} = \Sigma\mathbf{F} \text{ Total external force.}$$

Rotational motion

Total external couple = Rate of change of moment of momentum about a fixed point or mass centre,

$$\sum(\mathbf{r}\wedge\mathbf{F}) = \sum(\mathbf{r}\wedge m\ddot{\mathbf{r}})$$

$$= \frac{\mathrm{d}}{\mathrm{d}t}\sum(\mathbf{r}\wedge m\dot{\mathbf{r}})$$

$$= \bar{\mathbf{r}}\wedge M\ddot{\bar{\mathbf{r}}} + \sum(\mathbf{r}^*\wedge m\ddot{\mathbf{r}}^*)$$

Symbolically:

$\mathbf{G} = \dot{\mathbf{H}}.$ $\qquad \mathbf{H} = \Sigma(\mathbf{r}\wedge m\dot{\mathbf{r}})$ Total moment of momentum.

$= \dot{\bar{\mathbf{H}}} + \dot{\mathbf{H}}^*.$ $\qquad \mathbf{G} = \Sigma(\mathbf{r}\wedge\mathbf{F})$ Total external couple.

For laminas: $= \dot{\bar{\mathbf{H}}} + I\dot{\omega}\hat{\mathbf{k}}.$ $\qquad I = \Sigma(mr^2)$ Moment of inertia.

Momentum equations

Total external impulse = Change of linear momentum

Linear: $\Sigma\int\mathbf{F}\,\mathrm{d}t = [\Sigma m\dot{\mathbf{r}}].$

Symbolically: $\int \mathbf{P}\,dt = [\bar{\mathbf{L}}]$.

For jerks: $\Sigma \mathbf{J} = [\bar{\mathbf{L}}]$. $\qquad \mathbf{J} = \int \mathbf{F}\,dt$ for small t

Conservation: $\mathbf{P} = 0 \Leftrightarrow \mathbf{L} =$ constant.

Total moment of impulse = change of moment of momentum.

Rotational: $$\int (\mathbf{r} \wedge \mathbf{F})\,dt = \left[\sum (\mathbf{r} \wedge m\dot{\mathbf{r}})\right]$$
$$= [\bar{\mathbf{r}} \wedge M\dot{\bar{\mathbf{r}}}] + [\mathbf{r}^* \wedge m\dot{\mathbf{r}}^*].$$

Symbolically: $$\int \mathbf{G}\,dt = [\bar{\mathbf{H}}] + [\mathbf{H}^*]$$
$$= [\bar{\mathbf{H}}] + [I\omega\hat{\mathbf{k}}].$$

For jerks: $$\sum (\mathbf{r} \wedge \mathbf{J}) = [\bar{\mathbf{H}}] + [\mathbf{H}^*].$$

Conservation: $\mathbf{G} = \mathbf{0} \Leftrightarrow \mathbf{H} =$ constant.

Kinetic energy

Total external work done = change of kinetic energy

$$\sum \int \mathbf{F}\cdot d\mathbf{r} = \sum \left[\tfrac{1}{2} m\dot{r}^2\right]$$
$$= \left[\tfrac{1}{2} M\dot{\bar{r}}^2\right] + \left[\tfrac{1}{2} I\omega^2\right]$$
$$= [\bar{T}] + [T^*]. \qquad T = \sum \left(\tfrac{1}{2} m\dot{r}^2\right) \text{ Kinetic energy.}$$

Moment of inertia

Parallel axis rule: $I_O = I_G + M(OG)^2$.

For laminas: $I_z = I_x + I_y$.

Rigid bodies

Total external couple = Rate of change of moment of momentum.

$$\mathbf{G} = \begin{pmatrix} A & -F & -E \\ -F & B & -D \\ -E & -D & C \end{pmatrix} \dot{\boldsymbol{\omega}}. \qquad \begin{array}{ll} A = \Sigma m(y^2 + z^2) & D = \Sigma (myz). \\ B = \Sigma m(z^2 + x^2) & E = \Sigma (mzx). \\ C = \Sigma m(x^2 + y^2) & F = \Sigma (mxy). \end{array}$$

Symbolically: $= (\mathbf{I})\,\boldsymbol{\omega}$. $\qquad$ $(\mathbf{I})$ The inertia matrix.

In principal directions: $$= \begin{pmatrix} A & 0 & 0 \\ 0 & B & 0 \\ 0 & 0 & C \end{pmatrix} \dot{\boldsymbol{\omega}}.$$

About rotating axes: $= \dot{\mathbf{H}}' + \boldsymbol{\omega} \wedge \mathbf{H}'$

Euler:
$$\mathbf{G} = \begin{pmatrix} A'\dot{\omega}_x + (C' - B')\omega_y\omega_z \\ B'\dot{\omega}_y + (A' - C')\omega_z\omega_x \\ C'\dot{\omega}_z + (B' - A')\omega_x\omega_y \end{pmatrix}.$$

Gyroscope: $G_x = C'\omega_y\omega_z$.

Thus the motion of a body is completely determined by the equations of linear and rotational motion $\mathbf{P} = \dot{\mathbf{L}}$ and $\mathbf{G} = \dot{\mathbf{H}}$. They may be expressed in various forms for convenience of application. When integrated, as the momentum and energy equations, they can be of particular use.

Miscellaneous Exercises

These questions are all taken from the *O & C*, SMP *Further Mathematics* papers.

1. A particle is moved in the (x, y)-plane, in a field of force with components $(2x, y)$. If the particle is moved from $(0, 0)$ to (a, b) along a straight line, then from (a, b) to $(0, b)$ along the line $y = b$, and finally from $(0, b)$ back to $(0, 0)$ along the y-axis, find the work done.

Assuming that the work done during a movement from $(0, 0)$ to (x, y) is a function $W(x, y)$ of x, y, independent of the particular path taken, find an expression for $W(x, y)$. Illustrate by sketching some curves on which W takes a constant value. *(School Mathematics Project, 1966).*

2. Prove that the radius of curvature of the parabola $x = au^2$, $y = 2au$ at the point given by $u = t$ is $2a(1 + t^2)^{3/2}$.

Prove further that the circle whose centre is on the normal to the parabola where $u = t$, which touches the parabola at this point and lies inside the parabola, and whose radius is one quarter of the radius of curvature of the curve at this point, passes through the focus of the parabola.

(School Mathematics Project, 1966)

3. A smooth straight horizontal tube of some 400 cm in length is rigidly fixed at one end to a vertical axle rotating steadily at ½ revolution per second. A 30 g mass oscillates in simple harmonic motion within the tube so that at time t seconds its distance from the axle is $(4 + 3 \sin 2t)$ cm. Find the total work which has to be done on the axle during one complete oscillation of the mass.

By writing the position vector of the particle in the form $f(t)\mathbf{R}(t)$ where $\mathbf{R}(t)$ is a unit vector in suitably chosen coordinates derive an expression for the acceleration of the mass and find the times at which the radial component of the acceleration is zero. *(Adapted from School Mathematics Project, 1966)*

4. Define the instantaneous angular velocity $\boldsymbol{\omega}$ of a rigid body.

A satellite is moving with constant angular velocity $\boldsymbol{\omega}$ and in such a way that a certain point P of it has the constant velocity $\mathbf{v} \neq \mathbf{0}$. Prove that the velocity $\mathbf{V}$ of a point Q of the body is given by

$$\mathbf{V} = \mathbf{v} + \boldsymbol{\omega} \times (\mathbf{r}_q - \mathbf{r}_p),$$

where $\mathbf{r}_q$, $\mathbf{r}_p$ are the position vectors of Q and P respectively.

Prove that

$$\mathbf{v} \times \boldsymbol{\omega} . (\mathbf{r}_q - \mathbf{r}_p) = -\mathbf{v}^2$$

is a necessary condition that $\mathbf{V}$ is perpendicular to $\mathbf{v}$. Show that this condition cannot be satisfied if $\mathbf{v}$ is parallel to $\boldsymbol{\omega}$, and draw a diagram to illustrate why this is so. *(School Mathematics Project, 1966)*

5. If P is any point of a simple plane curve, and O is a fixed point on it, the arc length OP is denoted by s, being positive if P is on one side of O, and negative if P is on the other. Describe carefully what is meant by the curve having the property of 'a continuously-turning tangent'; and explain why this property is not sufficient for the existence of the curvature at every point.

For a plane curve on which the curvature K can be defined as a function $K(s)$ of s prove that the acute angle θ between the tangents at P and O can be written as

$$\theta = \left| \int_0^s K(t)\,dt + \pi N \right| ,$$

where N is a whole number to be suitably chosen.

Verify the correctness of this formula in the particular case of a circle.
(*School Mathematics Project, 1966*)

6. A boy is bowling a bicycle wheel of external radius r directly at a step of height h and he wants to estimate the bowling speed v at which the wheel will just surmount the step.

Describe briefly the mathematical model you would make to determine the speed v.

Give an argument to show that the final result of a detailed calculation of v will probably be expressible in the form

$$\frac{v^2}{gr} = f\left(\frac{h}{r}\right),$$

(*School Mathematics Project, 1966*)

7. A man of mass M stands at one end of a uniform plank of mass m and length $2l$ which is on a frozen pond. He walks to the other end in such a way that after time t he has moved a distance $k(1 - \cos t)$ relative to the plank. Find the speed of the plank when the man has walked half-way along it.

Find also the total distance relative to the ice which the man has moved by the time he reaches the other end. (*School Mathematics Project, 1967*)

8. A plane curve has cartesian coordinates given parametrically by

$$x = f(t), \qquad y = g(t), \qquad \text{for all } t,$$

where $f(t)$ and $g(t)$ are differentiable functions. Obtain the equation of the normal to the curve at the point t.

Write down the condition that the normal passes through the fixed point (a, b).

The curve is such that the normals at all points given by $t \geqslant t_0$ pass through the point (a, b). Show that the (x, y) equation of the curve for $t \geqslant t_0$ can be written as

$$(x-a)^2 + (y-b)^2 = (f(t_0) - a)^2 + (g(t_0) - b)^2.$$

Interpret this result geometrically. (*School Mathematics Project, 1967*)

9. The path traced out by the end of a length of cotton thread as it is unwound from a fixed cotton reel is ideally represented in terms of a parameter θ by the equations

$$x = r\cos\theta + r\theta\sin\theta$$

$$y = r\sin\theta + r\theta\cos\theta.$$

where r is a constant. Justify these ideal equations.

Prove that the normal to the curve with these equations is tangent to the circle

$$x^2 + y^2 = r^2,$$

and that the distance from the point of contact of the normal on this circle to the foot of the normal is

$$\left\{1 + \left(\frac{dy}{dx}\right)^2\right\}^{3/2} \Big/ \frac{d^2y}{dx^2}$$

(*School Mathamatics Project*, 1967)

10. A point P is said to describe an 'epicyclic' path if it moves in a plane, round a circle centre Q with constant speed whilst Q itself moves with constant speed round a circle with fixed centre O. Assuming $\overrightarrow{OQ}$ and $\overrightarrow{QP}$ rotate in the same direction with angular velocities in the ratio 1 : 4 sketch the epicyclic path of P.

Fixed rectangular axes Oxy are taken in a plane, together with two concentric circles centre O and radii r, s respectively, $r > s$. A point $A(x_A, y_A)$ moves round the outer circle at constant speed u, and a point B moves round the inner circle at constant speed v. Initially, at the time $t = 0$, $(x_A, y_A) = (r, 0)$, $(x_B, x_B) = (s, 0)$. Show that the path of the point with coordinates $(x_A - x_B, y_A - y_B)$ is epicyclic.

'Planets appear to observers on earth to stop and reverse their motions at regular intervals.' Comment.

(*School Mathematics Project*, 1967)

11. Three point-elements A, B, C of a lamina moving in its own plane are such that their position vectors are given, as functions of time t, by

$$\mathbf{r}_A = \mathbf{R}(t),$$

$$\mathbf{r}_B = \mathbf{R}(t) + a\,\mathbf{S}(t),$$

$$\mathbf{r}_C = \mathbf{R}(t) + b\,\mathbf{S}'(t)$$

where $\mathbf{S}(t)$ is a *unit* vector, $\mathbf{S}'(t)$ is its derivative with respect to time, and a, b are constants.

Prove that

(i) the angle subtended by BC at A is a right-angle;

(ii) the magnitude of the body's angular velocity is constant.

(*School Mathematics Project*, 1967)

12. Two stars, of masses m_1 and m_2, deemed to be unaffected by all other objects in the universe, are initially at a great distance apart and moving with velocities $\mathbf{u}_1$, $\mathbf{u}_2$. They come close enough to influence each other's motion and then separate to a great distance, their velocities then being $\mathbf{v}_1$, $\mathbf{v}_2$. Show on a single diagram the initial and final momenta of both stars, the impulse $\mathbf{I}$ of the force which m_1 exerts on m_2, and the total momentum $\mathbf{Q}$ of the system.

Explain why one would expect the initial and final kinetic energies of the system to be the same. On this assumption, prove that

$$\mathbf{I}.(\mathbf{U} + \mathbf{V}) = 0,$$

where $\mathbf{U}$, $\mathbf{V}$ are the velocities of m_2 relative to m_1 at the beginning and end of the period of effective interaction.

(*School Mathematics Project*, 1968)

13. A bead moves along a smooth helical wire which is such that the cartesian coordinates (x, y, z) of the bead are given by $(a\cos\theta,\ a\sin\theta,\ b\theta)$, where θ is a parameter depending on time t, and $\theta = 0$ when $t = 0$. Find the equation of the cylinder on which the helix lies.

The bead moves with constant speed. Prove that θ is directly proportional to time, that is, $\theta = \omega t$ where ω is a constant.

$\mathbf{F}$ is the total force which acts upon the bead (which is of mass m). Express $\mathbf{F}$ in its cartesian components as a function of t.

Prove that at each position of the bead $\mathbf{F}$ is perpendicular to the velocity $\mathbf{v}$ of the bead. *(School Mathematics Project, 1968)*

14. A sequence of vectors $\mathbf{v}_1, \mathbf{v}_2, \ldots$ is defined inductively by the equation.

$$\begin{cases} \mathbf{v}_1 = \mathbf{a} \times \mathbf{b}, \\ \mathbf{v}_{n+1} = \mathbf{v}_n \times \mathbf{b} \quad \text{for } n = 1, 2, \ldots, \end{cases}$$

where $\mathbf{a}$ and $\mathbf{b}$ are two given non-parallel vectors. Prove that, for $n = 1, 2, \ldots,$

(i) $\mathbf{v}_{n+2} = k\,\mathbf{v}_n$, where k is a scalar;

(ii) $\mathbf{v}_{2n} = \lambda_n\,\mathbf{a} + \mu_n\,\mathbf{b}$, where λ_n and μ_n are scalars depending on n.

Prove also that, if $\mu_n = 0$ for some n, then $\mathbf{a}.\mathbf{b} = 0$ and $\mu_n = 0$ for all n.

Note: It is not necessary to calculate the values of k, λ_n, μ_n.

(School Mathematics Project, 1968)

15. A uniform circular cylinder has radius r, mass m and moment of inertia I about its axis. It is placed with its axis horizontal at the top of a ramp inclined at an angle α to the horizontal. Find the accelerations of the cylinder down the ramp on the assumptions that the contact between the surfaces of the cylinder and the ramp is

(i) perfectly smooth;

(ii) perfectly rough.

Prove that the expression for the acceleration found in (ii) is in fact valid provided that the coefficient of friction is greater than

$$\frac{I\tan\alpha}{I + mr^2}.$$

Find also the acceleration in terms of the coefficient of friction μ when this condition is not satisfied. *(School Mathematics Project, 1968)*

16. Figure 1 shows a particle on the end of a string which is unwinding in a horizontal plane from a cylindrical reel of radius b whose axis is vertical. Initially the particle is in contact with the reel and is given a velocity away from the axis of the reel; after a time t the radius to the point where the string leaves the reel has rotated through an angle θ. $\hat{\mathbf{u}}$ and $\hat{\mathbf{n}}$ are unit vectors along and at right angles to this radius. Express the position vector of the particle, relative to the point in the plane of motion on the axis of the reel, in terms of b, θ, $\hat{\mathbf{u}}$ and $\hat{\mathbf{n}}$, and deduce its velocity and acceleration.

Supposing that the only force in the plane on the particle is the tension of the string, prove that θ is proportional to $\sqrt{t}$, and that the magnitude of the acceleration of the particle is inversely proportional to θ.

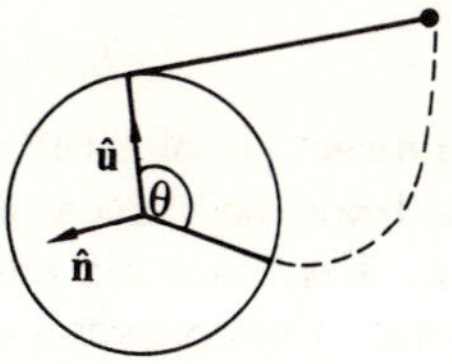

Fig. 1

(School Mathematics Project, 1969)

17. Write down expressions for the components of acceleration along the tangent and normal for a particle moving along a plane curve with speed v.

A particle moves with constant speed along the curve

$$y = ae^{x/b} \quad (a, b > 0).$$

Prove that the point of the curve at which its acceleration is greatest has co-ordinates

$$\left(\frac{b}{2}\log\frac{b^2}{2a^2}, \frac{b}{\sqrt{2}}\right)$$

(School Mathematics Project, 1969)

18. A particle of unit mass is attracted to a point O with a force $-9\mathbf{r}$, where $\mathbf{r}$ is the position vector of the particle relative to O. Initially the particle is at a point with position vector $16\mathbf{i}$ and moving with velocity $24\mathbf{j}$, where $\mathbf{i}$ and $\mathbf{j}$ are fixed unit vectors in perpendicular directions. Verify that the subsequent motion is described by the equation

$$\mathbf{r} = 16\mathbf{i}\cos 3t + 8\mathbf{j}\sin 3t,$$

and interpret this equation geometrically.

If there were also a resistance to motion of magnitude ten times the speed, obtain a differential equation for the motion and show that it has a solution of the form

$$\mathbf{r} = \mathbf{A}e^{-t} + \mathbf{B}e^{-9t}.$$

With the same initial conditions as before, find the values of $\mathbf{A}$ and $\mathbf{B}$, and investigate the nature of the motion for $t > 0$.

(School Mathematics Project, 1969)

19. A solid is rotated through an angle α in a clockwise sense about an axis through $O \cdot \mathbf{i}$ is a unit vector in the direction of the axis. The points whose position vectors relative to O are $\mathbf{r}$, $\mathbf{r}'$ are transformed to those whose position vectors are $\mathbf{R}$, $\mathbf{R}'$. Prove that

(i) $\mathbf{r} - \mathbf{r}' = t\hat{\mathbf{i}} \Rightarrow \mathbf{R} - \mathbf{R}' = t\hat{\mathbf{i}}$ for scalar t,

(ii) $\mathbf{r}.\hat{\mathbf{i}} = 0 \Rightarrow \mathbf{R} = \mathbf{r}\cos\alpha + \hat{\mathbf{i}} \times \mathbf{r}\sin\alpha$

By splitting **r** up into two vectors, parallel and perpendicular to $\hat{\mathbf{i}}$, deduce that in general

$$\mathbf{R} = \hat{\mathbf{i}}(\hat{\mathbf{i}}.\mathbf{r}) + \hat{\mathbf{i}} \times \mathbf{r}\sin\alpha - \hat{\mathbf{i}} \times (\hat{\mathbf{i}} \times \mathbf{r})\cos\alpha.$$

(School Mathematics Project, 1969)

20. **i**, **j**, **k** are unit vectors in the direction of three mutually perpendicular axes forming a right-handed set. Write down the values of $\mathbf{i} \times \mathbf{j}$, $\mathbf{j} \times \mathbf{k}$ and $\mathbf{i} \times \mathbf{k}$.

A cube has edges of length a. There are six edges which do not meet a given diagonal, joined together in a chain. Forces, each of magnitude F, act along these six edges. Find the force or couple needed to keep the cube in equilibrium if the senses in which these forces act round the chain are, consecutively, (i) ++++++, (ii) +−+−+−, (iii) ++−++−.

(School Mathematics Project, 1969)

21. Prove that a uniform disc rotating with angular speed ω about a stationary perpendicular axis through its centre has angular momentum $I\omega$ about any parallel axis, where I is the moment of inertia about the axis through the centre. (If you quote any general result about the angular momentum of a system you must prove it.)

A boy sits on a turntable which is free to rotate about a vertical axis, holding at arm's length l a bicycle wheel of mass M in a horizontal plane by the axle. Initially the turntable is at rest and the bicycle wheel has angular speed ω. He turns the bicycle wheel upside down so that it finally occupies the same position as before relative to himself. If the moment of inertia of the wheel about its axle is I, and that of the boy and turntable about the turntable pedestal is J, prove that in the subsequent motion the turntable rotates with angular speed

$$\frac{2I\omega}{J + Ml^2}.$$

Calculate also the change of kinetic energy of the system as a result of the manoeuvre. *(School Mathematics Project, 1969)*

Answers to Exercises

CHAPTER 1

Exercise A

1. $\mathbf{r} = 9\mathbf{i} + 6\mathbf{j}$,
   $\mathbf{v} = 6\mathbf{i} + 2\mathbf{j}$,
   $\mathbf{a} = 2\mathbf{i}$.

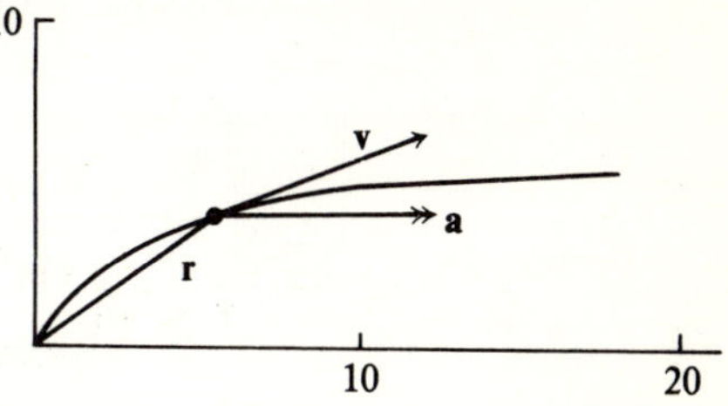

2. Ellipse, semi-axes 4 and 3, frequency 20.
   314°, $0{\cdot}16\,\pi^2$ when $t = 5(2n+1)$, $t = 10n$.

3. (a) Straight line, $\begin{pmatrix}2\\8\end{pmatrix}$, $\begin{pmatrix}0\\0\end{pmatrix}$.

   (b) Straight line, $\begin{pmatrix}5\\20\end{pmatrix}$, $\begin{pmatrix}0\\0\end{pmatrix}$.

   (c) Straight line, $\begin{pmatrix}5\\12\end{pmatrix}$, $\begin{pmatrix}0\\0\end{pmatrix}$.

   (d)

   $\mathbf{v} = \begin{pmatrix}24\\12\end{pmatrix}$ $\mathbf{a} = \begin{pmatrix}24\\6\end{pmatrix}$

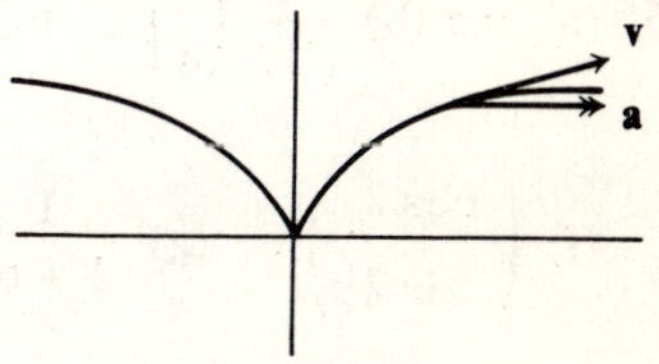

   (e) Circle, $\begin{pmatrix}3\cos 2\\-3\sin 2\end{pmatrix}$, $\begin{pmatrix}-3\sin 2\\-3\cos 2\end{pmatrix}$.

   (f) Circle, $\begin{pmatrix}6\cos 4\\-6\sin 4\end{pmatrix}$, $\begin{pmatrix}-12\sin 4\\-12\cos 4\end{pmatrix}$.

   (g) Circle, $\begin{pmatrix}-18/25\\-24/25\end{pmatrix}$, $\begin{pmatrix}24/125\\132/125\end{pmatrix}$

(h)

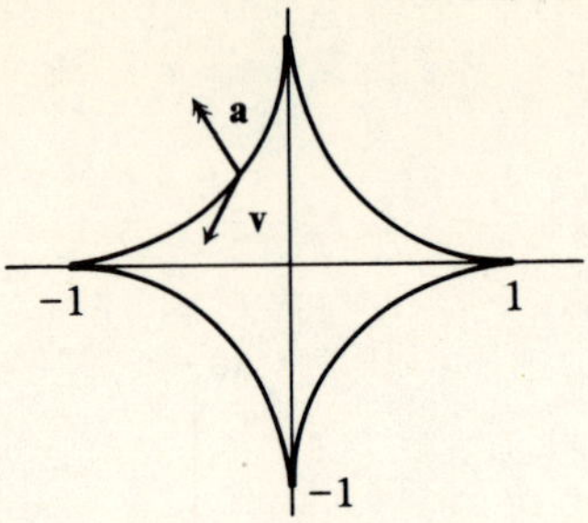

$$\mathbf{v} = 3\begin{pmatrix}\sin^2 2\cos 2\\ -\cos^2 2\sin 2\end{pmatrix},$$

$$|\mathbf{v}| = \tfrac{3}{2}\sin 4,$$

$$\mathbf{a} = 3\begin{pmatrix}\sin 2\cdot(2-3\sin^2 2)\\ \cos 2\cdot(2-3\cos^2 2)\end{pmatrix}.$$

4. (a) $y = 4x + 3$, (e) $x^2 + y^2 = 9$,

(b) $y = 4x + 3$, (f) $x^2 + y^2 = 9$,

(c) $y = \frac{12}{5}x$, (g) $x^2 + y^2 = 9$,

(d) $y = 3(\frac{1}{2}x)^{2/3}$, (h) $x^{2/3} + y^{2/3} = 1$,

(a), (b), (c), (d) are functions.

5. (a) and (b) $\dfrac{1}{\sqrt{17}}\begin{pmatrix}1\\4\end{pmatrix}$ (c) $\dfrac{1}{13}\begin{pmatrix}5\\12\end{pmatrix}$, (d) $\dfrac{1}{\sqrt{(1+p^2)}}\begin{pmatrix}p\\1\end{pmatrix}$, (e) $\begin{pmatrix}\cos p\\-\sin p\end{pmatrix}$,

(f) $\begin{pmatrix}\cos 2p\\-\sin 2p\end{pmatrix}$, (g) $\dfrac{1}{1+p^2}\begin{pmatrix}1-p^2\\-2p\end{pmatrix}$ (h) $\begin{pmatrix}\sin p\\-\cos p\end{pmatrix}$.

6. Circle, radius 5, centre (0, 5); towards centre.

7. (a) $(p,\ 2p+1)$, (b) $(p^2,\ 2p)$, (c) $(9p^3,\ 3p)$

(d) $(2\sin p,\ 2\cos p)$, (e) $(\sec p,\ \tan p)$.

8. (a) Line (b) Parabola with axis $y = 0$.

(c)

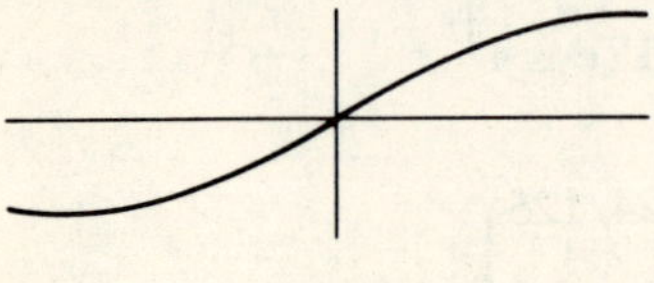

(d) Circle.

(e) Hyperbola

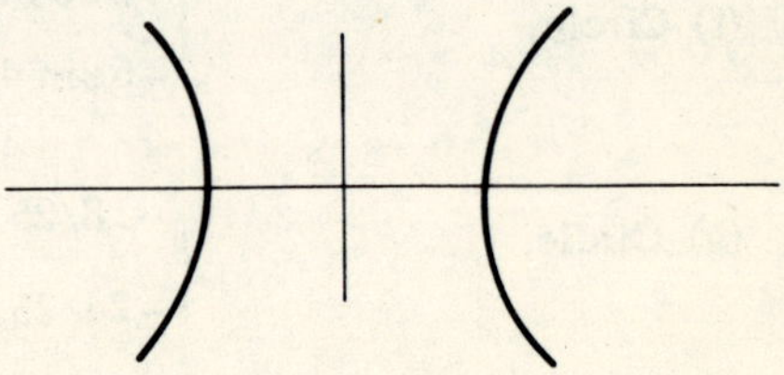

9. $3/\sqrt{5}$.

10. $(a \sin t,\ a \cos t)$ where $t = b \sin p$ (see Section 4).

11. $x = a(\alpha - \sin\alpha),\ y = a(1 - \cos\alpha)$.

12. The inverse of h must map the reals into the reals.

13. Helix (i.e. spring), speed $\sqrt{2}$.

Exercise B

1.

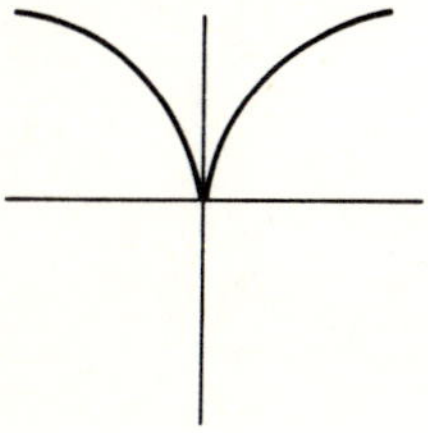

Zero velocity.

2.

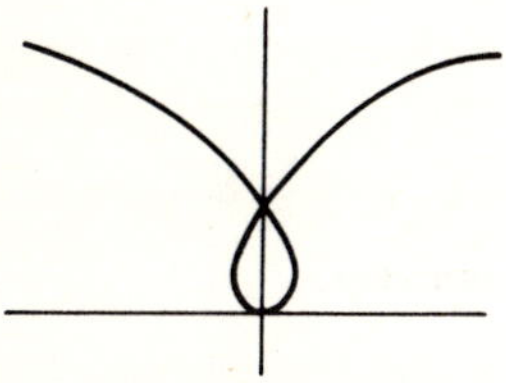

Acceleration $\dfrac{1}{\sqrt{40}}\begin{pmatrix}\pm 6\\ 2\end{pmatrix}$.

3.

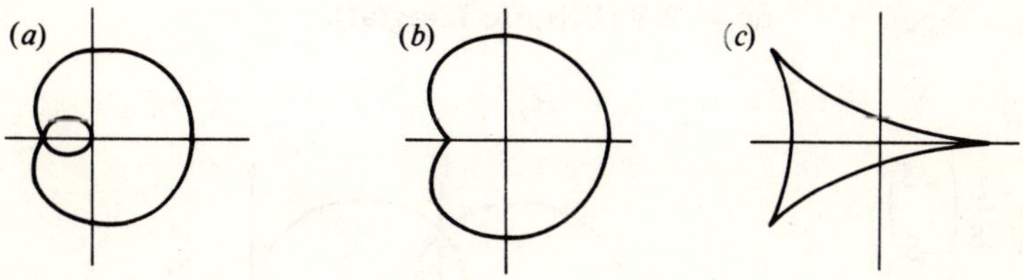

4.

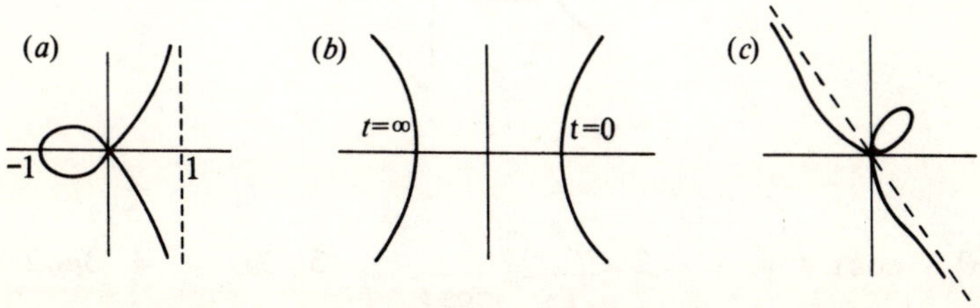

$$\begin{array}{cccc} t & 1 & -1 & 0, \\ \mathbf{v} & \begin{pmatrix}1\\1\end{pmatrix} & \begin{pmatrix}-1\\1\end{pmatrix} & \begin{pmatrix}0\\-1\end{pmatrix}, \\ \mathbf{a} & \begin{pmatrix}-1\\1\end{pmatrix} & \begin{pmatrix}-1\\-1\end{pmatrix} & \begin{pmatrix}4\\0\end{pmatrix}, \end{array} \qquad \begin{array}{ccc} t & 0 & \pm\infty, \\ \mathbf{v} & \begin{pmatrix}0\\1\end{pmatrix} & \begin{pmatrix}0\\0\end{pmatrix}, \\ \mathbf{a} & \begin{pmatrix}4\\2\end{pmatrix} & \begin{pmatrix}0\\0\end{pmatrix}, \end{array} \qquad \begin{array}{ccc} t & 0 & \pm\infty, \\ \mathbf{v} & \begin{pmatrix}1\\0\end{pmatrix} & \begin{pmatrix}0\\0\end{pmatrix}, \\ \mathbf{a} & \begin{pmatrix}0\\2\end{pmatrix} & \begin{pmatrix}0\\0\end{pmatrix}. \end{array}$$

5.

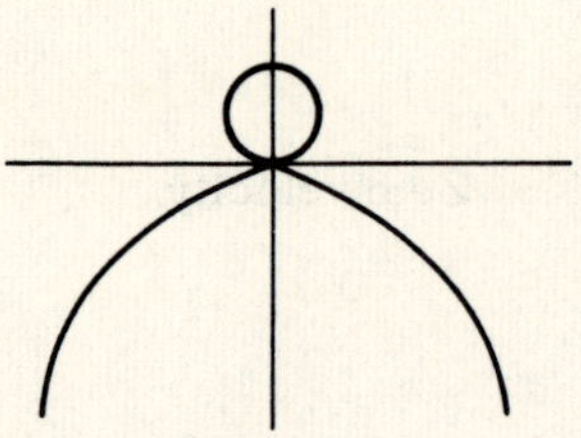

6. e.g. (a) $(p + \frac{3}{2}\sin\pi p,\ 1 + p + \frac{3}{2}\sin\pi p)$, (b) $[(p-1)^3, (p-1)^2]$.

Exercise C

1. $\sqrt{17}\,[x]$. **2.** $2[(1+p^2)^{3/2}]$. **3.** $[3p]$.

4. $[13p]$. **5.** e.g. $c[p]$, depending on choice of parameter.

6. $[4\sin\frac{1}{2}\pi]$. **7.** $1{\cdot}4 \times 10^4$.

8, $\sin\frac{1}{2}\theta = \frac{1}{3}\theta$, $\theta \approx 2\sqrt{2}^c$. **9.** $\frac{3}{4}a\cos 2p$.

10. $\int_0^{2\pi}(1 + 3\cos^2 p)^{1/2}\,dp \approx 9.9$ (Elliptic integral).

Exercise D

1. $\begin{pmatrix}0\\1\end{pmatrix}, \frac{-1}{\sqrt{28}}\begin{pmatrix}\sqrt{3}\\-5\end{pmatrix}$.

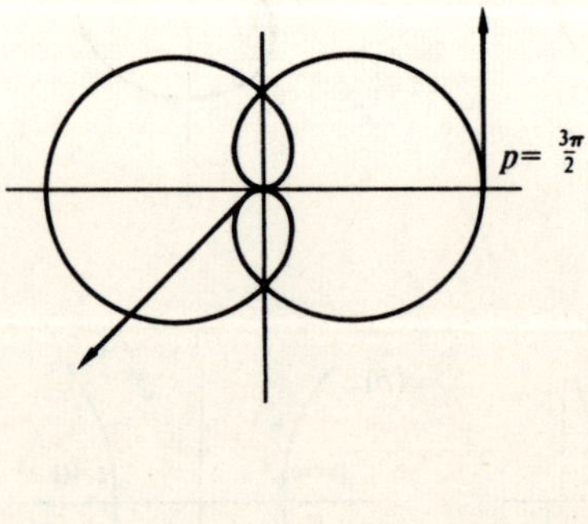

2. $v = 1$, $r\theta = \cos t \neq v$; $a = 2 \neq \frac{v^2}{r} = \frac{1}{\cos t}$. **3.** $3p$. **4.** $3p\sqrt{2}$. **5.** $2p$.

6. $2\sqrt{2}\,e^{\theta}$ **7.** $c\theta$.

8.

		t	$\frac{1}{3}\pi$	$\frac{2}{3}\pi$
v	Radial		0·5	–0·5
	Transverse		21·7	21·7
a	Radial		–43·5	–43·5
	Transverse		2	–2.

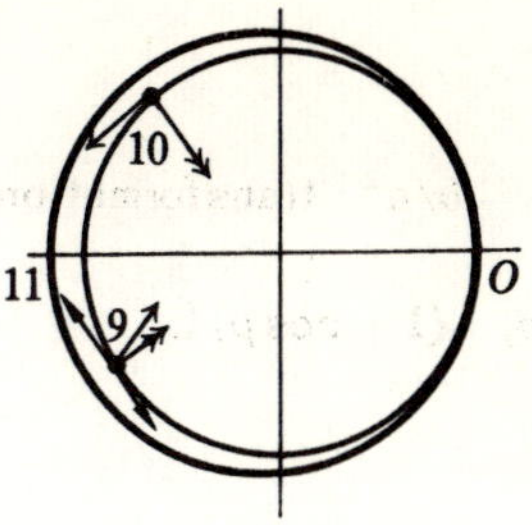

Exercise E

1. 0. **2.** $1/6p(1+p^2)^{3/2}$. **3.** $\frac{1}{3}$. **4.** 0. **5.** $\frac{1}{3}$. **6.** $\dfrac{1}{3\sqrt{2p}}$.

7. 1. **8.** $1/\sqrt{8}e^{\theta}$. **9.** $\dot{x} = \dfrac{13\sqrt{8}}{3}, \dot{y} = \dfrac{13}{3}$. **10.** $r = 24{\cdot}55,\ \theta = 15{\cdot}55$.

11. $x = \pm\left(\dfrac{2+\sqrt{14}}{15}\right) = \pm\, 0{\cdot}381$

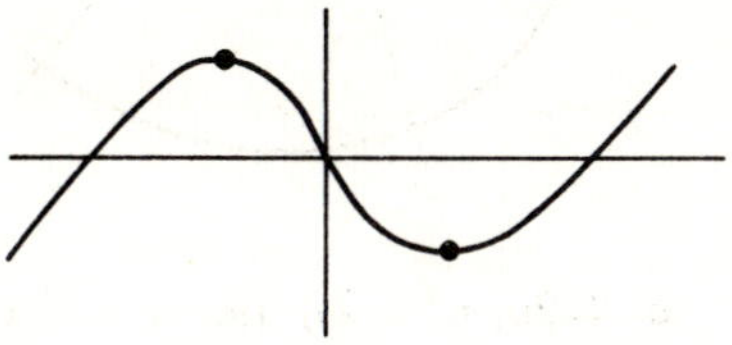

12. $\dfrac{16a}{3}\sin\dfrac{3\theta}{2},\ \dfrac{5}{16a}\sec\dfrac{3\theta}{2},\ 32a.$

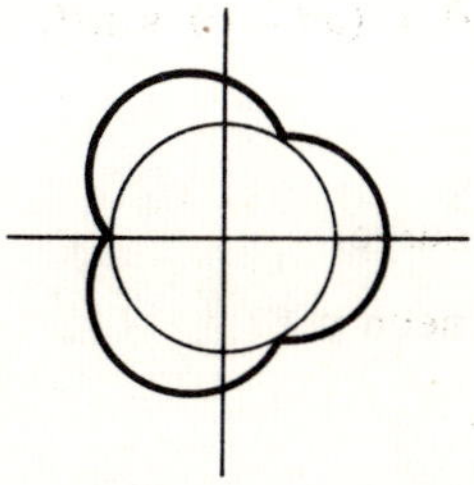

13. $-2/3a\sin 2t,\ 6a$

Exercise F

1. $\rho = \frac{16}{5}a\cos\frac{3}{2}\theta,\ (3a(4\cos\theta - \cos 4\theta)/5,\ 3a(4\sin\theta - \sin 4\theta)/5.$

2. $\rho = -\frac{3}{2}a\sin 2t,\ (a\cos t[(\cos^2 t + 3\sin^2 t)],\ a\sin t[\sin^2 t + 3\cos^2 t]).$

3. True.

4. $\psi = \theta + \phi$ where $\tan\phi = 1/k$.

$$\rho = \frac{ds}{d\psi} = \frac{ds}{d\theta}\cdot\frac{d\theta}{d\psi} = \frac{ds}{d\theta} = \sqrt{\left[\left(\frac{dr}{d\theta}\right)^2 + r^2\right]} = ae^{k\theta}\sqrt{(k + 1)} \propto r.$$

5. True

6. $-6p(1+p^2)^{3/2}$; $\{2p(3+4p^2), -3p^2(1+2p^2)\}$.

7. Same as Question 6 above.

Exercise G

1. $\frac{1}{2a}$. **2.** $-b/a^2$; transformation $y \to y - b$.

3. $\{p - \sin p, -(1 + \cos p)\}$.

4.

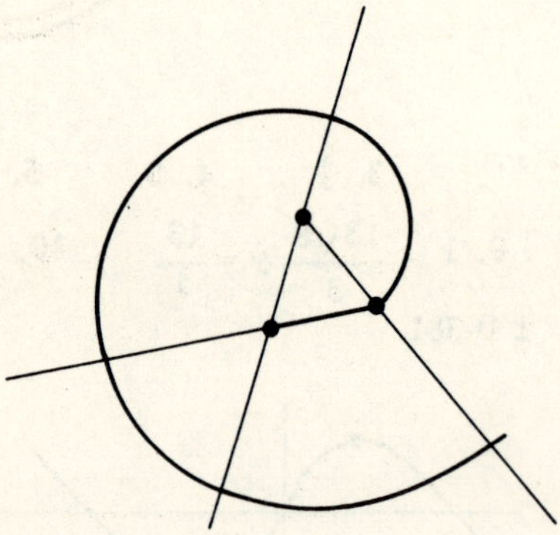

5. An equal cycloid. **6.** $(-2p, p^2 - 2)$, i.e. $y = \frac{1}{4}x - 2$.

7. $3p\begin{pmatrix}-\sin(\log p)\\ \cos(\log p)\end{pmatrix}$; *Note*: $\rho = 3\sqrt{2}p$.

8. Involute of a circle: $\{a\cos\theta + (a\theta - c)\sin\theta,\ a\sin\theta - (a\theta - c)\cos\theta\}$.

Miscellaneous Exercise

1. $\tan\psi = \sinh p$, for this curve.

2. $x = ap - \tanh p$, $y = a \operatorname{sech} p$.

3.

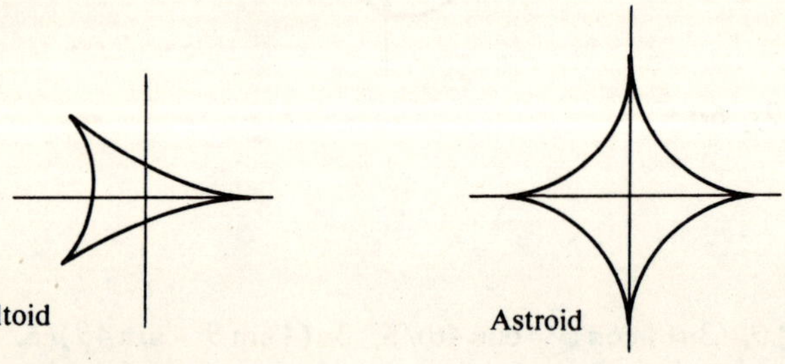

4. (a) Single point at origin.

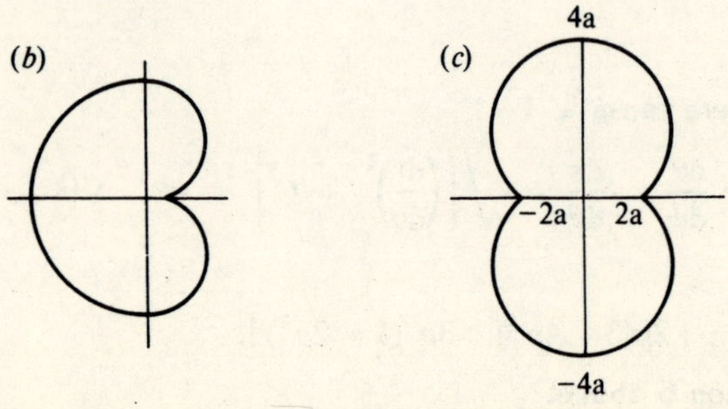

5. Spiral.

6.

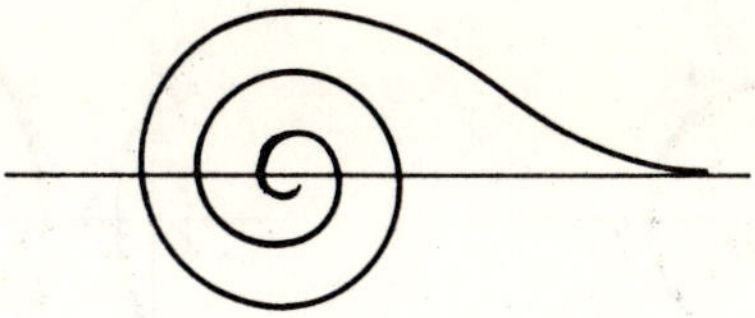

7. $[\sqrt{2}e^{\theta}]$, $\kappa = 1/\sqrt{2}\,r$.

8.

(a)

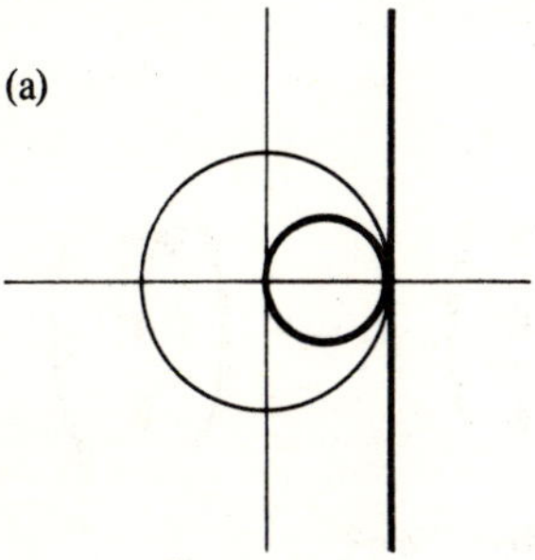

Circle, straight line

(b)

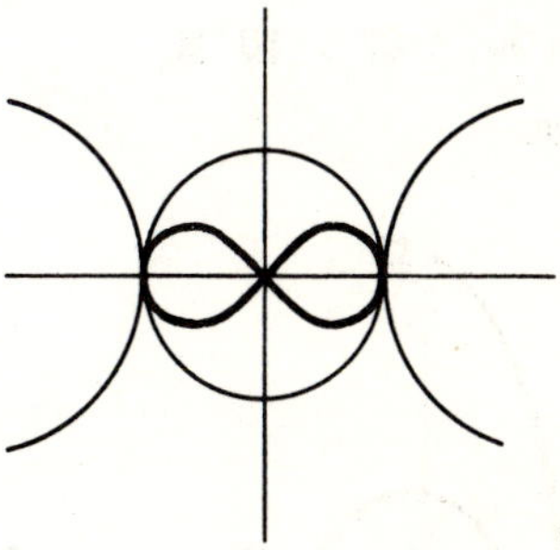

Lemniscate, hyperbola

9. Equiangular spiral, $s = \sqrt{2}e^{p}$.

10. Each $= 2\int_0^{\frac{1}{2}\pi} (a^2 + 6^2 + 2ab\cos\alpha)^{1/2}\ d\alpha.$

when $b = a$, ellipse reduces to straight line of length $4a$, covered twice.

11. $r^2 = a^2\cos 2\theta \Rightarrow r\,dr/d\theta = -a^2\sin 2\theta \Rightarrow \tan\phi = r\,d\theta/dr = -\cot 2\theta$. Hence $\phi = \pi/2 + 2\theta$ and $\psi = \pi/2 + 3\theta$, giving $\kappa = d\psi/ds = 3\sin\phi/r = 3r/a^2$. Lemniscate bends are used where the curvature is required to increase gradually from zero to a fixed amount. Strictly we should like $\kappa \propto s$; the curve that gives this is called *Cornu's Spiral*, and its equation is not elementary. The lemniscate is a close approximation to it and is used in practice.

12. Straight line through (1, 5, 4) in the direction of

$$\begin{pmatrix} 2 \\ -3 \\ 1 \end{pmatrix}$$

13. $x = a\cos p$, $y = a\sin p$, $z = bp$.

CHAPTER 2

Exercise A

1.

(a)

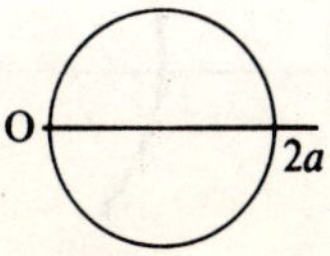

(b)

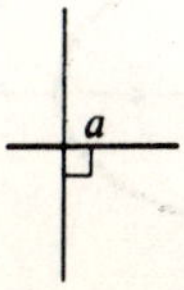

(c)

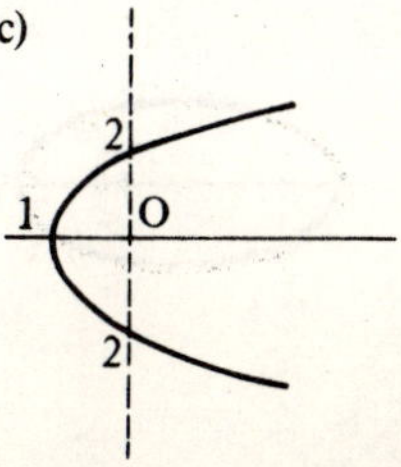

(*d*)

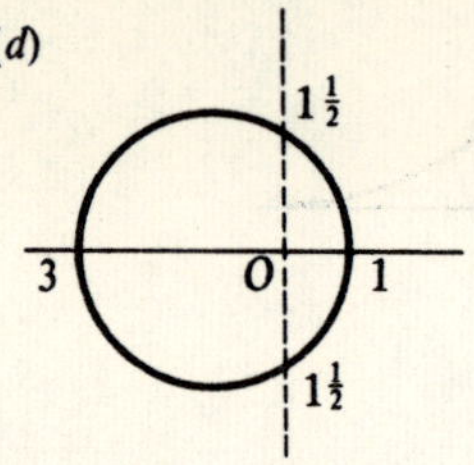

(*e*)

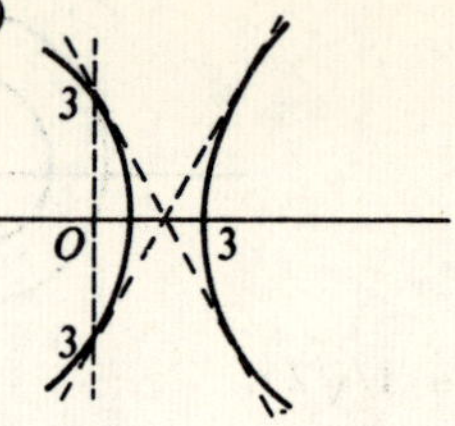

4. 27 100 km/hr, $6{\cdot}67 \times 10^2$N.

5. 95 minutes.

6.

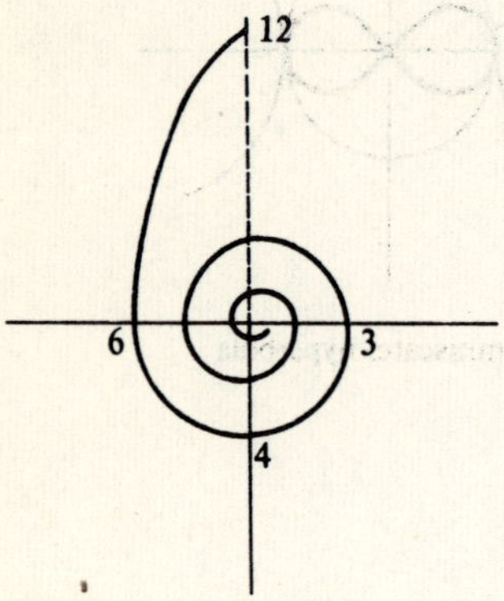

$$\mathbf{v} = \begin{pmatrix} 1 \\ \dfrac{-6\pi}{t} \end{pmatrix}, \quad \mathbf{a} = -\begin{pmatrix} \dfrac{36\pi^2}{t^3} \\ 0 \end{pmatrix}$$

Force $\dfrac{9\pi^2}{2}, \dfrac{4\pi^2}{3}$ centrally.

7. $k = 10$.

8. 27 400 km/h.

9. $c = 0 \Rightarrow$ min, $r = 8/5$; there is no max value and velocity $\to 0$ as $r \to \infty$.

10. Speed a parallel to $\theta = \pi$. Force $2\sqrt{2}a$.

11. Ratio $1 : \sqrt{2}$. Force $= \dfrac{h^2}{2r^2}\left[\cos\theta + \dfrac{2}{r}\right]$.

14. $u = \frac{1}{3}(2 + \cos\theta)$; when $\theta = \frac{1}{2}\pi$, $v = \frac{2}{3}\sqrt{5}$, $F = \frac{32}{27}$; when $\theta = \pi$, $v = \frac{2}{3}$, $F = \frac{8}{27}$

15. Straight line motion, hence no force.

17. $F = \dfrac{1350}{r^5}(r - 1)$.

18. Max 3. Speed 2. Min 2. Speed 3. $c = 0 \Rightarrow r = 0$, $v = 0$, i.e. no movement.

Exercise B

1.

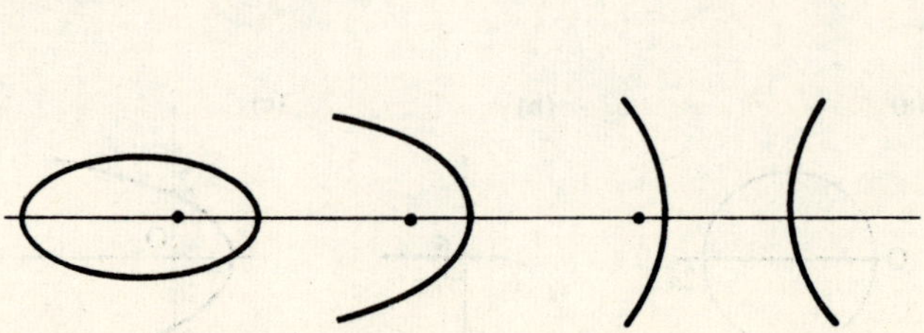

2.

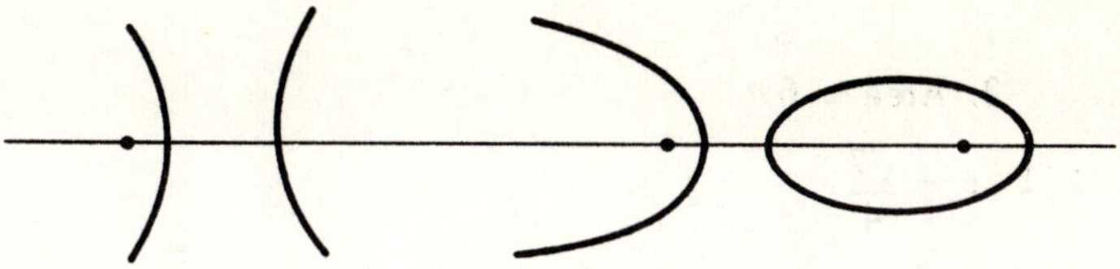

3.

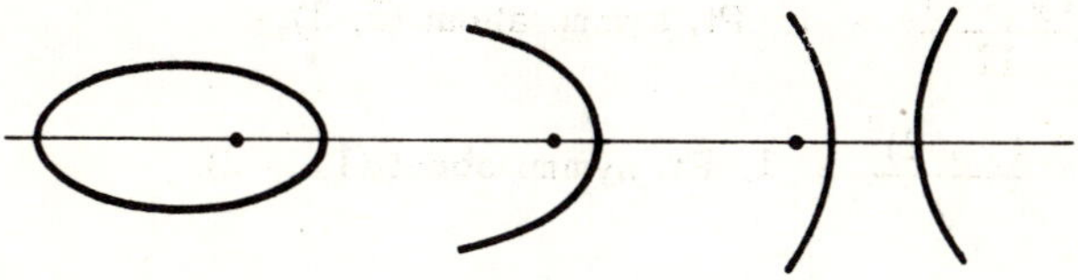

4. $a > b$, ellipse; $a = b$, parabola; $a < b$, hyperbola.

5.
$$-\frac{1}{r^2}\dot{r} = -k\sin\theta\,\dot{\theta}$$
$$\Rightarrow \dot{r} = hk\sin\theta$$
$$\Rightarrow \ddot{r} = hk\cos\theta\,\dot{\theta}$$
$$= \frac{h^2}{r^2}k\cos\theta$$
$$= \frac{h^2}{r^2}\left[\frac{1}{r} - \frac{\mu}{h^2}\right]$$
$$= \frac{h^2}{r^3} - \frac{\mu}{r^2}$$
$$= r\dot{\theta}^2 - \frac{\mu}{r^2}$$

Exercise C

1. $\frac{10}{9}$ and 10, ratio 9 : 1.
2. Apogee 8000 km, Perigee 7000 km. $112\,000 = r(15 + \cos\theta)$.
3. Curves as in Exercise A, Question 1 (c), (d), (e) rotated through 90°.
4. $e = 5$.
5. $\frac{3}{8}$ [*Note*: new apse is apogee equ. $1/r = (1 - \frac{3}{8}\cos\theta)$].
6. Reduced by factor $\sqrt{(2/3)}$.
7. Reduced by factor $2/\sqrt{5}$.
8. 9 : 4.
9. Direction $\theta = \pm\frac{\pi}{6}$, 4 units/s.
10. $l = a(1 + e)$, $h = av$, $v^2 < \; = \; > 2\mu/a$.
11. See Exercise B, Question 5.

Exercise D

2. $e = 3/5$. 3. Area $= 6\pi$.

4. $\frac{x^2}{16} + \frac{y^2}{9} = 1 \quad e = \frac{\sqrt{7}}{4}$.

5. $\frac{(x+1)^2}{9} + \frac{(y-2)^2}{4} = 1$.

6. $\frac{(x-5)^2}{4} - \frac{(y-3)^2}{12} = 1$. Pt. symm. about (5, 3).

7. $\frac{(x-3/2)^2}{9/4} + \frac{(y+2)^2}{2} = 1$. Pt. symm. about $(1\frac{1}{2}, -2)$.

Exercise E

7. $e = 1/\sqrt{2}$.

10. 19·5 m.

Exercise F

7. $r = \frac{a}{(\theta + 1)}$.

CHAPTER 3

Exercise A

1. $T = \sqrt{2}W$.

2. A strain would be set up at the centre of rotation.

3. 1 m. 4. $15\sqrt{2}/8$ kg. 5. 300 N.

6. It will topple first when the horizontal force equals half the weight.

7. $lF\sin\theta$. The same result is obtained using the obtuse angle.

Exercise B

1. $\begin{pmatrix} 70 \\ 0 \\ 0 \end{pmatrix}$ N m. $\begin{pmatrix} 70 \\ -250/\sqrt{2} \\ 250/\sqrt{2} \end{pmatrix}$ N m.

2. $|\mathbf{r} \wedge \mathbf{F}| = \sqrt{14}$, $|\mathbf{F}| = \sqrt{14}/30$. No, it can act along any tangent to a circle of radius 30 m, centre the origin, whose plane is perpendicular to

$$\begin{pmatrix} 2 \\ 3 \\ 1 \end{pmatrix}.$$

3. Instantaneous moment $\begin{pmatrix} -80 \\ 80 \\ 0 \end{pmatrix}$ N m.

No, because firing the first rocket can never affect the middle component and firing the second rocket always affects the third component, i.e. λ, μ do not exist so that

$$\lambda \begin{pmatrix} 70 \\ 0 \\ 0 \end{pmatrix} + \mu \begin{pmatrix} 0 \\ -250/\sqrt{2} \\ 250/\sqrt{2} \end{pmatrix} = \begin{pmatrix} -80 \\ 80 \\ 0 \end{pmatrix}.$$

4. $\begin{pmatrix} 0 \\ 6 \\ -3 \end{pmatrix}$ N m. The same answer is obtained for (10, 1, 2). Both points lie on the line of action of the force.

5. (a) $\begin{pmatrix} 14 \\ -2 \\ 9 \end{pmatrix}$ N m, (b) $\begin{pmatrix} 0 \\ 12 \\ 7 \end{pmatrix}$ N m.

6. (a) $\begin{pmatrix} 0 \\ -14 \\ 14 \end{pmatrix}$, (b) $\begin{pmatrix} \sqrt{\frac{2}{3}} \\ -\sqrt{\frac{2}{3}} \\ 0 \end{pmatrix}$, (c) $\begin{pmatrix} 4 \\ 4 \\ -4 \end{pmatrix}$,

7. (a) $\mathbf{r} \wedge \mathbf{F} = |\mathbf{r}| \cdot |\mathbf{F}|\,\hat{\mathbf{e}}$ (b) $\mathbf{r} \wedge \mathbf{F} = \mathbf{0}$ (c) $\mathbf{r} \wedge \mathbf{F} = -\mathbf{F} \wedge \mathbf{r}$.

8. If Q is fixed then $\mathbf{F}$ has a rotational effect only.

Exercise C

1. (a) $\begin{pmatrix} -1 \\ 1 \\ -2 \end{pmatrix}$, (b) $\begin{pmatrix} -26 \\ 38 \\ 15 \end{pmatrix}$.

2. $F_1 = \frac{1}{7}$, $F_2 = -\frac{4}{7}$. **3.** $\frac{2}{5}$ rad/s, 40 m/s. **4.** $T = 5\sqrt{29}/\sqrt{35}$.

5. (a) $T = \dfrac{5\sqrt{13}}{\sqrt{19}}$ (b) $T = \dfrac{25\sqrt{13}}{3\sqrt{35}}$.

7. The angular velocity is the same whatever point on the axis of rotation is taken as 'origin'.

8. From Question 7 it follows that (for all λ) $\mathbf{F}_2 = \mathbf{F}_1 + \lambda(\mathbf{r}_2 - \mathbf{r}_1)$

Exercise D

1. -7 units.

2. -8, maximum effect at $\pm\left(-\frac{1}{\sqrt{5}}, \frac{2}{\sqrt{5}}, 0\right)$,

minimum effect at $\pm\left(\frac{2}{\sqrt{5}}, \frac{1}{\sqrt{5}}, 0\right)$.

3. $F = 18\sqrt{3}$ units.

4. abc. Volume of a cuboid. Volume of parallelepiped. The volume is zero.

6. 280 units volume. 7. 6 units. 8. 266/6.

Exercise E

1. $17x - 2y + 5z = 18$. 2. $12x - y - 21z = 23$.

3. $\mathbf{r} = 2\hat{\mathbf{i}} - \hat{\mathbf{j}} - 5\hat{\mathbf{k}} + s(a\hat{\mathbf{i}} + b\hat{\mathbf{j}} + (3a + 2b)\hat{\mathbf{k}})$ (for all a and b).

4. No. 5. $\begin{pmatrix} 3 \\ 1 \\ 2 \end{pmatrix}$

7. $\mathbf{r} = \hat{\mathbf{i}} - 2\hat{\mathbf{j}} + 4\hat{\mathbf{k}} + s(-13\hat{\mathbf{i}} + 38\hat{\mathbf{j}} - 37\hat{\mathbf{k}})$.

8. $(\mathbf{r} - \mathbf{a})\cdot((\mathbf{a} - \mathbf{b})\wedge(\mathbf{b} - \mathbf{c})) = 0$ or equivalents.

10. $\cos^{-1}\frac{7}{\sqrt{(429 \times 314)}}$, $\cos^{-1}\frac{149}{\sqrt{(314 \times 550)}}$, $\cos^{-1}\frac{79}{\sqrt{(550 \times 429)}}$.

Exercise F

1. $-7\begin{pmatrix} 2 \\ 1 \\ 1 \end{pmatrix}$. 2. $12\begin{pmatrix} -9 \\ 5 \\ 22 \end{pmatrix}$. 3. $\frac{1}{12}\begin{pmatrix} \lambda \\ -\frac{1}{2} \\ 1-4\lambda \end{pmatrix}$ for any λ.

4. A force of $\begin{pmatrix} 7 \\ -4 \\ 8 \end{pmatrix}$ and a couple $\begin{pmatrix} 45 \\ 15 \\ -3 \end{pmatrix}$.

A force of $\begin{pmatrix} 7 \\ -4 \\ 8 \end{pmatrix}$ and a couple $\begin{pmatrix} -19 \\ 13 \\ 52 \end{pmatrix}$.

5. A force of $\begin{pmatrix} 2 \\ -2 \\ 2 \end{pmatrix}$ and a couple of $\begin{pmatrix} 3 \\ -1 \\ -4 \end{pmatrix}$.

Yes, because these vectors are perpendicular. The line of the force is

$$\begin{pmatrix} \lambda \\ 2-\lambda \\ -\frac{1}{2}+\lambda \end{pmatrix}$$

i.e. through $(0, 2, -\frac{1}{2})$.

6. A force of $\begin{pmatrix} 12 \\ 6 \\ 8 \end{pmatrix}$ and a couple $\begin{pmatrix} 0 \\ 2 \\ -1 \end{pmatrix}$.

The equivalent force acts at $\frac{1}{12}(0, 1\frac{8}{61}, 1\frac{55}{61})$ and the couple is

$$\frac{1}{61}\begin{pmatrix} 12 \\ 6 \\ 8 \end{pmatrix}.$$

7. $\sum_i \mathbf{F}_i = \mathbf{0}$ and $\sum_i \mathbf{r}_i \wedge \mathbf{F}_i = \mathbf{0}$ for *one* point.

8. No.

9. $\lambda = 1$ and the force acts through $(1, -1, 0)$.

CHAPTER 4

Exercise A

1. It moves vertically downwards.

2. $\bar{\mathbf{r}} = \dfrac{m_1}{M}\mathbf{r}_1 + \dfrac{m_2}{M}\mathbf{r}_2 + \dfrac{m_3}{M}\mathbf{r}_3$.

Coplanar since $\dfrac{m_1}{M} + \dfrac{m_2}{M} + \dfrac{m_3}{M} = 1$.

$\bar{\mathbf{r}} = 2\mathbf{r}_1 + 3\mathbf{r}_2 + 4\mathbf{r}_3 \Rightarrow P_1C$ divides P_2P_3 in ratio 4 : 3.

3. No, we can only locate their mass centre. (a) No. (b) Yes.

4. Mass centre motion unchanges. Tip rotates about mass centre, so does not rise so rapidly.

5. $\sum m(\ddot{\mathbf{a}} + \ddot{\mathbf{a}}^*) = M\ddot{\bar{\mathbf{r}}} \Rightarrow \sum (m\ddot{\mathbf{a}}^*) + M\ddot{\mathbf{a}} = M\ddot{\bar{\mathbf{r}}}$,

$\dot{\mathbf{a}} = \dot{\bar{\mathbf{r}}} \Rightarrow \ddot{\mathbf{a}} = \ddot{\bar{\mathbf{r}}} \Rightarrow \sum (m\ddot{\mathbf{a}}^*) = \mathbf{0}$.

6. Grip point furthest from cone mass centre.

7. Idealise the jumper as a rubber block $2 \times \frac{1}{2} \times \frac{1}{2}$ m which when bent double will have a mass centre almost $\frac{1}{2}$ m below the bar. The mass centre moves in a parabola of unalterable dimensions once the ground is left.
[See *Mechanics of Athletics* by G. Dyson]

Exercise B

1. Mr^2. 2. $Mv^2\sqrt{(a^2+h^2)}/a^2$.

3. 54 N. Dancers treated as particles. Still 1 rad/s and 54 N.

4. $l/(l-c)$

Exercise C

2. Still $2:\sqrt{3}$. 3. $\dfrac{1}{4}\dfrac{g}{\pi^2}$ or $\dfrac{3}{16}\dfrac{g}{\pi^2}$.

Exercise D

1. Ma^2. 2. Ma^2. 3. $\frac{1}{3}Ml^2$, $\frac{1}{3}Ml^2\sin^2\alpha$.

4. $\frac{2}{5}Ma^2$. 5. $\frac{1}{12}Mb^2$, $\frac{1}{12}Ml^2$. 6. $\frac{1}{12}M(l^2+b^2)$.

7. $I_z + \sum m(x^2+y^2) = \sum mx^2 + \sum my^2 = I_x + I_y$. 8. $\frac{3}{2}Ma^2$, $\frac{7}{5}Ma^2$.

9. $\frac{1}{3}Mb^2$, $\frac{1}{3}M(l^2+b^2)$. 10. $\frac{1}{2}Ma^2 + M(a+l)^2 + \frac{1}{3}ml^2$.

11. (i) F/M along the x-axis, rF/I about the y-axis (if **F** in the xz-plane),
(ii) F/M along the x-axis, F/Mr about the x-axis, $lF/2I$ about the z-axis.

12. $\frac{1}{3}MR^2$.

Exercise E

1. $5(L-G)/2Mr^2$. 2. $4:1$. 3. $(l^2+b^2):l^2$.

4. $2(T_1 - T_2)/Mr$. 5. $2g/11r$.

6. 10 rad/s^2. Inertia of pedals and chain ignored.

Exercise F

1. (a)

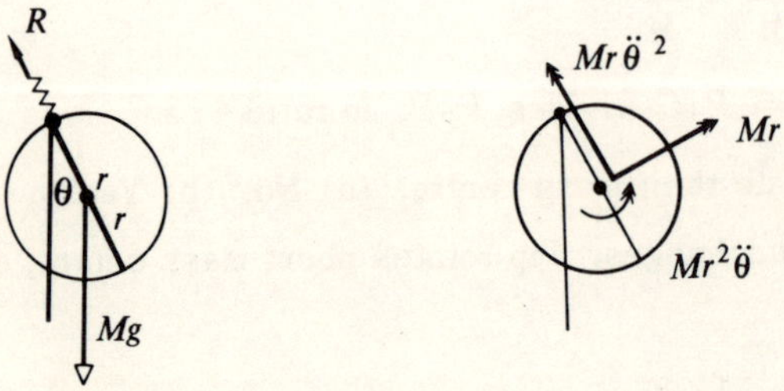

(b)

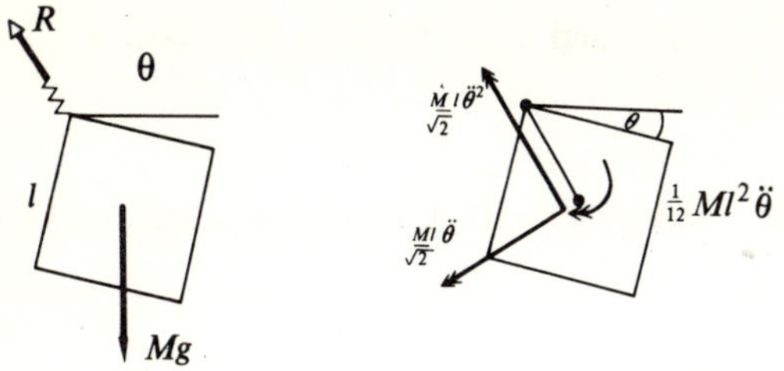

(c)

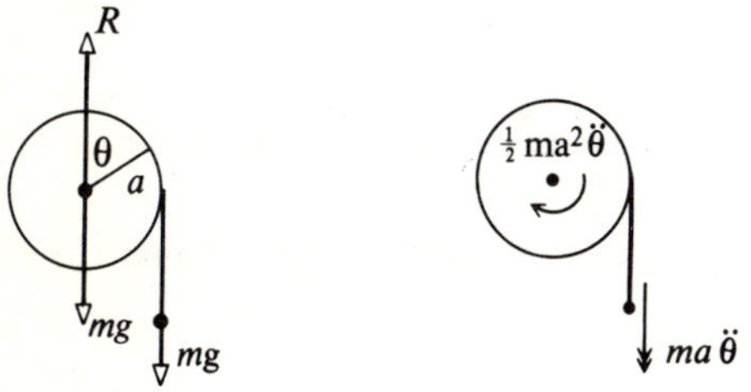

2. (a) $2\pi\frac{\sqrt{(2r)}}{g}$, (b) $\frac{5}{2}Mg$

(c) $\frac{2}{3}g$, $\frac{4}{3}mg$, (d) $2\pi\sqrt{\left\{\frac{3022a}{66g}\right\}}$, 0

3. Three times as great.

Exercise G

1. 2400 rad/s.

2. He rotates with acceleration T/I.

3. $(I_1\omega_1 + I_2\omega_2)/(I_1 + I_2)$, $I_1I_2|\omega_1 - \omega_2|/L(I_1 + I_2)$.

4. $\frac{1}{2}\omega$. **5.** $LT/2I$. **6.** 31/14 rev/s.

(d)

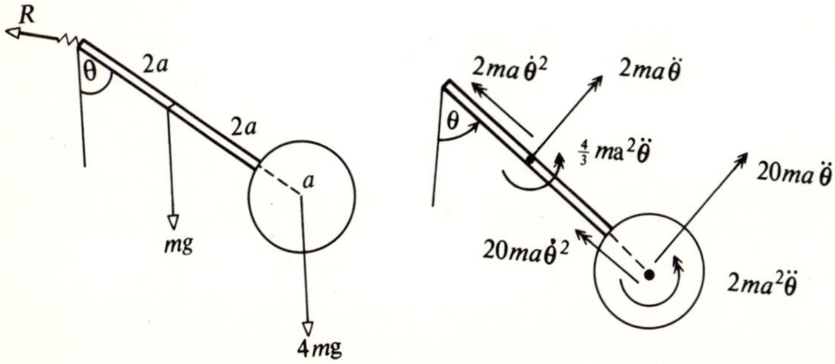

7. $\dfrac{mR^2 - mR\,v/\omega}{I + mR^2}$ where $I = \dfrac{8}{15}\rho\pi R^5$ and $\omega = 2\pi/(24 \times 60 \times 60)$.

8. 8 N s, 7·6 rad/s.

9. $6\,mhv/(3mh^2 = Ml^2)$, $Mmlv(2l - 3h)/(mh^2 + Ml^2)$. Minimum when $h = \frac{2}{3}l$, $\frac{2}{3}$ of the way down the blade.

10. Velocity of mass centre $= \dfrac{3m}{5m + 2m}$ **v**, angular speed $= \dfrac{9mv}{(5m + 2M)a}$.

11. $\tan^{-1}\{\frac{7}{5}\,e\tan\alpha\}$ to the ground.

12. (i) Vel. A = Vel. C = 0, Vel. $B \doteq$ **v**; mass centre constant velocity $\frac{1}{3}$ **v**. A and C rotate about B with angular speed v/l.

(ii) Speed A = speed C = $\frac{15}{43}v$ towards B, Vel. $B = \frac{25}{43}$**v**. A and C rotate about B with angular speed $\frac{16}{43}(v/l)$.

13. Mass centre moves perpendicular to AB with speed (i) $I/2m$, (ii) $I/3m$. AB rotates about mass centre with angular speed (i) I/lm, (ii) I/lm.

Exercise H

1. $\cos^{-1}\left\{1 - \dfrac{m^2v^2}{2gl(m+M)^2}\right\}$. 2. 0·2036 kg cm^2, 2 220 rad/s.

3. $\dfrac{6m\sqrt{(2gh)}}{M + 3m}\,l$, $\dfrac{M + 3m}{6m}\,l$.

4. (i) $\sqrt{[M^2V^2 - 2mMvV\cos\theta + m^2v^2]}/(M - m)$.

(ii) $-\dfrac{mM}{2(M - m)}\{(V - v)^2 + 2vV(1 - \cos\theta)\}$. Gain.

5. 2·02 rev/s. 67 N m. 6. 2 : 1 , 1 : 1. 7. $(\sqrt{133}/16)l\omega$.

(ignoring work done by gravity on his arms).

INDEX

Acceleration 1, 12, 14, 18–19, 23
  and central force 27
  angular 99, 103, 106, 107
  linear 107
  mass 103, 106
Addition of vector products 57, 83–4
Angular acceleration 99, 103, 106, 107
Angular momentum 76
  of rigid bodies 97
Angular velocity 11, 65, 98, 117, 127
  constant 122
  vector 65
Apogee 37, 48
Apse 31, 36, 47–8
Apsidal distance 31
Arc length 11, 19, 20
Area, rate of description of 28, 51
Areal speed 28, 51
Argand diagram 22
Axis of rotation. *See* Rotation
Axis of symmetry 128

Cardioid 22
Cartesian coordinates 7, 16
Catenary 23
Central force 27, 28, 33
  and acceleration 27
  function of distance 31
  motion under 35, 46–51
  particle moving under 29
Centre of curvature 17–18, 24
Centre of gravity 92
Centroid 88
Circle of curvature 17, 24
Coefficient of restitution 112
Components 62, 84
Conics 35, 51
  cartesian equation of 40
  central 43; focal properties and symmetry of 43–5
  chord of 36
  eccentricity of 35
  focus-directrix definition 35
  focus-directrix property 42–4
  geometrical properties of 42
  major axis of 43
  minor axis of 43
  polar equation of 35, 51
  tangent property of 42–3
  types of 36
Couples 58, 77, 84, 93, 127
Cross product 56
Curvature 13–16, 24
  centre of 17–18, 24
  circle of 17, 24
  radius of 17
Curve(s), in terms of parametric functions 2, 4
  length of 6–9, 24
  motion on a 13
  properties of 22–3
Cusps 5
Cycloid 5, 22
Cylinder, moment of inertia of 100

Degrees of freedom 1
Derivative, of non-unit vector 10
  of unit vector 10
Differential geometry 1–26
Directrix 35
Distance along a curve 6
Distributive Law 63, 68, 75, 84
Dot product 56
Dynamics of particles 75–7

Earth's gravitational attraction 1
Eccentricity 51
  of conic 35
Einstein 37
Ellipse 35–7, 43, 44, 49, 51
  cartesian equation 40
  length of 44
Energy equation 115, 117, 119
Epicycloid 22
Equiangular spiral 19, 23
Euler's equations 126, 127, 132

Evolute 20–1, 24
External forces 87, 95, 96, 103

Focus 35, 51
Force(s), acting on particle 28
  and orbit 28
  central. *See* Central force
  exerted on satellite 28
  external 87, 95, 96, 103
  internal 87
  point of application of 56
  systems of 77–8; application to single particle 78–80

Gravitation, Newton's Law of 32
Gravitational attraction 91
  rotational effect of 92
Gravitational constant 33
Gyroscope 129, 132

Hyperbola 35, 36, 38, 43, 44, 51
  cartesian equation 41
Hypocycloid 22

Impulse 109, 118
  moment of 109
Inclination 96
Inertia matrix 122
Internal forces 87
Intersection of planes 73–5
Intrinsic equation 23
Inverse square law, motion under 33
  of attraction 32–4, 37
Involute 19–20, 24

Jerks 110–11, 131

Kepler 39
Kinematics 1
  polar 27
Kinetic energy 113–20, 131
  and mass centre 115
  and work done 114–17
  applications 116–19

Laminas 98–100, 105, 106
Latus rectum 36, 51
Length, of arc. *See* Arc length
  of curve 6–9, 24
Linear momentum 90
Linear motion 87, 130
  equations for 130, 132
Locus of a point 2

Mass-acceleration 106
  problems in 2-dimensions 103
Mass centre 87–9, 95, 102, 117
  and kinetic energy 115
  motion relative to 90
  rotation relative to 104
Moment of force 53–7
  and system of particles 92
  resultant 58
Moment of impulse 109
Moment of inertia 99–100, 131
  additive property of 100–1
  definition 98
  of cylinder 100
  of flywheel 116–17
  of solid body 101
Moment of momentum 76, 93, 104, 121
  rate of change of 103
Moments as vectors 55
Momentum 109–13
  angular 76; of rigid bodies 97
  linear 90
  moment of 76, 93, 104, 121; rate of change of 103
Momentum equations 130
Moon probes 27
Motion, on a curve 13
  under central force 46–51
  see also Linear motion; Rotational motion

Newton's Interaction Law 93
Newton's Law of Gravitation 32
Newton's Laws of Motion 36
Newton's Second Law 75–7, 87
  rotational analogue to 99
Newton's Third Law 87
Nodes 4–5
Non-unit vector, derivative of 10
Normal unit vector 13

Notation 23, 130

Orbits 33, 46–50
and force 28
types under gravitational attraction 36
Origin, choice of 105

Parabola 35, 36, 51
cartesian equation 41
properties of 45–6
Parallel axis rule 101
Parameters, special 8, 15, 24
Parametric functions 1, 2, 21
curves in terms of 2, 4
Parametric representation 2
Particle(s), dynamics of 75–7
force acting on 28
moving under central force 29
notation 130
rotational motion of system of 86
system of 92
velocity of 30
Pendulum 96
Perigee 37, 48
Period 95–7
Periodic functions 2
Plane, equation of 71–3, 85
intersection of 73–5
of rotation 54
Planets 33, 36, 39
Point of application of force 56
Point of inflexion 14
Point symmetry 43
Polar coordinates 9, 16
Polar kinematics 27
Position vector 66
Precession 129
Principle axes 123, 125, 127, 128
Principle directions 124
Pythagoras's Theorem 7

Radius of curvature 17
Radius of gyration 102
Ratio theorem 43
Restitution, coefficient of 112
Resultant moments of forces 58
Resultant turning effect 59, 83
Right-Hand Corkscrew Rule 56, 59
Rigid bodies 86–132
angular momentum of 97
definition of 89
mass centre of 89
rotational motion of 86
summary of equations 130
three-dimensional motion of 120–30; applications 126–9
Rotation, axis of 65–7, 125: non-perpendicular 69–70; perpendicular 55
plane of 54
relative to mass centre 104
Rotational effect 84
of applied forces 52, 75
Rotational motion 9, 52, 76, 91, 130
fundamental equation for 93, 95–6, 130
of rigid bodies 86
of space craft 86
of system of particles 86
particular cases of 52

Satellites 27, 28, 33, 36, 37, 48, 75
Scalar product 56
Scalar triple product 68–9
Serret–Frenet formulae 26
Sign convention 8
Simple harmonic motion 96, 97
Simpson's rule 9
Slipping 107–8
Solid body, moment of inertia of 101
Solid body model 95
Space craft 52, 65, 128
rotational motion of 86
Space station 77–9, 94
Spiral 22–3
equiangular 19, 23
Standard deviation 102
System of forces 77–8
application to single particle 78–80
System of particles and moments of forces 92

Three-dimensional motion of rigid bodies 120–30
applications 126–9

Torque 93
Tractrix 24
Transverse unit vector 10
Trochoid 4–5
Turning effect 52, 53, 55–7, 69, 78, 93
  resultant 59, 83
  total 83
Turning moment 77–8, 83

Unit tangent 13
Unit vectors 1, 7, 23, 62–5
  derivative of 10
  normal 13
  transverse 10

Vector angular velocity 65
Vector products 52–85
  addition of 57, 83–4
  component form 62, 84
  definition of 56, 62, 84
  determinant form 63–4
  geometrical applications 71–5
  notion 56
  properties of 62–8, 84
  summary 84
Vector triple product 75
Vectors, moments as 55
Velocity 23
  of particle 30

Work done and kinetic energy 114–17
Wrench 80–1, 85